BUILDING ENTOPIA

Books in This Series

ANTHROPOPOLIS City for Human Development by C. A. Doxiadis *et al.*

ECUMENOPOLIS The Inevitable City of the Future by C. A. Doxiadis
and J. G. Papaioannou

BUILDING ENTOPIA by C. A. Doxiadis

ACTION for Human Settlements by C. A. Doxiadis

BUILDING ENTOPIA

C.A. DOXIADIS

W · W · NORTON & COMPANY · INC · New York

Library of Congress Cataloging in Publication Data
Doxiadēs, Cōnstantinos Apostolou, 1913–1975.
    Building entopia.
    Bibliography: p.
    Includes index.
    1. Cities and towns.   2. Cities and towns—
Planning—1945–   I. Title.
HT119.D69   1977   301.36'3   76–25455
ISBN 0–393–08362–4

1 2 3 4 5 6 7 8 9 0

To Anthy, Cali, Eufrosyne and Apostolos

Preface

This is the third of the four "red" books which try to help the understanding of what will happen to our human settlements and what we can do to save them. It deals with the problem of how, in order to avoid disasters, we can turn *Ecumenopolis*, the Inevitable City of the Future (second book) into *Anthropopolis*, the Humane City that we need for Human Development (first book). This book is called *Building Entopia* because it deals with the general ideas about future developments that we need. It deals with the way we can really build Entopia, the city of dreams that can come true, and not remain unrealistic. The fourth book is dedicated to the way in which we can move from talking and writing about ideas, dreams and theories towards action, and will be called *Action for Human Settlements*.

Building Entopia is addressed to all those who are related to the City of Anthropos:
— to the child who must understand it and someday ameliorate it
— to all its inhabitants who live or come to the city because they prefer it to the village, and then suffer with it and cry
— to all its builders, from those building a small home to big industries or highways
— to all who advise on its formation, from the decorator, the architect, the engineer, the planner, the ecologist, the environmentalist
— to all who take the final decisions, from the mayor and his counselors, to the leaders of states, nations and our globe.

I do not present a utopia, for which there is no place, but an *Entopia* (Part One) for which there is a place on our globe (on Mars I would act differently). For this reason I start by explaining in a realistic way that certain characteristics, such as the dimensions of the City of the Future, are inevitable because of the explosion of science and technology. We cannot avoid them any more than the farmers could avoid the formation of the village once they decided to cultivate the soil and to abandon hunting. If we want to build and not only talk, we must be realists.

However, inevitable larger dimensions do not necessarily mean lower quality. We are confused because we forget that Florence was of higher quality than the villages that preceded it, and Paris of the second half of the 19th century was much better than smaller French cities. This is why, after speaking about the inevitable, I proceed and clarify the desirable city. This is the main subject of this book: to demonstrate very clearly what is the desirable and feasible city, what is a real *Entopia* and how it can be really built. If we want to build it, we must conceive it very clearly and set it as our goal. Even very large and expensive cathedrals have been built once they were properly conceived; in spite of great difficulties and lack of financial means they were eventually completed.

Following the concept of the inevitable dimensions and desirable quality of our Entopia, I will clarify how we can go about achieving our goal, and how we will move from the suffering city of the present to the city of the future that we set as our goal. To achieve this, I present the solution for every spatial unit (Part Two), from the smallest to the largest ones, and then the steps leading to it both in the case of new cities and in the case of existing cities and other settlements of all sorts.

Each spatial unit should be studied separately in order to be understood, but this is not enough as, if we do not have the proper city, even though we build the best home or neighborhood, our life will not be happy. For this reason I will continue by presenting Entopia as a system of life with its elements and as a whole (Part Three). This is the most difficult part because it is the most complex one and because though we may conceive the best home, if it is not conceived as a cell of a system, its value within the city is lost.

I present these concepts and proposals in order to help us to escape from the great explosion we are in and the great confusion that it has caused in our minds. We need to understand what we can do and how. Otherwise we will never do it. This book is intended to help the process for the big change and the revolution that we need in order to build the City of Anthropos, our great master, in the best possible way. Unless we face the problem of how the city of the future should be built we will never achieve anything.

For all those who speak today of quality of life I have to answer a basic question: do we really add quality to our life by building Entopia? My answer is as follows: the physical structure cannot alone change our life, but as Freud said "Anatomy is destiny". If we build the proper city we will not, for example, change the political system overnight. If there is a dictatorship or corrupt government it will remain. Gradually, however, people living in the proper city will become more humane, they will have higher quality and more choices and this will help them to fight for freedom, honesty and everything else that developed and civilized people need. Anatomy is indeed destiny. Let us ameliorate the anatomy of our city and our destiny will be a much better one.

Entopia will not be built tomorrow, but we have to start the process by laying foundations — the only possible way to do so is to conceive properly the most desirable and feasible City of Anthropos and the steps leading to it. This is what I have done here and I have been patiently waiting to turn 60 in order to do it, so as not to present some "big ideas" or serve my personal needs for self-expression and satisfaction. This is only personal art. I am trying to serve Anthropos by using my human experience of 60 years and my professional one of 40 years. This is not a book intended to save the world, but to build a better City of Anthropos.

It has been written by a bricklayer.

Table of contents

List of illustrations

Part One

The concept of Entopia

1. Ecumenopolis

The Inevitable City of the Future

The realistic view of the City of the Future accepts that it will be a global city. This does not mean that it will cover the whole globe — only a very small part of the globe can and will be covered[1] — but it will be a system of human settlements encircling the whole globe, made up of several types of cities and other settlements of all types interconnected into broader urbanized areas like the ones we today call megalopolises. It will consist of parts with very different densities ranging from very high to very low, and of continuous built-up areas as well as separate areas interconnected by several types of transportation and communication lines.

This global City of Anthropos is the Ecumenopolis[2] or the city of the inhabited globe. At night we can get a general picture of it, because on a global scale the lights give us the best picture of the total system created by Anthropos (Fig. 1) and properly transmit to us the notion of the very different densities that such a city has. We will gradually see how this happens in smaller scales, starting with the smaller ones and finishing with the structure of the whole system. Ecumenopolis, or the global City of Anthropos, consists of all possible types of human settlements, from the smallest and most isolated ones and including hamlets and villages, towns and cities, metropolises, megalopolises and eperopolises. In the past, however, a village or town was in complete isolation in relation to the big city; in the future they will form all together one urbanized system — the system of Ecumenopolis.

After clarifying the notion of "city" which includes all human settlements, we have to clarify the notion of "future". One basic reason for the great confusion we are in is that we do not specify what we mean by future, and thus there is no way of understanding each other. The future I present here is not tomorrow morning — by then the only possible change will have been in the mind of the reader. Nor is it simply a few days, weeks, months or years. The future begins now and lasts over a few generations, up to the year 2121, by which time Ecumenopolis will have reached its maximum dimensions, and then a few more generations up to the 23rd century by which time Ecumenopolis may have the best quality that Anthropos has ever dreamt about.

It is clear that I speak of a maximum of a few centuries because beyond this the future may be completely unpredictable, especially because of the huge unpredictable changes which science and technology may bring on this globe. I thus wish to make very clear that I am not speaking either of the impossible changes of tomorrow when we cannot demolish existing buildings even if we have the financial and technical means, or of a future as distant as 40 billion years when some physicists expect the inevitable collapse of the whole universe when it will turn into "black holes".

If there is any doubt about the inevitability of Ecumenopolis I will remind the reader that the same doubts must have existed in the minds of the hunters when farming was invented and some people started speaking of the creation of villages and much later when people conceived a new city, like Theseus who conceived Athens, at a time when most farmers still thought of the villages as the only natural settlement. Even a few centuries after the creation of the city of Athens, Aristotle had to defend it as a natural phenomenon[3] and this proves that the human mind does not easily and quickly accept great and radical changes in the system of human life, although it accepts any small-size technological invention like photography or television immediately.

If we do not set goals there is no hope of ameliorating the system of our life. New needs and new scientific and technological progress will cause the city to acquire some new and better parts. But as a whole it will become worse and worse. The overall concept of the proper solution is our only hope as long as it combines the idealistic and realistic view and can become our goal.

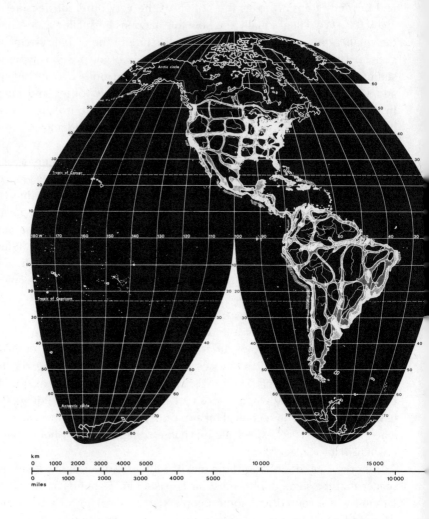

km
0 1000 2000 3000 4000 5000   10 000   15 000
0 1000 2000 3000 4000 5000
miles

1.   **Ecumenopolis at night**

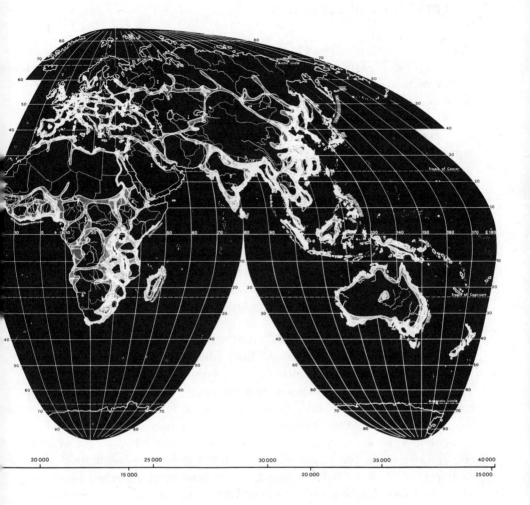

The principles of dimensions

Doubts are a natural reaction to such a big change and thus I will explain why Ecumenopolis is inevitable. It took us fifteen years of research work at the Athens Center of Ekistics to find Ecumenopolis and to justify it; this work has been presented from 1961 on in a series of documents, articles and addresses as a challenge for objections and comments. The conclusions are presented in the book *Ecumenopolis: the Inevitable City of the Future*[4] which is a short presentation of a great number of research efforts. What I present in this chapter is only the very general conclusion drawn from this long and hard effort.

Ecumenopolis is inevitable and can be predicted because in creating his settlements Anthropos has always been guided by five basic principles[5] which have not changed since the beginning of his history. Anthropos himself has not really changed basically for at least 40,000 years and not at all for the last 10,000 years and is not changing today. This means, as scientific research has proved, that he will not change in the future we are speaking about. His principles will not, therefore, change either. In this way we can predict how Anthropos will act in developing his settlements and thus we will gradually understand what is inevitable and what is not.

The location and the basic dimensions of Anthropos's settlements have always been defined by the first two of the five basic principles.

The first principle is the maximization of Anthropos's potential contacts (Fig. 2). This means that when a hunter searched for a cave, he selected the one giving him more chances to get water from a river, wood for his fires, stones for his tools and which would be as close to the animals he hunted as possible. When he became a farmer, he built his home as close to the land he was cultivating, and to water, wood, etc. as possible. As an urban dweller he had to be close to sources of food, water and wood, and also as close as possible to a larger city where he might sell the pots he produced and where he might buy some other products. When he created larger cities he selected locations increasing his choices of communicating with wider areas, and thus he preferred the coastal sites or sites on navigable rivers, etc. There is no case where a successful and surviving settlement has not been guided by this principle.

The second principle is the minimization of the effort and energy required for the function of any settlement. This is why hunters' bands could not exceed 100 persons: this would have required a much larger territory to find enough animals, and this meant they would have had to walk for weeks to find enough food. This is also why villages did not exceed 1,000 persons, as farmers could not walk more than one hour to their fields every day in order to save energy for cultivation. In the same way the size of towns and cities was also defined and all sorts of roads and other networks were created. People do not climb over a hill if there is a valley near by they can use instead (Fig. 3).

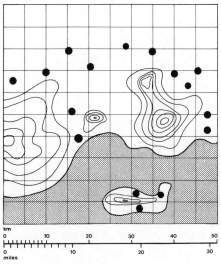

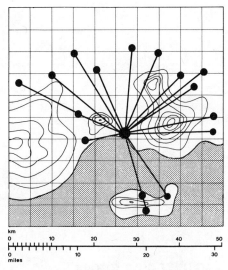

given certain conditions in a certain area

Anthropos will select the location which allows a maximum of potential contacts

2. first principle: maximization of potential contacts

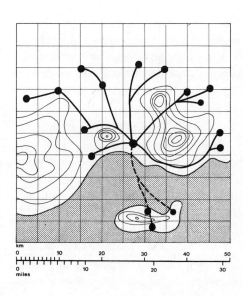

at a minimum of effort in terms of energy, time and cost

3. second principle: minimization of effort in terms of energy, time and cost

The changing forces

Because of these principles we moved after 1825, which we consider as the birth date of the contemporary settlements[6], towards metropolises and megalopolises. In the future there will be more and more metropolises and megalopolises which will form eperopolises and Ecumenopolis. The reason for the change is that, although guided by the same principles, Anthropos now deals with new forces in terms of energy and technology, economy and organization and thus the global container is increasing its capacity and can support an increasing population.

The population increase to date and the most probable increase in our future (always under the assumption that no unpredictable change takes place) shows that we are in the middle of a population explosion (Fig. 4) which will slow down and lead to a levelling off of the present population of 3.8 billion to around 20 billion by 2150.

The corresponding change in the global economy demonstrates that although the average per capita income is today $423 it has enormously increased since the pre-industrial age and will reach at least $12,000 by the 22nd century by which time it may again level off as it did quite some time after the agricultural revolution (Fig. 5).

Such changes are based on a continuing increase of energy production and consumption, which in spite of the present oil crisis will continue going upwards (Fig. 6) especially in the 21st century, by which time both nuclear fusion and the use of solar energy will have been realized and thus a much easier progress will be possible. No pessimism is justified since we must remember what people could predict before the invention of the steam engine and the use of mineral oil. Technology, which is definitely progressing, is leading towards new possibilities in this field of energy which influences many of Anthropos's activities.

4. **the present population will level off by 2150**

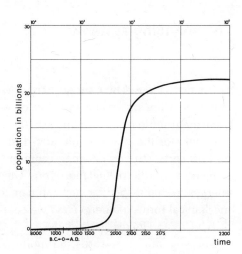

5. **average per capita income will increase enormously until the 22nd century**

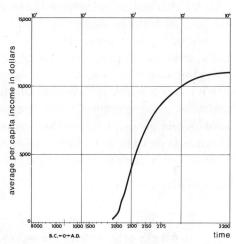

6. **global per capita energy consumption will continue to increase, especially in the 21st century**

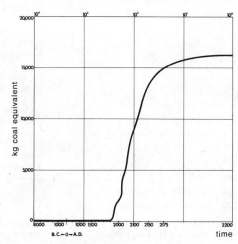

9

The changing systems

The activity altered by energy changes which directly influences the human settlements is the increasing mobility of Anthropos who created and lived in his
permanent settlements for almost 10,000 years simply by walking and very seldom
(and only for those who could afford it) using the power of the horse to ride or
pull his carts. The real change came in 1825 when the first railway carried passengers in northern England. Thus we moved from a uni-speed city (human
energy) to multi-speed cities (human, railway, motorcar, airplane, and other
mechanical forms of energy) and we continue to move towards a greater number
of vehicles and increasing speeds.

Once we moved towards the multi-speed city, the conditions of human settlements changed completely and new systems of life were created. Where in
the past settlements always consisted of isolated built-up areas in territories
covered by farms or forests (Fig. 7a) they were gradually interconnected (Fig. 7c)
and in this way new cores were created (Fig. 7d) and Anthropos moved from the
notion of isolated built-up areas to the notion of areas interconnected (Fig. 7e)
into broader and broader systems. In this way the change was, is and will be
continuous even in settlements not increasing in population, but with increasing
incomes and energy, because these increases give people the chance to move
far out or to move in from outlying cities and villages and our settlements become
more and more complex systems of life.

7. **from a city of pedestrians to an urban system**

● built-up areas
— paved road
▬ machine transportation
⚟ 10-minute kinetic field
✖ overlapping kinetic field
• a new center is created
•— directions of easier traffic

a. in the past we had small isolated cities of
pedestrians

b. which grow in concentric circles without
touching each other

c. when machine transportation began, people
started moving out of the cities

d. until they had moved out so far from two
neighboring cities that they created a new one
between them answering the needs of people
coming from both cities;

e. this new center of growth

f. led to new connections with other cities, and an
urban system was born.

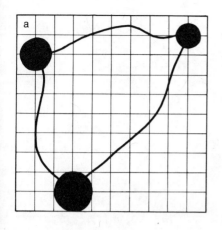

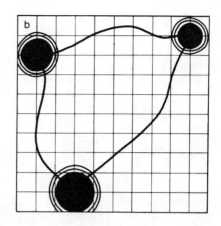

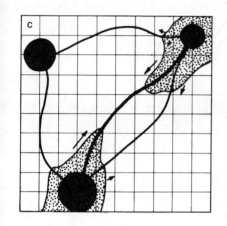

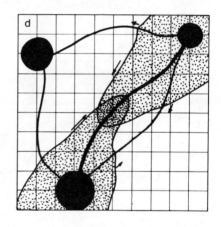

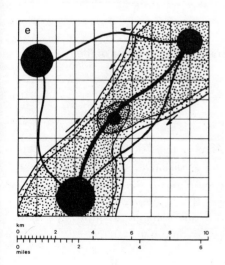

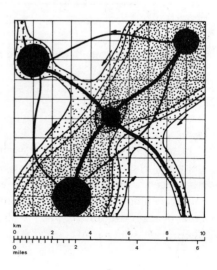

km
0   2   4   6   8   10
0   2   4   6
miles

km
0   2   4   6   8   10
0   2   4   6
miles

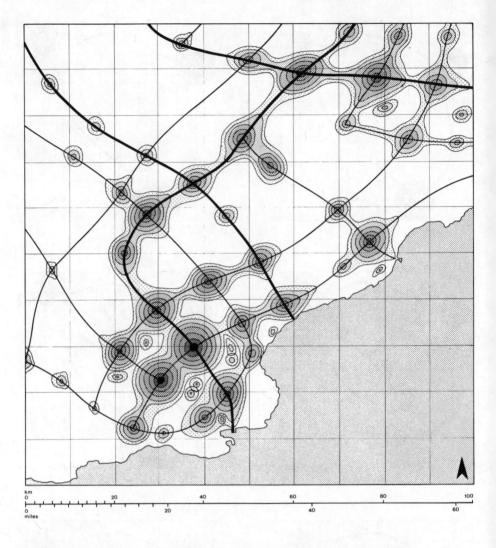

km
0   20   40   60   80   100

0   20   40   60
miles

8.   **our settlements become more and more complex systems of life**

In this way we can see how we moved from systems of isolated human settlements, even quite often within walls, lying at distances of many kilometers
from each other towards completely new systems of closely interconnected
human settlements, which grow continuously. This is the great change from the
polis or static city of the past, to dynapolis[7] or the dynamically growing city of
the present, which leads from a single city towards an urban system (Fig. 8).

12

The changing dimensions

The result of changing mobility and the formation of new systems is two-fold. First there is the immense growth of the built-up areas as we can see in the case of London which was probably the first modern city, having around 1800 a continuous built-up area containing one million people. Now, following the multi-speed systems, London has reached around 10 million. In the four phases of the evolution of London's central built-up area, we see how the city begins as a system of one core and several unconnected parts (Fig. 9a) and ends up as a continuous built-up area (Fig. 9d). What is now only central London was a system of

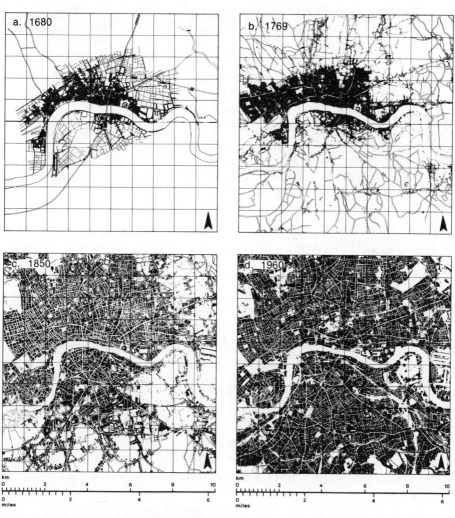

9.   evolution of London (England)

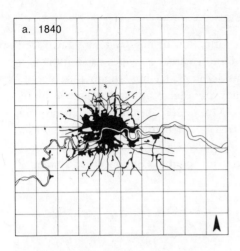

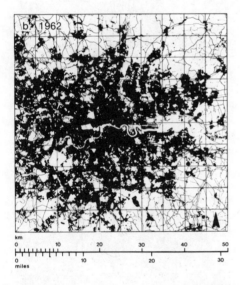

10.   evolution of London (England)

many settlements 200 and even 100 years ago. In this way we moved from the city to the metropolis which has a very densely built-up core.

The same phenomenon appears later in a much larger scale. We first examined a typical size of a total territory (built-up and cultivated) of an average town or city, that is 10 × 10 km (6 × 6 mi.) and saw how it turned into a built-up area. We now turn to London again, but in an area which is 25 times larger, that is 50 × 50 km (30 × 30 mi.) and we see that what happened in the smaller area from the 16th to the 19th century now happens from the 19th century onwards (Fig. 10).

The changes are huge in terms of dimensions.

The second result of changing mobility and formation of new systems is that the city is no longer limited to the built-up areas, as we had thought so far. Today the built-up area is only a small part of the city, existing from ancient times to our days. The real city is the whole territory within which people move every day. This always had a radius of about 5 km (3 mi.) corresponding to one hour's walk for Anthropos. We can see that even London was limited to such an area up to the 19th century (Fig. 9) until the machines came in and the radius increased continuously. In this way we now have people moving daily far beyond the former territory of their cities and reaching other cities where they work, are educated, entertained, etc. An example is Syracuse, New York, U.S.A., (Fig. 11), where some people even move daily towards the cities of Rome, Utica, etc.

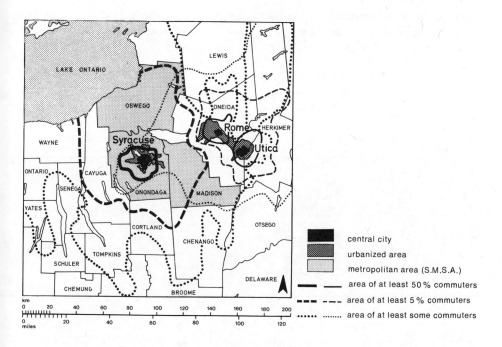

11.   Syracuse, New York (U.S.A.), 1960

Even this scale is not yet sufficiently large to demonstrate how far out the real city is. A specific case is the study of the commuting fields of eleven American cities (not the largest ones) which shows how far people were commuting in 1960 (Fig. 12). The record was then 127 miles in Albuquerque, N. Mexico, but the continuous increase has brought us now to about 150 miles.

In the same way we can follow the second result of the great changes: in specific cases like Detroit, which is no longer limited to the city itself (Fig. 13) as it was 150 years ago, nor is it limited to the urbanized or the metropolitan area but covers a much larger one as people move daily between all cities, townships and villages that we see on this map. Anthropos has moved from the typical township of 10 × 10 km (6 × 6 mi.) of 150 years ago towards areas which are several hundreds of times larger. In this way we moved from metropolis to larger Daily Urban Systems (DUS).

In such a way we can safely predict that the increasing dimensions and mobility which brought us from a city area included in the 10 × 10 km (6 × 6 mi.) frame to areas requiring a 500 × 500 km (300 × 300 mi.) map, will unify the megalopolises such as the northeastern megalopolis of the U.S.A. already analyzed by J. Gottmann[8] and the Great Lakes Megalopolis[9] (Fig. 14) which is already creating systems connecting parts like Chicago with Milwaukee in the North or Cleveland with Akron and Pittsburgh in the South and will be connected into a complete system in one or two generations. In this way it becomes clear how we move from larger Daily Urban Systems (DUS) to megalopolis.

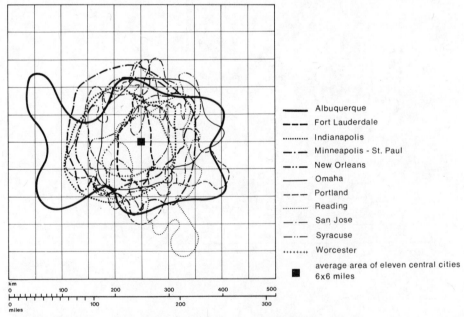

Legend:
— Albuquerque
— — — Fort Lauderdale
·········· Indianapolis
—·— Minneapolis - St. Paul
—··— New Orleans
——— Omaha
— — — Portland
·········· Reading
—·— San Jose
—··— Syracuse
·········· Worcester
■ average area of eleven central cities 6x6 miles

km
0   100   200   300   400   500

0   100   200   300
miles

12.   commuting fields of eleven American cities in 1960

16

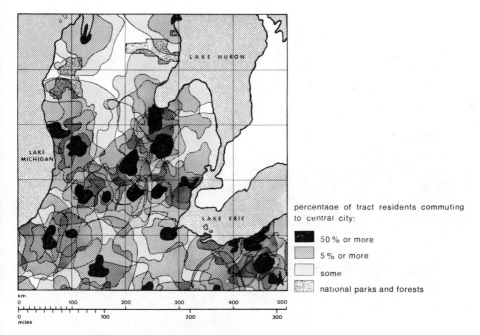

percentage of tract residents commuting
to central city:

■ 50 % or more

▨ 5 % or more

☐ some

▨ national parks and forests

km
0   100   200   300   400   500

0   100   200   300
miles

**13.   Urban Detroit Area (U.S.A.), 1960
the daily urban systems are no longer confined to the city or the metropolis**

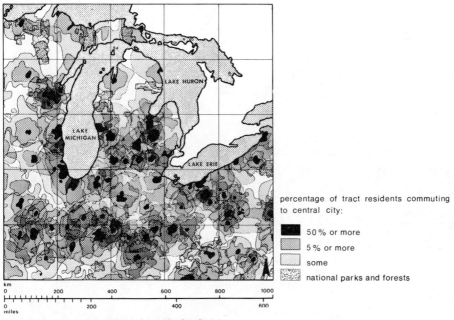

percentage of tract residents commuting
to central city:

■ 50 % or more

☐ 5 % or more

☐ some

▨ national parks and forests

km
0   200   400   600   800   1000

0   200   400   600
miles

14.   Great Lakes Megalopolis (U.S.A.)

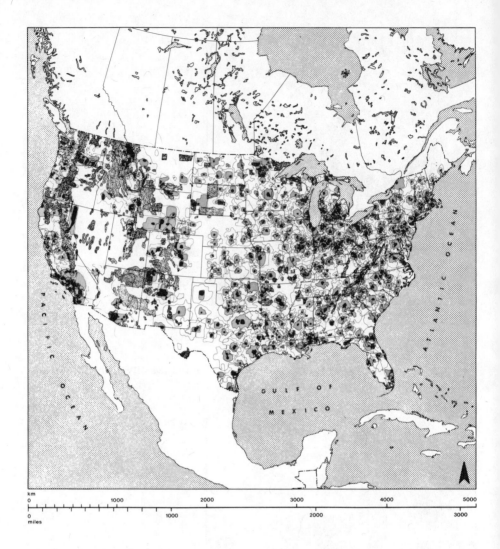

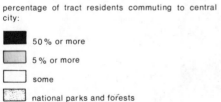

percentage of tract residents commuting to central
city:

▮ 50% or more

▨ 5% or more

☐ some

▥ national parks and forests

15.   the emerging urbanized continent, or eperopolis

18

When the megalopolises of the U.S.A. take shape in the northeastern part, in the Great Lakes region, in Florida, in California, etc. then we will gradually begin to see the emerging urbanized continent or eperopolis (Fig. 15) which will become a part of Ecumenopolis. In this way Anthropos will have made one more step towards the last human settlement which is the global Ecumenopolis in terms of dimensions of human settlements (Fig. 1).

Conclusion: Because humanity has entered a new era of science and industry, Ecumenopolis is as inevitable as the village after the agricultural revolution. The changing systems and dimensions of human settlements lead to a completely new global system.

2. The great danger

The changing quality

To speak about the dimensions of our cities is not enough. We know very well that our cities grow, but they are also in a big crisis. We have to be realists and recognize that this crisis exists on a global scale. We all suffer today in our large and growing cities, but we do not know why and thus we cannot solve our problems. Suffering from a disease does not mean that we even understand its causes. We should not think that there is only one kind of suffering such as we hear and read a lot about in the high-income countries, because there are more people who suffer even more in other parts of the world. Suffering in cities is really a global problem, and I cannot mention any city which does not suffer a great deal in its own way. It is true that we begin to protest against social problems and this is natural: every disease causes cries and screams from those who feel the pain; and these infected parts become swollen and painful and suffer more. We even cry in the streets about our diseases. This is a good sign, because if we do not develop higher temperatures and fever we will not recognize the existence of the real disease and there will be no hope for any cure. Do not mothers cry when their children are seriously ill? Do they not call for doctors? Thus quite often, especially when we are rich, we call on surgeons to help us and they cut through our cities as much as they can. But surgery is not always a cure, especially if the surgeon is not also a general practitioner or if he has not asked the advice of a wise doctor. Too many surgical operations have made the situation worse in many of our cities. They have increased the social problems, they have spoiled Nature.and they have harmed the whole system of life. Because of growth of population, income and energy and because of the disease in the central city, our cities first grow all around in a disorganized way, like a cancer eating-up the countryside; and then also in towers which create many additional problems for the city and eliminate all our existing values. Thus our cities change and suffer more.

This situation will continue with our growing settlements because we are not prepared to face their problems either in central cities or in the countryside both in high-income or low-income countries. The problems will be many, beginning with economic ones (our cities are not economically conceived at all) continuing with social ones (people in the past were equal in the streets and now only those with motorcars are in control), with political and administrative ones (a great confusion of where we belong) and many technological ones (like pollution by machines) and cultural ones (like loss of existing human scale).

The trends of increasing dimensions will continue and this means all existing problems will be multiplied in an enormous way. It is time that we understood that Ecumenopolis was really born in 1825 as a result of science and technology and we are halfway towards its completion in terms of dimensions. But if it is leading us towards such a crisis why don't we stop it? We simply cannot, anymore than we can reverse the law of gravity. We have no way of reversing the two principles that guide Anthropos towards the formation of Ecumenopolis.

I hear one remark often: "But in the past the same principles kept us in smaller cities with less problems". I can answer it in the following way: the problems of today did not exist in the cities of the past, but most of them had other problems, particularly of health and safety, which we usually forget. Second, if we insist on returning to the cities of the past I have only one method which I have proposed to several governments[10]; but it has always been rejected. It consists of two approaches as follows: my first was to kill all the scientists and all the engineers in one night, and to close all the universities so that no new minds could be trained to develop new technologies. This was considered to be unreasonable. Then I suggested that we should build high walls around all the cities of the world, and paint all the urban dwellers red and all the rural dwellers green, so that every night the police could chase all the rural dwellers out of the city. This may sound like a joke, but emperors and tyrants have tried it in history, and they have failed. In modern China, it is stated that every October they have to send out of Peking over two hundred thousand people who have entered the city without a permit.

We can close this discussion in a very clear way: the Ecumenopolis *is* inevitable. The present trends demonstrate that there is a very big danger in it: the creation of very bad conditions of life if there is no action for a better city. There is even a prediction that, "a baby born this year in one of the 50 largest cities in America has a 2% chance of being murdered"[11]. Our great mistake is that we ignore and overlook this danger and thus instead of preparing for Ecumenopolis so that it happens in the best possible way, we let it happen in the worst one.

This is our failure: not Ecumenopolis, but our complete ignorance of it. Its dimensions are inevitable but who said that larger settlements have to be worse than smaller ones? There is no reason why a larger system should be worse than a small one, any more than an Anthropos should be worse than a mouse or an elephant worse than an Anthropos. Dimensions are not connected with efficiency of the system; they simply make it more difficult.

The reasons for quality change

There are many reasons why people, guided by their two principles, swarm the large cities where quality of life has been lost. The one basic reason that explains all losses of quality is the great confusion created by the huge change of dimensions and systems taking place at such a great and unexpected speed that Anthropos does not understand its meaning, does not take the necessary measures and suffers from future shock as Alvin Toffler defined it[12]. Because of these changes Anthropos has greater choices, but lives in a system of greater complexity.

To understand the changing complexity which has an impact on every aspect of life and every element of the city we should follow the evolution of an area of 100 × 100 km (60 × 60 mi.). When this area was inhabited by farmers only (Fig. 16), the territory covered daily did not exceed 20 sq. km (8 sq. mi) and the number of all possible human contacts did not exceed one thousand. When the first towns were created (Fig. 17) the area was increased to 100 sq. km (40 sq. mi.) and the possible contacts reached many thousands.

After 1825, when the railway joined the human settlements, the territories covered daily increased enormously (Fig. 18) and the possible contacts reached tens and hundreds of thousands by special connections in certain directions.

Gradually more and more railway lines were created and the overlapping of kinetic fields created more complex systems (Fig. 19) without any great increase of territories (as long as speeds did not increase), but with greater increase in possible contacts. The result was a new system of much greater complexity.

Then came the automobile and later the airplane. By 1925, that is one hundred

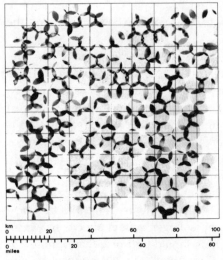

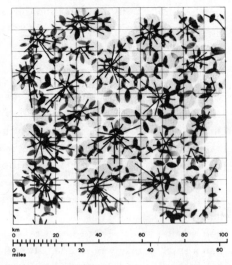

16. area inhabited by farmers only

17. area with farming and the first towns

22

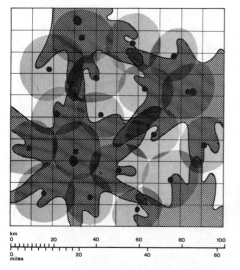

18. territories increased enormously due to railway

19. overlapping kinetic fields create more complex systems

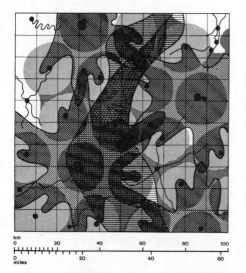

20. new means of transportation mean that people move in all possible directions

21. continuously increasing complexity

years after the railway was developed, people were moving in three revolutionary ways, and no longer on prearranged lines but in all possible directions. The result was a continuously increasing complexity (Figs. 20, 21) in every respect.

This is the main reason for quality change: whereas in the past Anthropos was used to deal with certain forces and a limited number of people within a limited natural and man-made environment and he could either be adjusted to it or — in very few cases — escape from it, he now deals with so many forces which change so quickly that he cannot find a way for adjustment and balance and escape no longer gives him the choice of better human settlements. Even the islands of the Pacific have lost their virginity through booming tourism.

The principles of quality

When we see this failure of Anthropos to face the new complexity and create quality we ask how he achieved it in the past.

When we understand Anthropos and follow his evolution we find that he is not guided only by the two principles (see p. 6) of coming together with others in order to maximize his potential contacts (first principle) and minimizing his efforts (second principle). While doing so Anthropos understands that he needs some protection from big pressures. The third principle is to optimize Anthropos's protective space. When speaking to each other people stand at the proper distance as defined by whether they like each other or not, how loudly they speak, whether one smells, etc. (Fig. 22). If a person sees a criminal he increases his distance. When building his home he tries to avoid the noise of the street. When building his village or town he does it on a hill if there are enemies around or in the middle of the plain if there are none (Fig. 23). In this way Anthropos increases his safety, his happiness and his freedom to live longer and develop better. His civilization lives longer and moves ahead.

The conflict created by the overplay of the first two principles with the third one leads to additional principles. Coming together is not enough for happiness and safety. There is a need for continuity of safety and happiness. Anthropos's fourth principle is therefore to bring a balance between the elements of his settlements: between Nature, Anthropos, Society, Shells and Networks (Fig. 24). How else could his village or his city-state survive without enough areas for food production, forests for wildlife, hunting and timber? How else could he be happy in his home, road or neighborhood? In this way he increases his safety from his enemies, but also avoids elimination of his own natural resources and traditional values.

All four principles are very important, but one may lead in a different direction from the others and thus the most important principle arises: leading to balance and harmony. This is the fifth principle of balance between the other four (Fig. 25). Anthropos has always been guided by his four principles, but the situation was constantly changing — he was a hunter, a farmer, a cattle-breeder, a merchant, a craftsman or a leader. The dangers from Nature were always different in winter or summer, and from his fellow men, etc. Sometimes defense was more important and sometimes commerce and industry, or culture and religion. In this way he managed to survive and to develop civilizations by

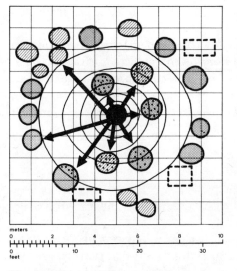

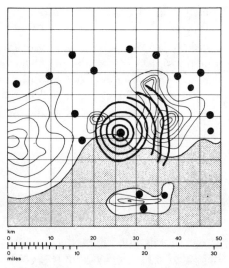

meters
0   2   4   6   8   10
0   10   20   30
feet

km
0   10   20   30   40   50
0   10   20   30
miles

22. third principle: optimization of Anthropos's protective space when he is alone

23. third principle: optimization of Anthropos's protective space when he builds his settlements

- ⬤ Anthropos
- ⬤ Nature
- ⬤ other elements
- ▬▬ Shells
- ▬▬ Society
- ▬▬ direct human contacts
- ▬ ▬ other contacts

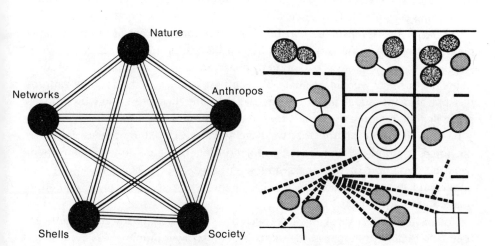

24. fourth principle: optimization of the quality of Anthropos's relationship with his system of life

25. fifth principle: optimization in the synthesis of all principles

25

adjusting all his principles into a system conditioned by his permanent and temporary needs.

If there is any doubt as to the possibility of a balance being developed between four principles which present differences and even conflicts, such as between minimization of energy (second principle) and protective space (third principle), the answer has been given by Heraclitus: "the fairest harmony springs from difference"[13] and by the examples of so many successful villages and cities of the past which we admire.

Evaluation of quality

It is a very difficult task to evaluate quality as it is very complex and can be seen, measured and evaluated in many ways.

We should not forget that in the usual exchange between people, quality depends on the person who is speaking and on his own real objectivity, which is quite often questionable. In a Gallup Poll report it is mentioned that 51% of Americans believe that unidentified flying objects are real[14]. We should never forget that a scientific approach intended to serve Anthropos needs an objective measurement. If, for example, we study the city in terms of the fourth principle of balance between the five elements, we can describe it not as an ideal city (Fig. 18), but as it really is (Fig. 26). In such a general way we can look at the whole situation on the basis of the five principles that guide the human settlements and we can proceed to the evaluation of any situation. This can be done on the basis of the satisfaction of Anthropos as an individual, or even better by the additional factor of equality between individuals as it is not enough to have an average person satisfied since there is a distribution of people among many unequal groups. The average may be satisfactory for some but not for very many people. We have to be sure that all human beings, no matter what their social status, race, religion, sex, development phase and health condition, have equal rights. In this way we can evaluate both the satisfaction of the average Anthropos but also the equal rights between all humans to express their own needs and only then measure the results for the whole system (Fig. 27).

Beyond the static picture that we have seen, we can study the evolution of the forces created by Anthropos (population, energy, etc.) and compare them with the evolution of happiness and safety (Fig. 28). In such a way we can understand the alternatives which exist for the future and we can be guided in our action for our city.

Conclusion: because of the unexpected changes leading towards Ecumenopolis, the quality of human settlements is getting lower in many ways, but there is no proof that this loss of quality is inevitable. Ecumenopolis is inevitable because of the first two principles, but its quality depends on Anthropos's ability to follow the other three principles.

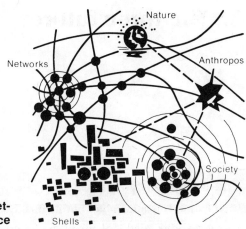

26. **the five elements of human settlements are now out of balance**

principles	satisfaction of average Anthropos	equality among Anthropoi	result
first			
second			
third			
fourth			
fifth			

□ increase
in relation to present

▨ decrease
in relation to present

■ high decrease
in relation to present

27. **the fulfilment of Anthropos's desires in terms of satisfaction and equality**

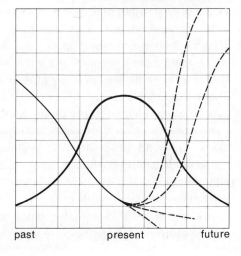

── rate of change of quality

━━ rate of growth of forces

28. **evolution of forces created by Anthropos and of happiness and safety**

past   present   future

3. The three futures

The desirability approach

Ecumenopolis is inevitable, but its quality depends on Anthropos's ability. Now we must clarify what is really desirable for Anthropos. It is clear that his desires are expressed by the five principles, and that the first two change dimensions and systems. How can we understand the meaning of the other three and how to serve them?

Any effort to define what is desirable for Anthropos is very difficult and most confusing. In the past people spoke mostly of happiness, but now their attention has been turned more to "quality of life". There are many efforts made for the clarification of this term, but even when I read some of the best ones[15] since every author presents his personal view and there is no agreement on the meaning of quality, I cannot draw any conclusions. When I study some official statements such as the declaration on the human environment submitted to the Stockholm Conference in 1972, I still find no clear agreement about what we mean when speaking of happiness or quality, about environment or human settlements. It seems that this is a phase of a great confusion we are in.

I have personal views on how we can get out of this confusion by creating a systematic approach for the system of our life[16] but this is another subject and I will not deal with it here as it is of a more general nature than our subject.

This confusion is not only related to our subject of cities. It is much more general and covers every aspect of our life, especially since the Second World War. By the middle of our century, mankind, and not only a few intellectuals as before, started to open its eyes to many phenomena, such as a global view of many problems like famine or war, to the existence of a whole universal cosmos and to new problems created by expanding human knowledge or the expanding population. Because of such an explosion of knowledge the view of our world is not always right and not at all total. We make many mistakes as when we call our whole globe a village, which it is not, as it has no single characteristic of a village, either in dimensions or in conditions of life. Our globe is a system which is nine and ten times higher in scale of order and complexity as we can see from the ekistic logarithmic scale[17]. Even from the point of view of communications the globe is not the same as a village, because in the village every one can speak and transmit messages to everyone else, but to transmit messages throughout the globe you have to be in power or to pay a lot. Let us clarify these confusing issues in our minds.

This confusion can also be seen in the arts, for example, where many able people are experimenting in many ways, as in music, for a new type of synthesis such as a computer-produced one. The similar phenomena, futurism and cubism in painting, started half a century earlier and were followed by many corresponding expressions up to the present where painters like Jackson Pollock transmit an image of extreme confusion. By now there is no single sector of human life, economic, social, political, technological or cultural where we do not witness a great explosion as we can see in Figure 29, demonstrating how a city is broken by the explosion. It is quite clear that we have many benefits from it, and this is why it has to continue[18]. But we suffer from it and this is why we have lost the cultural synthesis and balance of our systems of life which existed in the past. We need only remember that when a system, especially a physical one, is balanced this does not mean that it guarantees equality to all people. Balance is one thing and justice is another.

This great confusion does not yet allow a clear definition of desirability, but we must proceed and clarify our views on this question in order to define the road we will follow. In this respect we can clearly see the existence of three futures as represented by our present knowledge and efforts. These are the futures of the bad city or dystopia, the non-feasible city or utopia, and the desirable and feasible city or Entopia[19].

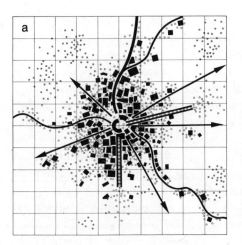 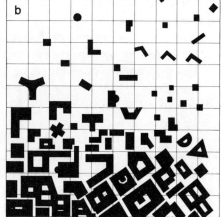

29.   the city is broken by the explosion of forces

Dystopia or the bad city

This future is the result of the continuation of present trends and means a real disaster for Anthropos. There is no doubt that because of the explosion we break and destroy the values created in the past. We know this and we are beginning to protest. These values are deep in our hearts but we do not respect them in actual practice. There is a saying in Japan that "we would like to grow old and die in Kyoto", but at the same time multi-storied buildings are being built in the old part of the city which loses its value. There is a reason for this failure: we think that the value is contained only in the appearance of the old parts and that we can design more fashionable ones. But the real value of many older parts of cities is that they represent the human scale and we cannot abandon it unless we want to turn into ants or bees. It is characteristic that we are studying how Anthropos may some day return to where he came from and live in the water. Is this not a sign of a broader confusion which leads more and more towards a bad city?

Some people state that the reason we continue moving towards the bad city is technology, but the truth is that we have achieved a lot through modern technology for our cities. Never before did Anthropos have such good means of transport as the modern motorcar or any such well-built, well-heated or cooled, well-connected and served houses. The technological progress is huge. When we place all these extraordinary achievements together, however (Fig. 30) we can see where we have failed: by bringing together all the elements of progress into a meaningless and inhuman system of life. I present this view of the city at night because one of the things we forget is that electricity has brought a very strong fourth dimension into our cities. During the day, when we are very high up, and do not hear the noise (although we do receive a part and suffer from it) we see a three-dimensional city, but at night it becomes a four-dimensional one. The three-dimensional jungle that we build is really a multi-dimensional one which does not at all serve many of our needs.

Anthropos, home, human scale and peace have disappeared, as we can see at night from a multi-storied building. We cannot see people, but only buildings and machines with continuously changing lights. Why do we believe we can become human if this is the message that we receive? Why do we believe that children growing in such a city can look at our world in a human way?

We should not forget that Anthropos began to develop as a special animal when he moved out of the jungle and into the savannah and that the continuation of present trends leads again towards a jungle. Such a solution will bring us into the city as children see it now (Fig. 31)[20]. This will be the result of a continuing explosion without any control. Sectors will progress, but over all there will be a real disaster for the City of Anthropos. Some scientists who predict disasters by the 21st and 22nd centuries really have this in their minds: progress in many ways but without overall guidance[21].

30. progress has created a mean-ingless and inhuman system

31. the city as seen by a child

Utopia or the non-feasible city

This is the future that most "experts" talk about today. Some consider utopia to be the city of dreams by confusing it with eftopia (the good city), but they do not know what good city means. Others propose some ideals like *Walden Two*, but they do not mention that this escape to small cities is an infeasible solution as it is against the first two principles of Anthropos.

Most of these efforts of our era, since confusion started, prove that we do not understand the real values of the past and the achievements of Anthropos, and we try to create many things in our cities which do not serve our human needs in a humane way. We only have to look at most of the proposals for the cities of the future or look at what we create on many occasions and will understand how Anthropos is forgotten. I do not need to mention all our problems in human settlements as everybody suffers from them, but I can mention some which are not yet understood.

Proposals for the cities of the future are by now unbelievable both in terms of feasibility and desirability. Up to a generation ago, people were at least proposing utopias of escape from the suffering city which had a certain value and quality like *Walden Two* by B.F. Skinner or *Island* by Aldous Huxley[22]. The problem was then that such utopias concentrated on quality and forgot the first two principles guiding by necessity to larger settlements. They created the problem of unrealistic solutions but they gave the proper image of quality and this was a definite contribution justifying the saying of Oscar Wilde "a map (of the world) that does not include Utopia is not worth glancing at, for it leaves out the one country at which humanity is always landing. And when humanity lands there, it looks out, and seeing a better country, sets sail. Progress is the realization of Utopias"[23]. Now the situation is tragic and this proves that we have reached the maximum of confusion. People propose that we settle into great moving machines replacing our cities or in aerial clusters in space or inside pyramids in the desert or floating islands. These proposals can no longer be called u-topias or ef-topias (desirable cities); they are the real dys-topias (non-desirable cities) which manage also not to be feasible. What happens to Anthropos inside these machines and huge pyramids? Nobody explains it. And why do we present them to the public in our museums and praise them when we know that Anthropos can never build them except at a cost 10 to 100 times higher than normal? We are really confused and this is expressed also by some efforts made to give prizes in architectural competitions to designs which do not serve Anthropos at all.

This is not the only aspect of the confusion created by these new proposals. It is very good that we cannot afford to pay for these cities, because if we build them Anthropos will suffer as never before. In an environment which may consist of beautiful rooms and homes in a huge pyramid the life of Anthropos will be tragic, because we will be deprived of any possibility of walking in the street and meeting people and interacting with them.

There are similar proposals for the creation of cities consisting only of multi-story buildings, or skyscrapers which do scrape the sky, but do not serve Anthropos, as is beginning to be understood now[24]. This has already begun and is even worse when some people try to turn the whole elevation of such buildings into a great mirror which presents many other views of the city and thus confuses the mind completely by the continuously changing images. We cannot hope to remain quiet in a city if we hear unbearable noise, and it is very clear by now that we suffer so much in our cities we get completely confused and thus try to find solutions of a different kind — forgetting what Anthropos has learned after thousands of years of experimenting in building human settlements. The great mistake is that we try to build single projects, buildings and settlements and not human settlements.

It has become clear that what was called in the past a utopia now prevails in the minds of many "experts" and it is really a dys-utopia, a both bad and infeasible city. I attack the first notion, but as the second proves that this city will be never built, we should not waste time and energy on it. It is much more important to concentrate on the dystopia of the first future that is under way and being built at great speed.

Entopia or the desirable and feasible city

This is the third future which must become our goal. If we are realists we can see two major possible roads for the future of the City of Anthropos, since the utopian one has been eliminated. The *first* road is to let only the first two principles guide Anthropos as happens today. In such a case we will have an Ecumenopolis of very bad quality, even worse than the present situation in megalopolises such as the northeastern American and the Japanese megalopolis.

The *second* road is to let all five principles guide Anthropos as happened in the past in those settlements which were successful and we admire. Ecumenopolis will then be the very successful human city.

This last statement demonstrates what is really happening today. As we are in an explosion, we are guided by the first two principles only, but we begin to feel the problems of this limited guidance.

In this way it becomes clear that the road we have to follow is the second one. We must be guided by all five principles, and thus we will be able to create better human settlements than in the past since we now dispose of greater forces. Our failure is that we forget all principles. If we now open our eyes we can see clearly the road leading to an Ecumenopolis which is a feasible and desirable city.

We can be optimists and believe in our city because we found Anthropos our great master and we decided to follow his principles. This demands a realistic approach, that is to let the explosion continue as long as Anthropos needs it, but instead of letting it get out of control (dystopian future) to bring it under control, to guide the explosion and understand it better. This is the road to Entopia, the feasible and desirable city.

The goals of Entopia

Once we have selected Entopia out of the three futures to be the realistic and inevitable city, we have to define the goals of Entopia, our desirable and feasible city. As the city defines in many ways the future of Anthropos, its formation has to be directly connected to him. Though a city has to be adjusted to geography, topography etc., these forces condition it, but not its goal.

If there is any question as to how important the impact of the city on Anthropos really is and if we are not to be lost in the general but vague statement of Churchill, we shape our buildings and our buildings shape us, we have to turn to biology. From it we learn that organisms do have inherent tendencies to evolve in fixed directions regardless of the environment, but that "The most promising clue seems to lie in the interrelationship between organism and environment and not in one or the other of these alone. This functional interrelationship is adaptation, one of the major features of evolution of life"[25]. In our case of the interrelationship of Anthropos and city we speak of extra-organic adaptation which "adjusts the individual to the physical, psychological, and economic world. It allows him to survive in spite of the unfavorable conditions of his environment"[26].

Entopia must be the city which helps Anthropos to proceed to an extra-organic adaptation for his own benefit. Whether it also helps in the long run for an intra-organic adaptation is beyond the frame of this study and of my capacities.

The big question is how can the city help Anthropos for his own benefit; that is, what is the main goal of the entopian city? From history and from what has been said and discussed, my conclusion is that the goal of the city is:

To make people happy and safe as Aristotle has defined. But the goal of the city is also: *To help people for human development* as we must add today because Aristotle was speaking of Anthropos living in a static world and therefore happiness and safety were the only satisfactory goals. Today we live in a changing world and we have the great task of helping Anthropos to develop in a human way so that he does not adapt to an inhuman city and suffer from it, but develops in a way enabling him to control the situation and adapt the city to his basic need to remain human and develop in the best possible way. In *Anthropopolis: City for Human Development*[27], we explain this third goal and all its aspects which are usually forgotten in their relation to space, creativity etc.

There is though a fourth goal which is so important that it has to be stated separately as a fourth goal. It is the goal: *To help people to be equal* as we do not speak only of an average person but of all mankind and we must be sure that we do not work for one Anthropos, but for all. This means that the city must also be the city of people of equal rights, or Isopolis[28].

It becomes clear that Entopia has the four goals of making Anthropos: *happy, safe, develop humanly, have equal rights.*

To reach our goals we have to define the following points:
— What is going to happen in any case?
— What do we want to happen?
— What is best for us, to be optimists or pessimists?

The first point means that we have to be realists. Imagine talking to some hunters about 10,000 years ago, when farming was first developed, about their future settlements. The older ones would insist that they would remain in their caves forever while women and some youngsters turning into farmers would very clearly say that they would settle in the plain in the middle of their fields. This is how their villages were born. Some thousands of years later everybody would only speak of villages, but a few merchants and a priest spoke of a town which was not only created, but also became the center of all the villages.

The time has come for us to understand the effect of the revolution created by science and technology for our settlements, and face them in a realistic way. This is definitely our first obligation and if we try to avoid predicting the predictable because something unpredictable might occur, this is clear cowardice.

The second point means that after clarifying what will happen in a realistic way we must be clear in our minds what we wish to happen. Science and technology cannot and should not be stopped as they serve Anthropos in every possible way. The question is how we want things to happen and towards what end. Another obligation is to clarify in our minds what we really desire our city to be. How can we create an airplane if we do not define its carrying capacity, speed, safety, etc? But we still try to speak of cities without clarifying what they have to achieve as well as their specifications.

The third point is whether we should be optimists or pessimists when facing the realistic and desirable future. The answer depends on us, on our character, on our decisions and on our courage. If we are pessimists our future will be definitely worse — no pessimist can ameliorate situations. If we are optimists our future will be definitely better, provided that we are also realists. The pessimists see our cities in the future with more machines, more pollution, more crime, more, more, etc. and they are not wrong, because if we do not act in time, something like this will certainly happen — any city will be controlled by machines and pollution by 1984, and by the year 2000 it will be completely inhuman in every respect. If we are optimists we can definitely create much better cities, not only better new cities but also improved existing ones. As a builder of 40 years experience I am completely convinced that if we are pessimists we condemn our cities and there is no hope for them.

My optimism is not only based on my personal experience but also on the long human experience which includes admirable cities like Teotihuacan, classical Athens, 15th century Peking, Renaissance Florence and many others created by Anthropos. In the same way we must remember that biologists like René Dubos clearly tell us that "the symbiotic interplay between man and nature can generate ecosystems more diversified and more interesting than those occurring in the state of wilderness"[29]. This interplay has been very successful many times in the past in the many plains and hillsides we now tend to destroy because of the present revolution. But this interplay can definitely be changed and I completely agree with the great historian Arnold Toynbee that our century will be remembered for "having been the first age since the dawn of civilization. . . in which people dared to think it practicable to make the benefits of civilization available to the whole human race"[30].

It is very clear now that if we want to reach our goals we need:
— to have knowledge and courage to predict the inevitable
— to have knowledge, courage and imagination to predict the desirable
— to be optimists about Anthropos's ability to solve his own problems.

We need knowledge, courage and imagination to predict what should and can happen to our cities with a realistic optimum for our Entopia. I use these forces here to help us deal with cities.

Out of the confusion

To reach our goals and to see how we can create Entopia we must escape from our present confusion. We must use knowledge, courage and imagination and we must clarify what we mean by happiness, safety, development and equality — which is a much broader and clearer goal than the quality of life we usually speak about — as well as we can. For, not only are we in the middle of a great confusion, but also the issue is a very difficult and complex one. We need only think that we relate quality of life today mostly to natural environment, but it is also very much related to segregation and integration, to social systems of life from isolated villages to over-pressured ghettos, etc. we can see the need to clarify the whole issue as well as we can.

This clarification means the imperative need to give an answer to the questions:
Who represents our interest.
What is our subject.
Where is our area of concern.
When are we speaking about.
How can we face the future.
This is the road I will follow from now on.

With such a road we have to face the problem of the following cities:
— the existing and suffering cities
— the existing cities, even if they do not suffer today
— the new cities to be created tomorrow
— the future cities.

This means that we must define the process of the evolution of all our settlements and not speak of some few settlements with a monumental appearance. The only monument of the future, the big cathedral that we need, is Ecumenopolis as an Entopia, the global City of Anthropos and not of the feudal lords.

In dealing with cities described above we have therefore to develop:
— therapy for the suffering cities
— preventive medicine for all, including the non-suffering cities
— proper conception for the new cities, leading to a prescriptive and creative method.

In all these efforts, we have to follow a diagram as in Figure 32. In such a case we define the most probable trend and the degree of probable changes. In the

feasibility	A	B	C
	continuation of present trends	easy changes	possible changes
desirability			
1 desirable	no need of action	evaluation in relation to A1	evaluation in relation to A1, B1
2 acceptable	need of action towards B1, C1	need of action towards 1	need of action towards 1
3 non-desirable	imperative need of action towards 1,2	imperative need of action towards 1,2	imperative need of action towards 1,2

32. feasibility and desirability

same way, we also clarify the alternatives from the most desirable to the non-desirable ones and the conclusions are clear: we see where there is an imperative need for action and in what direction. To scream against the many highways is not enough and to stop them is wrong. What we need is to turn them from undesirable to desirable ones.

It is time that we learned how to turn our attention towards what we can really do to ameliorate the conditions within our city and get ourselves out of the crisis we are in. This means to turn towards the desirable conditions of life and see whether we can create them as our entopian Ecumenopolis, that is with all of the existing human settlements as well as with all the new ones which will be parts of it.

4. Definition of Entopia

Who is the master?

When we build a city we must answer the most basic question as for any type of project: who is the master whom we have to serve? We must remember that we do not work for ourselves and the only master in a city is Anthropos with a capital A. It is necessary to clarify that we speak of the human animal and not only Man, the male animal. In Greek (an ancient inheritance) the word for Man is Anthropos but it comprises all human animals and has nothing to do with male or female, young or old, or any other partial expression such as homosexual, disabled,

Thus, I will not speak of any particular fashion, or for any locality, culture, civilization or any special type of Anthropos. These are variations of the basic trends serving Anthropos. The picture of the evolution of human trends does not contain any straight lines. As for any other biological phenomenon, an Anthropos's daily behavior, his blood circulation or his mood, the way he walks or rests, the way he dresses or designs, form a continuously changing curve (Fig. 33) as can be learned from many studies like *Body Time*[32]. There are periods when these fluctuations are small, and others, like our present time, when they are big. Individuals become my concern when I have a specific client, and then I try to understand as much as possible the existing variations in order to serve my master. In this book, though, I have only one great master, Anthropos, and I try to forget all the partial characteristics of any specific man, woman, or child and I concentrate on the basic characteristics of Anthropos only (Fig. 33), and the basic line which can serve everyone on our globe.

Who is Anthropos? In terms of art, architecture and city building we like to use Leonardo's presentation of him (Fig. 34) and it is a useful one, but it only presents his body. This has been done many times in many ways, from the prehistoric Anthropos in Val Camonica[33], the Indian square representing Anthropos, the ancient Greek measure of Anthropos, the medieval and Renaissance designs, Le Corbusier's Anthropos as a modulus, up to the medical doctor's and anatomist's presentation of Anthropos. All these designs are excellent as symbols but they do not transmit the message that real Anthropos is the center of a system and covers the central part with his body, a larger part with his body and direct feelings (the human bubble of Edward T. Hall)[34], an even larger one with his sense of smell and even larger ones with his hearing or screaming and with his sight (Fig. 35). In this way the real Anthropos is the center of a system of spheres which also reaches beyond what we see with our eyes, as it goes as far out as modern science allows, and even beyond when Anthropos imagines the whole cosmos (Fig. 36).

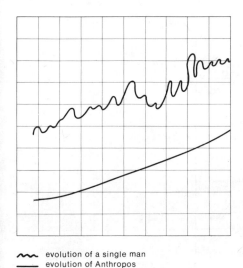

~~~ evolution of a single man
——— evolution of Anthropos

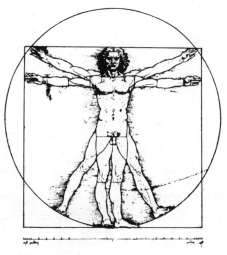

33. the difference between any individual and our great master, **Anthropos**

34. Anthropos as Leonardo da Vinci drew him

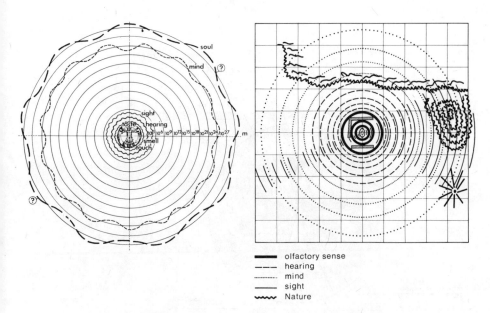

olfactory sense
––– hearing
.... mind
——— sight
~~~ Nature

35. Anthropos reaches beyond his body with his senses

36. Anthropos is the center of a system of spheres reaching out even to the whole cosmos

development phases	name of phases	ages
12	old age	76 - 100
11	early old age	61 - 75
10	real adulthood	41 - 60
9	middle adulthood	26 - 40
8	young adulthood	19 - 25
7	adolescence	13 - 18
6	school age	6 - 12
5	preschool (play age, strider, early childhood)	2.5 - 5
4	toddler	16 - 30 months
3	infant	7 - 15 months
2	breast dependence	0 - 6 months
1	prenatal or fetal	-9 months - 0

37.   the twelve phases of human development

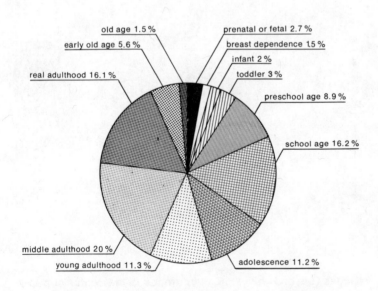

38.   the global population by development phases

Even when we speak of Anthropos only, and not of any race or type of person, we have to remember that Anthropos is born, grows and dies and during his lifetime he changes in size, dimensions and abilities continuously. During these periods Anthropos has different needs and we have to remember to take into consideration:

— development phases,
— disabled people (there are many),
— sex (there are many types).

The important variations of the needs of Anthropos are created by all these phenomena. I presented my conclusions on the first phenomenon, development phases, in my book *Anthropopolis: City for Human Development*[35]. I studied several types of development phases as presented by different cultures and experts and I came to the conclusion that we have to study Anthropos in at least twelve basic phases of his life (Fig. 37), from the prenatal or fetal one which is so often forgotten, to very old age. The global population can be analyzed by percentages in every phase (Fig. 38) which range from 2.7% in the prenatal to 20% in middle adulthood and 1.5% in real old age. No matter what the percentage is, all phases are of equal importance and no effort should be allowed to be implemented if any one of them has been forgotten.

For disabled people only special studies can guide us because of the very many types of disability.

As regards the sexual groups, I do not have any signs that the city should be different in its basic structure for any sexual type. Their differences refer more to fashions and detailed behavior which does not affect the general characteristics of the city as a system of life. This elaboration has to take place in every single case.

It becomes clear that we can now see Anthropos in a rational way and try to measure his relation to the system of life created by the city. It is clear that I speak of the rational relationships. This does not mean at all that there are no irrational relationships or that there will not be any. It seems that Anthropos needs them at times, but it is not my goal here to present them. This is another aspect of the City of Anthropos, but it has to be dealt with in a different way, mostly case by case.

I clarify here very strongly that I speak about Anthropos as our master in all phases of his life and his rational expressions and relations to his city.

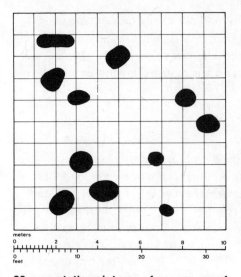

39. a static picture of a group of people as usually given in plans

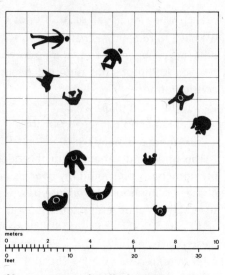

40. a more detailed picture of the same group of people

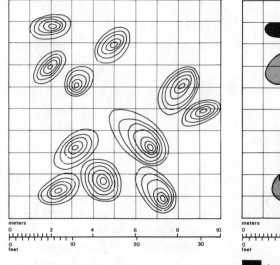

41. a picture of the bubbles of the same group of people

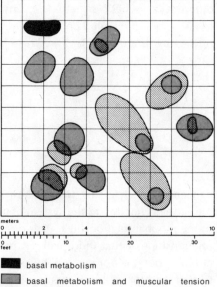

■ basal metabolism

▨ basal metabolism and muscular tension

▨ energy spent for muscular activity

42. a better picture of the same group is given by energy measurements

On the basis of what has already been explained I define that we must visualize Anthropos in space not in the usual artistic way, nor as a single body. We can present him showing the part of space that is covered by his body (Fig. 39) or by a better presentation of his body in order to transmit the message of movement (Fig. 40) or by his bubbles which demonstrate his movement (Fig. 41) and even better by the energy that people produce (Fig. 42).

When we see these pictures together we understand that the first one is a static one and presents people as though they were statues. The second one helps towards the understanding of the needs created by movement, but it is only the third one that demonstrates the space needed by any person whether sleeping, sitting or walking. Finally it is only the fourth one that reminds us that the two small children (lower right in Fig. 42) create the greatest problem because they play and run screaming towards their mother who lies on a sofa.

Only when we manage to combine and create the image of Anthropos as a moving system which has many needs and creates different situations in different ways, one expression of which is energy, can we be certain that we have understood him properly and can serve all his needs in space.

What is the subject?

Once we know the master, it is time that we clarify the subject also. I speak of the City of Anthropos and I also explain that it really comprises all types of human settlements which until 1825 were isolated from each other, but since then have become more and more interconnected into larger and larger urban systems. Some people think of the city as the built-up area only, others as the megalopolis and by now it really begins to be everything. Because of the great confusion around this subject I clarify the following points.

One: The city or polis which has become a dynapolis[36] is much more complex than anyone supposes because it consists of many dimensions: the three spatial dimensions, additional energy (see pp. 8, 9) the dimensions of time, of senses (Fig. 35), etc. and because of the present explosion which changes them all.

Two: When I speak of the City of Anthropos I do mean the whole system of human settlements, because the explosion unifies them more and more with every day that passes.

The next question is, then: What are the elements forming the city? Again we live in a confusion. When I ask anyone to give me an answer as to whether the city is: monuments, housing, shops, social groups, racial groups, individuals, highways, railways, factories, downtown, suburbs, parks, forests, universities, schools, churches, temples, etc. I receive many more answers than my questions or the words I mention.

In reality our city is a very complex organism consisting of all previously mentioned parts and many many others. We can understand it only when we classify these parts properly, as medicine classifies our complex organism by parts like head, body, arms, legs, etc. or by systems like the peptic, cardiovascular, nervous, etc. In this way we begin to understand our organism and later to locate our diseases.

In order to understand and remember the very complex organism of the city, we must understand that it consists of five elements: Nature, Anthropos, Society, Shells and Networks and each one of them acts on itself in a positive or negative way as well as on all the others (Fig. 43).

But if I ask people their view on widening a street in order to ease the traffic, the answers will be positive from the technological point of view, negative from the social and cultural one and will be deferred by political leaders at least until an economic study can be carried out. In this way we see that the city does not only consist of five elements but also depends on the five economic, social, political, technical and cultural forces (Fig. 44).

If the city consists of all human settlements and since we know they start with a single piece of furniture, room and house and end with the global city, of what units do we have to speak? What is our subject? The answer is very clear: our subject includes all the units of the human settlements from the smallest ones which are furniture, room and house to the megalopolis, the eperopolis or urbanized continent and Ecumenopolis. If there is any doubt about this we have to remember that we cannot study Anthropos unless we study all his parts down to his cells, because suffering may not be connected with broken bones but infection of cells.

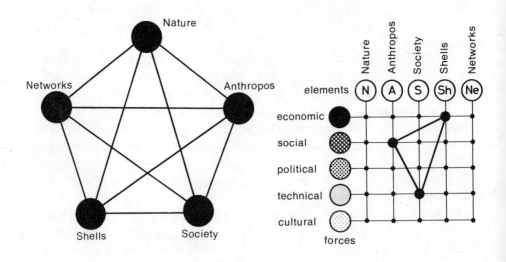

43.   the five elements of human settlements

44.   the five elements and the five forces of human settlements

To study the city systematically we have to understand that it consists of the following fifteen units and their corresponding populations[37]:

1. furniture — 1
2. room — 2
3. house — 5
4. housegroup — 40
5. small neighborhood — 250
6. neighborhood — 1,500
7. small polis — 10,000
8. polis — 75,000
9. small metropolis — 500,000
10. metropolis — 4 million
11. small megalopolis — 25 million
12. megalopolis — 150 million
13. small eperopolis — 1,000 million
14. eperopolis — 7,500 million
15. Ecumenopolis — 50,000 million

We can conceive the whole city as a system consisting of five elements, five forces and fifteen spatial units (Fig. 45). To demonstrate how difficult it is to cover the whole system, I experimentally prepared grids during some special symposia where experts spoke of the city showing what part of the city was covered by the discussions, and found that finally only a very small part of a huge grid was covered[38]. In this way we reach the point of understanding that our city is much more complex than we think and this is why we are confused. We have to proceed and clarify how we can face all its possible aspects in a systematic way.

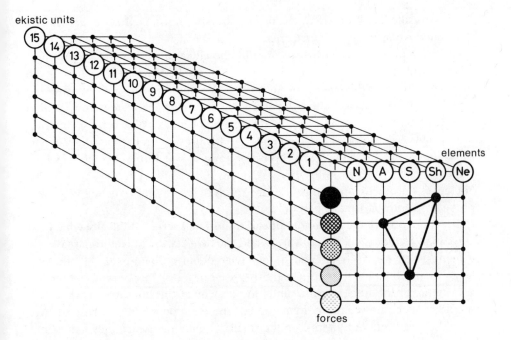

45. **the five elements, the five forces and the fifteen ekistic units make up the system of the city**

Where do we concentrate?

As the city is so complex we have to concentrate on very specific areas in order to again avoid the confusion. The first clarification is that unless we always keep in mind all five forces (economic, social, political, technical and cultural) we will make grave mistakes by forgetting either the feasibility or desirability aspect.

My position is therefore clear: on everything I propose I will take all five forces as first criteria into consideration as much as I know and I can.

I cannot leave any one of the five elements out. Even a room cannot exist for Anthropos if Nature, at least in the form of atmospheric air and oxygen, does not exist in it.

I therefore take into consideration all five elements in the following way. Human settlements are composed of different parts, from the parts created by Anthropos, like the densely built-up areas, to the parts where Anthropos has changed the flora and cultivates them to those not touched by him which he uses in many indirect ways, either by simply visiting them or only using the oxygen they produce. They are all parts of human settlements[39] but their character differs, depending on how much Anthropos interferes. In this sense we can divide the city into four major types of areas:

1. The natural areas or *Naturareas*.
2. The cultivated areas or *Cultivareas*.
3. The so-called built-up areas, mostly used by Anthropos, or *Anthropareas*.
4. The industrial areas or *Industrareas*.

Although my effort is always inspired by the city as a complete system (otherwise we will fail), in this book I will concentrate on the built-up areas, that is the areas mostly under the control of Anthropos, the Anthropareas and Industrareas, and their relationship to Cultivareas and Naturareas. My goal here is how to build a better city and not how to populate or administer it. Within these built-up areas I always consider all five elements, and I express them in their physical part of Nature, Shells and Networks. This is the physical structure of the city of which I speak. The master is Anthropos as an individual and as represented by his Society as a group of interactions and the result of his action in city building is the physical or Anthroposmade part of it.

The four types of areas cannot appear in the small scales of the city which has very small Naturareas and Cultivareas and thus we start with Anthropareas only (Chapters 6-9), we reach the Industrareas in larger units (Chapters 10, 11) and then when we reach the metropolis (Chapter 12) we can see all four areas together.

In terms of the fifteen spatial units the answer to the question of where we should concentrate is a more difficult one. There are people who advise that we should concentrate our interest on the small communities which they name anti-polis, or the opposite of the city, and others who always speak of the existence of the "invisible" city connecting the people by communications only. They are both wrong because the city can be seen in these ways and in many more.

As an example we can see how every person can now conceive his city. Some people conceive it as the built-up area (Fig. 46a), others as the area defined by administrative boundaries (Fig. 46b), but an urban dweller can see it as a much larger system (Fig. 46c), and a modern farmer as a complex system (Fig. 46d), within which the farmers and the members of their families commute. There are certainly many views of the city.

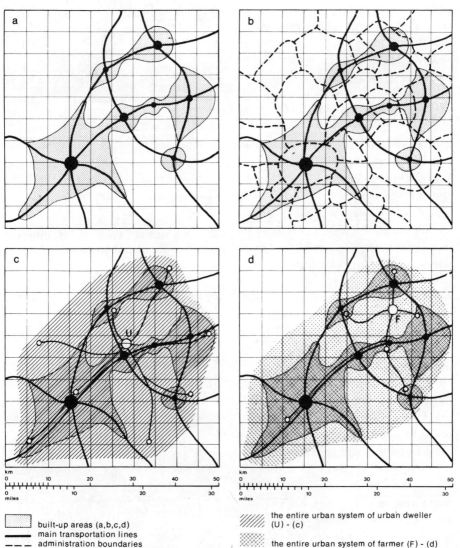

built-up areas (a,b,c,d)
main transportation lines
administration boundaries

the entire urban system of urban dweller
(U) - (c)

the entire urban system of farmer (F) - (d)

46.   several views of the "city"

We can understand how many more views of the city exist if we remember that Anthropos over the weekend quite often does not move in the same area as his daily movement, but further out and many people with a second home consider this broader area as part of the outskirts of their city. Many people also move farther out once a month and even once a year. In this way, our system of life or our city can be seen as a Daily Urban System (DUS) or a Weekly Urban System (WUS) or a Monthly Urban System (MUS) or an Annual Urban System (AUS) or a Lifetime Urban System (LUS). These systems or cities do not coincide (Fig. 47) for every person, but they are systems.

A different way of looking at the complexity of the problem of how far the city reaches is given by one of its social aspects, the institutions to which people belong. It is clear that any Anthropos has direct connection with his room, home, neighborhood, community, etc., but also belongs to institutions like family, club, church, professional or business organization, etc. The first connections are related to space, but this is not necessarily true for the institutions. If we superimpose them in space we can see that more often than not they do not coincide (Fig. 48). Thus the conclusion is clear: the city can be seen in very many ways in terms of space and area and we have to find the way to study it as systematically as possible, and to concentrate on those units which are important.

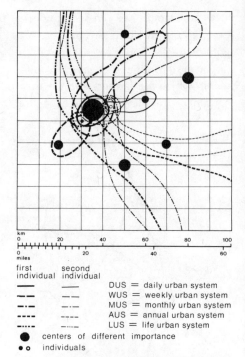

first individual / second individual

DUS = daily urban system
WUS = weekly urban system
MUS = monthly urban system
AUS = annual urban system
LUS = life urban system

● centers of different importance
● ○ individuals

47. the urban systems of different people do not coincide

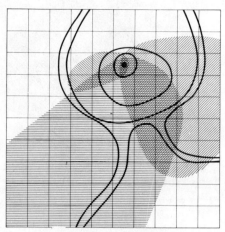

● Anthropos, house, neighborhood, and community are shown by continuous lines
▨ area of his club
▨ area of his church
▨ area of his professional institution

48. the "city" and its institutions

There is no way for anyone to concentrate on any single spatial unit for a very simple reason. No one lives any longer within one room, house or small unit. Even sick people have to be examined in hospitals and thus are taken out into much larger spatial units and centers. There are no more isolated monasteries and the number of people in prisons is gradually being reduced.

Looking at how much of our time we spend in the different spatial units (Fig. 49) we understand that 40% of our time is spent in our room, decreasing to a very small percentage in larger units[40]. But we have to remember that our life within our room depends on our home life and our satisfaction in it can be upset by noise or lack of facilities in the neighborhood. This means that life in any unit also depends on conditions in the larger one.

Every person has a direct interest in obtaining quality and satisfaction within the smaller units where he spends the largest part of his life but this is also true for the larger centers because his education, health, safety, etc., depend on much larger units.

The conclusion is clear: we have to deal with the city as a system of life consisting of all sizes of spatial units. If we do not, we will not be speaking of anything concrete and we will be lost in a jungle. When we speak of quality and desirability it is not the question of one unit, but of the whole system.

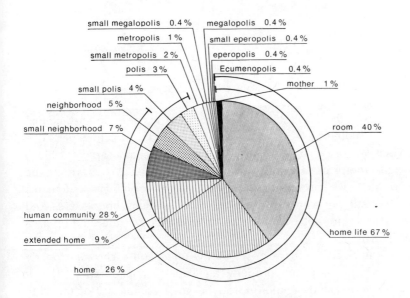

49. lifetime spent in different units of space

We have to deal with all the units of space which form the city in an equal way and I propose a systematic approach beginning in the next chapter. To make the task easier for the reader I will present the fifteen units (which is the proper scientific number) in ten chapters (6-15) by putting two units together in some chapters as follows:

furniture	ekistic unit 1
room	ekistic unit 2
house	ekistic unit 3
housegroup	ekistic unit 4
neighborhood	ekistic unit 5, 6
polis	ekistic unit 7, 8
metropolis	ekistic unit 9, 10
megalopolis	ekistic unit 11, 12
eperopolis	ekistic unit 13, 14
Ecumenopolis	ekistic unit 15

In this sense when I speak of city from now on I do mean every unit given above from the housegroup to Ecumenopolis because every one of us looks at his city in a different way.

In order to deal with these ten units in the proper way we must understand that they depend on each other very much, as each one forms the structural parts of a larger one. When we see a house (Fig. 50) we can see it either as a part of the block or as consisting of rooms or of rooms, furniture and a garden. When we see the built-up area of a city we can see it as a part of a system of human settlements (Fig. 51) or as consisting of blocks or of blocks, roads, gardens, houses, etc. And this is not all as these presentations are two-dimensional, but the built-up area is three-dimensional.

The conclusion is clear: we have to see all the units, and each one properly inserted into the larger one and properly built-up by smaller ones. This is ekistic synthesis, whose study demonstrates the great complexity of this situation because the laws of synthesis and the forces of each unit change from one to the other[41]. In this book I present the ten units by properly using my experience of ekistic synthesis.

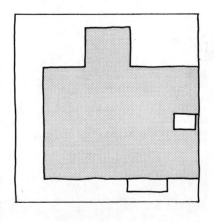

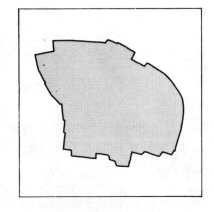

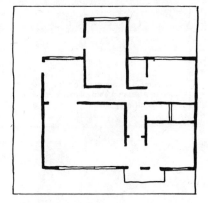

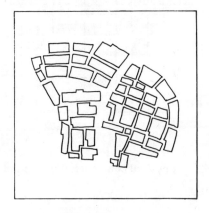

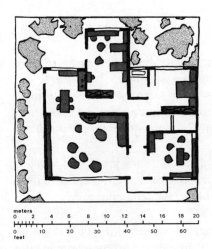

meters
0 2 4 6 8 10 12 14 16 18 20

0   10   20   30   40   50   60
feet

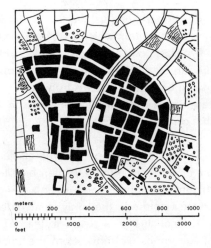

meters
0   200   400   600   800   1000

0   1000   2000   3000
feet

50. a house can be seen as part of a block, or of rooms, furniture and garden

51. a city can be part of a system of human settlements, or consisting of blocks, roads, etc.

ekistic unit	1 Anthropos	2 room	3 house	4 housegroup	5 small neighborhood	6 neighborhood	7 small polis	8 polis	9 small metropolis	10 metropolis	11 small megalopolis	12 megalopolis	13 small eperopolis	14 eperopolis	15 Ecumenopolis
scales in meters															
100,000,000															
50,000,000															5
20,000,000														5	
10,000,000												2	2		
5,000,000															
2,000,000												5			
1,000,000											2				
500,000															
200,000									5						
100,000															
50,000								5							
20,000										2					
10,000							2								
5,000						2,5									
2,000															
1,000				4											
500			5												
200															
100															
50		5													
20		2													
10	2														
5															
2															
1															
chapter	6	7	8	9	10		11		12		13		14		15

the numbers appearing on the grid indicate the relationship of each scale with the one directly smaller

52. physical scales used in each chapter

To properly understand the dimensions of the ten units we can study the physical scales within which we can insert them (Fig. 52).

One last point needs clarification: in dealing with the ten units do we start from the largest or the smallest one? Turning to the best synthesis that we can see, that of biological systems from cells to organisms, we learn that there is no single case where synthesis did not start from the bottom and move upwards. This is how the cell was created and how we moved from uni-cellular to multi-cellular organisms.

The same has happened with all human settlements: they grew from small to big at a certain rhythm. When people like Genghis Khan tried to speed up the rhythm and conquer and organize a continent in a few generations, they did not create a synthesis, they only created disasters.

The conclusion is clear: to lead to the proper synthesis of the desirable City of Anthropos we move from the smallest unit, furniture, to Ecumenopolis, the largest one. On the basis of this approach I will start with the furniture at 2 m (6.8 ft) and 5 m (16.8 ft), proceed to larger and larger scales to end up with Ecumenopolis at 50 thousand km (30 thousand mi.).

When is the future?

This basic question has already been answered, defining the inevitable City of the Future as the future in a few generations' time up to 2121 A.D. (Chapter 3). This is the future I will further clarify here. Not tomorrow morning. It is the whole process which is starting now in our minds, that will be expressed in a few years with the first models of furniture which will influence production in large numbers more and more. For houses and neighborhoods it will take longer as the larger the unit the more people are involved and it takes longer to realize it. Cities will take a generation and metropolises and megalopolises will start the process by the end of our century and realize their projects in the 21st century. By 2100 even Ecumenopolis can achieve its goals.

This is the realistic future I speak about. The reasons which will delay implementation, even if the decision is taken tomorrow, are related to the huge investment in many peoples' ideas, energy, money, legal rights and structures which exist in human settlements. Such are the real forces that people existing today will disappear in three generations, but buildings will last longer (Fig. 53) and even more so the facilities, rights of way, etc. The creative conceptions will decide the more distant future, provided we start them in time.

conceptions
rights of way
facilities
buildings
people

53. forces of the present as projected into the future

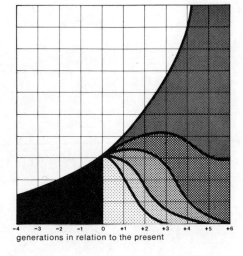

generations in relation to the present

On this basis, we can see the four basic futures we always deal with, the constant, declining, continuing and creative futures (Fig. 54)[42] and then connect them with the probabilities and desirabilities which exist (Fig. 55) and proceed to our predictions on Entopia.

Of course, I must clarify that when I speak of the four futures I am referring to the general and average situations of Anthropos and city in general. If instead of this we speak of a specific case, then there is also a fifth future, the unexpected one. The human may die, the house may be burnt and a whole city may be destroyed by war or earthquake. This again is the difference between general conditions and the single cases which are much more unpredictable than the general trends.

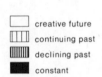

☐ creative future
▥ continuing past
▨ declining past
■ constant

54. the four futures of human settlements

generations in relation to the present

criteria / futures	probable	desirable	feasible
constant			
declining			
continuing			
creative			
total			

55. the four futures and the three criteria approach

54

The Anthropocosmos model

We have seen that our "City" consists of five elements, can be influenced by five forces and divided into fifteen spatial units, and all of them form a complex three-dimensional model (Fig. 45). But even this does not cover the whole situation because it leaves the dimension of time and the desirability and feasibility criteria out. When we add them all together, we reach a much more complete model of the city which consists of:

— elements
— spatial dimensions
— time dimensions
— forces
— criteria

as we can see in Figure 56. This is the Anthropocosmos model which covers our globe and if need be goes beyond it (ekistic unit 16 and more) to the Cosmos. We look at it on the basis of Anthropos's interests and not those of ants, etc. This is why it is called the Anthropocosmos model and guides our efforts and makes them systematic[43].

This is therefore the model of the city which creates the frame for the answers to so many confusing questions. If we want to face our problems and build the city we desire we must define where we stand on such a model and what we do for each of its units of interest to Anthropos. This is the task ahead.

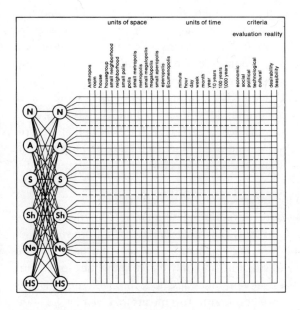

56.   the Anthropocosmos model

5. The road to Entopia

How we create

Once we have clarified our master, our subject and where and when we should act, we must clarify how we create our city. We have to be very careful about this point, because if we make mistakes we will not pay for them simply in terms of money, but with our own lives, since our buildings shape them, as Winston Churchill said. We cannot demolish what we built overnight in the same way as we can take the painting that we dislike out of our room. Building in a city means many commitments lasting for at least several decades.

We cannot allow any mistakes any more than medicine allows experimentation with new drugs on any individual unless there is scientific proof that they will not harm the patient. In medicine, before it became a science, the only approach was the witch-doctor approach. Every witch-doctor came up with new ideas, he spoke to the moon, he danced around the sick person and touched him with the bones of a fox and the feathers of an eagle — something like this now happens with our cities. People come up with "clever" ideas to build pyramids in the desert or artificial islands on the sea — they seem like magic solutions and some sick people pay attention to them. But no sick city has tried them — or will ever try them. The reason is that our cities are living organisms which are 10,000 years old and cannot be changed by magic solutions. They have to be helped to develop better, as every good physician or psychiatrist tries to help his patient.

This is our great task: to build better cities, by ameliorating the existing ones (therapy), by expanding the existing ones (development), and by creating new ones (birth) in order to prepare for ourselves a better life in the immediate future, to help our children and grandchildren achieve a much better life and to create an entopian Ecumenopolis where Anthropos can be happy, safe, equal and better developed.

To succeed we have to keep the following four very basic rules:

One: We have to know what our cities, or better, human settlements, are. We have to be very well informed about how they grow and why they are successful or not. We cannot speak of their form and appearance only as we usually do. We have to speak of their function and structure and only then of how they look. Our life is not limited to what our eyes see and much less to fashionable design. It is much more complex and much more important. This means that we have to learn the biology, anatomy, pathology and cure of human settlements and to develop the medicine for our cities. All these methods belong to *ekistics*, the science of human settlements. We say human settlements and not only cities, which are adults of old times but youngsters for our time, because real medicine starts with the prenatal phase and ends after the death, and the diagnosis of death, of the individual. This is what we have to create, the scientific approach to help our cities.

Two: We have to be creative when thinking about the future, not in order to impress public opinion, but in order to serve Anthropos. This means to imagine how we can ameliorate the human settlements created by Anthropos in all their parts or how we can continue the biological process by changes done in the best possible way. It is a step further, since in prescriptive action which decides our future we do not have to copy the past but to respect the principles and laws that we learn from it and ameliorate the situation. When we speak of creativity we need the overall inventive concept and then very special inventions, not for their own sake but for the sake of the improvement of our life.

Three: Beyond learning first and then thinking creatively, we must have the courage to act — human settlements are not created by Nature, in which case ecology would be enough, but by Anthropos following the principles and laws of Nature and of himself. Rules One and Two, are valueless unless we implement them in practice, both to serve Anthropos and to have him test our rules.

Four: We have to be very specific in every case as is a clinical doctor. What our cities need is a good medical doctor who can examine them, make the proper diagnosis and call the cardiologist, the surgeon, the psychiatrist, the physiotherapist, etc. and the nurses who can tell each specialist what his patient really needs and guide them towards cure and therapy by very careful steps for every dangerous symptom because each patient needs his own cure. Good medicine knows that the therapy depends on the patient, who may be allergic to some antibiotics and may be saved by some very old creams such as those made of zinc which have been used for centuries. We do not learn only from medicine the need to deal separately with each case, but also from biology, as Paul Weiss tells us: "The only scientific way to deal with adaptation is to get the facts for each case. Only after the facts are known is it possible to tell just how much of the adaptedness of a given phenomenon is due to inherited evolutionary prearrangements, and how much to direct adjustive interactions. This ratio varies greatly and unpredictably from species to species, from function to function, from unit to unit."[44]

The conclusion is clear, in order to succeed we have to:
— know our subject in depth,
— imagine its evolution in a creative way,
— have the courage to act,
— distinguish every single case.

In this way we can serve our master both as the global phenomenon of Anthropos and his city and as every single individual organism of humans and their settlements.

Towards specific proposals

To serve our goal I present in this book the solutions corresponding to all four rules in order to give the best global image, especially on the basis of rules One and Two, with only some few details of the third rule as this requires another big study for action, or of the fourth one as this requires concentration on very specific cases. I have applied all these rules in practice over the last 40 years and this is why, following the presentation of my general proposals (rules One and Two) I sometimes mention a specific example (rules Three and Four) not as *the* solution, but as one case out of the many existing on a global scale; that is as a single illustration of how the basic solution relying on the first two rules can be applied to one specific case by applying the third rule. I will not deal with any extreme case like spatial satellites or building in the polar zones or in the Sahara. I give the solutions that can serve Anthropos in any part of our globe, although in every place they have to be completely adjusted to local conditions.

What I propose has one basic characteristic: it is a part of the whole system of our life expressed in human settlements. I use ekistics, the science of human settlements, because Anthropos usually tends to create pieces of a whole system. This has been very well expressed by Paul Valéry, representing Eupalinos the great ancient builder who said: "Man, I assert, fabricates by abstraction, ignoring and forgetting a great part of the qualities of what he uses, and concerning himself solely with clear and definite conditions, which can most often be simultaneously satisfied, not by a single material, but by several kinds" and "The artisan cannot do his work without violating or disarranging an order by the forces which he applies to matter in order to adapt it to the idea he wishes to imitate, and to the usage he intends. He is therefore inevitably led to produce objects of which the whole is always a degree below the level of their parts."[45]

What I propose is a synthesis of the elements and the parts of our city.

The proposal is based on the proper application of all five principles and serves all five forces, as I will explain in the following section using one example for each force.

The proposal is then very specific in Part Two, with ten chapters, each of which presents one or two ekistic units.

From wasting to saving energy

The economic aspect is usually forgotten in city building because of the current economic explosion. The result is that the city becomes much more expensive in terms of energy, money, time, etc. and much more difficult in terms of person-to-person complete contacts. We now certainly have many more opportunities for contacts by several means, but the distance between people remains a reality. No matter whether we cover it by walking, driving, telephoning, supplying electricity, etc., when the distance increases we pay much more for it than we believe.

I use the example of how many cities are
still building houses next to each other in
the wrong way in order to demonstrate how
we have to change the situation and satisfy
human needs in terms of economic forces.
The solution I propose also satisfies many
other needs, such as social contacts, privacy,
etc. but here I emphasize the economic one
which is forgotten, although it is a very important one which is better understood when
expressed as energy.

The solution we need is to fill the gaps
between houses as these gaps do not serve
any human needs that cannot be served by
a wall and space which otherwise could be
used is wasted.

When houses are far apart, the corridor in
between is of no real use to anyone (Fig.
57a). Forty percent of the total space in the
whole globe is lost (Fig. 57b). The houses
have to be brought closer together as was
done in the past; this is necessary, but not
satisfactory in terms of construction, danger
from fire, noise, etc. (Fig. 57c). We need a
system of separating walls, saving 40 percent
of space, increasing safety from fire or attack,
increasing privacy, decreasing noise and dis-
turbance and serving better in terms of quality related to industrial desires (Fig. 57d).

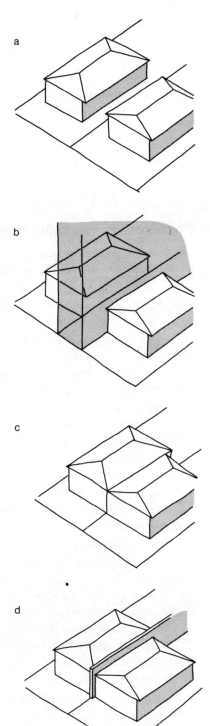

57.   from wasting to saving space

From social inequality to equality

The social aspect in city-building is now completely overlooked. In the past, people managed to create balanced cities where everyone had equal rights in the streets and in building their houses. The economy, the technology and the balance that people managed to create led, for example, to cities with houses of equal heights. Some few cities had one-story buildings, many two or three-story ones and those cities squeezed within walls or becoming too large moved up to five or six stories, with slight variations from part to part. Now many cities allow those who have large plots or special financial privileges to create skyscrapers while their neighbors remain down below. This is, among other things, a great social injustice.

There is an imperative need for a great change. This would be the definition that all citizens who own land do not own the sky and they cannot scrape it. They only own the space up to three stories high (10 m, 33 ft) and two stories underground (6.60 m, 22 ft).

The space above the third story (10 m, 33 ft) should belong to the community up to a certain height, to the city beyond the community's level, and to the nation beyond the city level, etc.[46] We cannot build the Anthropopolis by allowing anyone who can manage it to exploit space and create social injustices. It also has to be the city of equal people or Isopolis[47] as this is one of the four basic goals (see Chapter 3).

From the balance of the past (Fig. 58) we have been led to the great injustice of the present. Anthropos now spoils what he managed to create in the past by allowing some owners to rise above the city (Fig. 59). We have to create a new balance where only buildings belonging to the city, that is to all citizens, can rise above the others. In the future, there is an imperative need for social balance which is also the basis for a balance between Nature, Society and Anthropos. This will be the entopian Isopolis (Fig. 60). In this way we have both social justice and the symbolism that no single owner can rise above the others; only the common facilities of the City of Anthropos can and this can happen in a certain order.

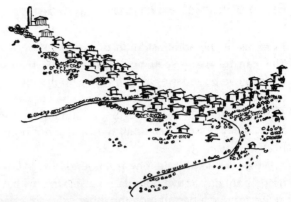

58. Anthropos has always created a social balance in his cities

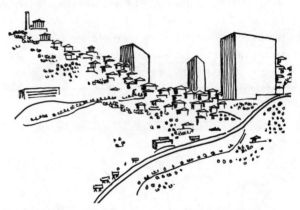

59. there is a loss of balance today in our cities

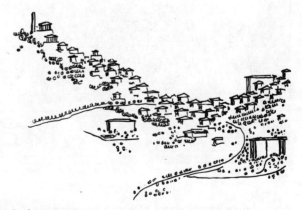

60. we must create a new balance

From administrative chaos to order

In terms of the administration of our cities we are in a really chaotic situation. This can be easily seen by placing on the map of your own city its own administrative boundaries as well as the boundaries of the authorities or companies for water, sewage, gas, electricity, safety, etc., as well as the boundaries of your own territories of interest beginning with infants and ending with very old people. There is no coincidence at all between these boundaries — everywhere we live in chaotic systems.

Where in the past the physical boundaries, like hills and rivers, were very often used as administrative boundaries also, we now have highways which cut the city in two leaving a part of it on the other side. In order to visit our former neighbors or to send police or fire services to serve them, we must go around for many miles.

In the future we badly need an administrative reorganization so that boundaries of all sorts coincide and this will help us identify where we are and how we can receive all possible services in the best and most economic way. This means that we have to remember that we are masters of our own room, together with our family of our own home and its garden and courtyard, with our neighbors of our neighborhood (why should the mayor of 5 million people decide about the fountain we want to create?) and so on.

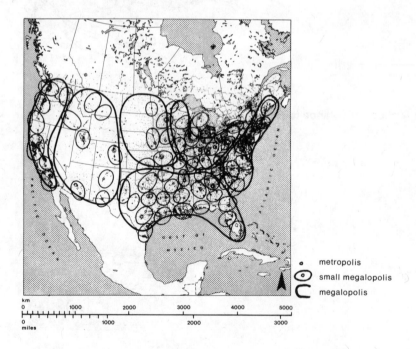

metropolis
small megalopolis
megalopolis

61.   hierarchical levels of urban America

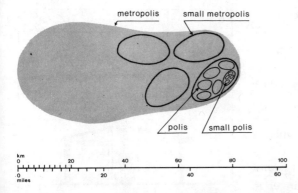

metropolis small metropolis

polis small polis

km
0   20   40   60   80   100

0   20   40   60
miles

62. hierarchical levels of metropolis

This means that we have to remember that our city now exists in many sizes. Looking at the U.S.A. we move from the federal city or megalopolis to the small megalopolis, to the present Daily Urban Systems, or metropolis, to small metropolis (Fig. 61), polis, small polis, neighborhood, etc. (Fig. 62).

This is the pattern we have to conceive and carry out at all scales. Every citizen should have much more freedom than today (as we will see) to move around and in order to help him achieve it we need the best possible organization of our city. This is our great task.

From technological disorder to order

We will be no more successful with the technological aspect than with the others if we speak of part of the city (like telecommunications where the progress is excellent) instead of the city as a total system. We need a very great change: instead of letting technology influence our city and our life by chance and necessity (to copy old Democritus who is now so much remembered by biology) as now happens, we have to guide it towards our goals.

To achieve this and influence the technologists on what our city needs from them, we have to tell them what the city is going to be and what we expect from them. This is one of the partial goals of this book, to tell the inventors and industry about our total goal and give them examples of what we mean in some parts and elements of the city. I cannot tell everything we need technologically in one book. What I will do is give in the following chapters a clear indication of what we need on several occasions from furniture to global transportation and how we have to develop it. I certainly do not describe all the technological advances of our future city because many are unpredictable even as concepts, but I give the frame of the radical changes we need.

I do not believe that we have completely understood what automation can do for us. One example is the "auto-mobile." It is not yet a real "auto-mobile" because it needs a driver to guide it by committing his whole human system (body, eyes, ears, hands, legs, etc.). We badly need the real "auto-mobile" where we can just push buttons for where exactly we want to go and then go to sleep or read and think while the "auto-mobile" takes us there.

We have to conceive the real revolution that real automation can create and face properly the many things that can be turned to automation. Not

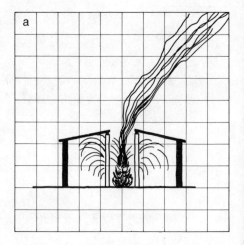

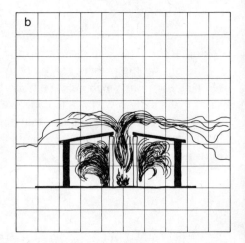

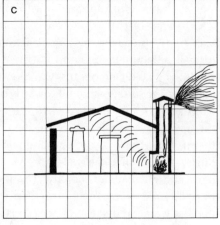

63. with his present technology Anthropos can solve many problems

a. one explosion begins
b. pollution follows
c. technology solves the problem

only liquids, but solids (beginning with letters and small packages) will move in pipes reaching our houses. There is no reason why later we will not receive everything by a bubble arriving automatically through special channels and bringing the new equipment we ordered.

For those who have become pessimists now because of the recent awareness of great pollution, I will remind them that the greatest pollution Anthropos has ever faced was the smoke from his fireplace until the day of the chimneys came (Fig. 63). Anthropos first allowed the invention of fire to pollute his caves and huts. Then the no-fire movement started and technologists invented the fireplace. We are now in a similar phase in our cities. Technology explodes and takes everything far out[48], and thus some people begin to turn against technology; but the only real solution is not to stop progress in the explosion that takes place now (see Fig. 29 and corresponding text), but to guide the explosion for the benefit of our cities (Fig. 64).

In the next chapters I will propose specifically some of the automated parts of the city, and to distinguish them from the ones existing now I prefix the word "auto." Thus, I will propose the auto-furniture versus the furniture we now have, the auto-mobile versus the motorcar we now have and others. Our city will rely on many auto-parts.

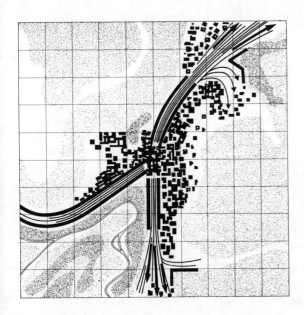

64.   our cities need guidance for their growth instead of the chaotic situation of the present and the "stop growth" slogans

From broken cultures to a human culture

The cultural aspect is completely overlooked today with the exception of the proper movements to save some older and still existing cultural expressions which, up to a certain degree is reasonably possible. It is true that many individuals try to create their own cultures in art, architecture, etc. but that is not a solution as cultures have never been created by individuals, even by very strong tyrants, but only by Anthropos. This demonstrates clearly that if we wish to help towards the creation of the new culture we need, we must help Anthropos save and express himself in the best possible way.

He has to save himself because some companies do not even remember his existence unless he is in a motorcar. One company advertises tires which throw more water on the sidewalks to make driving safer and the other presents cars running through old narrow streets without leaving any space for the pedestrian to survive.

In order to demonstrate how we have to achieve this in the city, I select here the example of streets which in the past were the corridors connecting people to each other, from babies to old and disabled people. This happened in a very natural way because Anthropos was the master of street and square; that is of all public spaces (Fig. 65). Now he is only a slave squeezed between machines and walls (Fig. 66).

The great change we need is the transition from the street of the present to two completely different types of streets, that is the human ones or hustreets and the mechanical ones or mecstreets (Fig. 67). We will see how this can be achieved later, but what is important now is to understand that the notion of street where Anthropos is completely mixed with machines has to be replaced by a system of hustreets and mecstreets. We cannot drink water when we mix it with petrol, and this is why we cannot remain humans when we mix with machines. If there is any doubt about the feasibility of this idea we have to remember that we used to mix water and sewage with Anthropos in his streets, but they are now separated in underground pipes; we also used to see all sorts of cables and pipes in the streets (Fig. 68) and on our walls, but we no longer see them. We start by mixing things until we open our eyes and separate them properly.

Towards an entopian synthesis

It now becomes clear that Ecumenopolis is inevitable and its quality depends on us. If we do not let it just happen, but guide it, Ecumenopolis can turn into an Entopia, the desirable and feasible Anthropopolis.

Ecumenopolis is now happening and brings its five elements into a great conflict, physically expressed by the lack of balance between them and by the great conflict between the four types of areas covering our globe. Where in the past

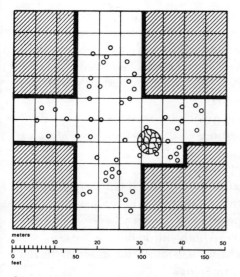

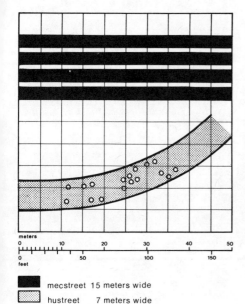

mecstreet 15 meters wide
hustreet 7 meters wide

67. we must create hustreets and
    mecstreets

68. Broadway, New York (U.S.A.),
    1887

we only had Naturareas and later also Cultivareas, which were closely related to Naturareas, we now have Anthropareas and especially Industrareas which invade and spoil the first two. This leads to disaster, but there is no reason for this to continue as their feasible balance conditions the quality that we need.

For this reason in the ten chapters of Part Two I will present, starting with room and ending with Ecumenopolis, the following:

— The five basic elements, that is Nature, Anthropos, Society, Shells, Networks.
— The four basic areas in which they are expressed, that is Naturareas, Cultivareas, Anthropareas, Industrareas.
— The interrelationship between elements and areas.

In every chapter, depending on the size of the unit that it represents, I will explain the elements and areas that matter most. For a room I have to discuss noise, but not in Ecumenopolis as it does not spread so far out. In a megalopolis I speak of Industrareas which do not exist in the neighborhood. In this way we can follow the basic characteristic of every spatial unit, form gradually the image of the total entopian synthesis and be guided in building Entopia.

Part Two

The parts of Entopia

6. The furniture

Ekistic Population Scale	Name of unit	Population range	Ekistic units covering this chapter	Kinetic field	Com. class	Ekistic unit
1	Furniture		░░░░░░░	a		1
2	Room			b		2
5	House	3 - 15		c		3
40	Housegroup	15 - 100		d	I	4
250	Small Neighborhood	100 - 750		e	II	5
1,500	Neighborhood	750 - 5,000		f	III	6
10,000	Small Polis	5,000 - 30,000		g	IV	7
75,000	Polis	30,000 -200,000		A	V	8
500,000	Small Metropolis	200,000 - 1.5 M		B	VI	9
4 M	Metropolis	1.5 M- 10 M		C	VII	10
25 M	Small Megalopolis	10 M- 75 M		D	VIII	11
150 M	Megalopolis	75 M- 500 M		E	IX	12
1,000 M	Small Eperopolis	500 M- 3,000 M		F	X	13
7,500 M	Eperopolis	3,000 M- 20,000 M		G	XI	14
50,000 M	Ecumenopolis	20,000 M and more		H	XII	15

The present situation

If we do not understand furniture we cannot understand the city, because we miss the understanding of room, house, block, etc. Anthropos started without furniture, sitting on the soil or on rocks; then he developed, as far as we know, several types of "furniture" through using carpets and floor mats to sit on and gradually sofas and beds — even for his dinners as in ancient Greece. Then he used chairs — perhaps they were first limited to kings and lords — but gradually they were used by everyone. In China, we know that this happened in their golden era, beginning in the South from the 7th century A.D. The time came when Anthropos was used to and basically had to sit on a chair, armchair, sofa, etc., made either of wood or stone, that is inflexible or very flexible as they were formed by piling many pillows even on an inflexible frame.

Today we are in the phase where we experiment with several types, ranging from very old to very new ones, harder or softer or inflexible and much more flexible ones.

Some of them will survive, but not all. On the other hand we are forgetting some pieces which were very useful, such as the adjustable rocking chair of bent beechwood (Fig. 69) which developed in the first half of the 19th century and was very much used until the first quarter of the 20th century, but has been almost abandoned today.

What happens today is a mixture of the past, as we admire or use furniture of the past either because of its esthetic or financial value, and of the desire for change which leads to all types of variations some of which are very good and others very unreasonable and only used because they are considered fashionable. The result is that we are in an area of transition. We will gradually move away from it because, for example, some of us like to sit on the floor for a change, but history and physiology have proved that Anthropos also needs to sit in a chair, armchair or sofa in order to relax his body.

If we look at the present efforts as experiments and avoid following them just because they are different and fashionable, we will learn what we need and what we need to develop in the future.

The big lesson so far is that we do not need only one type of furniture for sitting, but several in order not to become stiff or to have only standardized positions of our body and its movements.

There are several efforts being made today to develop appropriate types of chairs. An example are those "ergonomically" designed for people who work sitting in them long hours and there are others designed in a very simple way for those who will sit up to ten minutes in an airport, and others conceived as folding chairs to save space when they are not used. We could call many of these efforts for new types of chairs useful experiments in the big laboratory of our life. The same is valid for our beds, tables and shelves where many efforts are also being made which I can again call only experimental ones.

The conclusion is that we need many variations and we cannot have them all in our own home. This is our problem.

69.   rocking chair

The furniture of the future

The furniture of the future will serve all human needs in a much more efficient way than the furniture of the present. The basic criteria will be to serve:

— the body in the best possible way by giving it more choices,
— the muscles by not forcing them to work for what machines can do automatically, so that the body will exercise only on what it likes,
— the eyes by not overloading the brain with too many messages at the same time,
— the ears by not creating noises,
— the nose by not creating any smells from materials, paints etc.,
— the fingers by giving Anthropos the chance to enjoy what is touchable.

Some of the walls will be covered by auto-shelves which will serve many more purposes than at present. Figure 70 illustrates the auto-shelves as they appear at a moment of work when the room owner wants to look at the books (left), hear and read the last financial information through television (center), receive information from his office to compare with the official news (right of center) in special equipment printing this information, and compare all these with his notes on his auto-table (lower right) in order to take decisions.

At the same time he can push buttons to have his slides projected showing the inside of his village (upper left) and his family (upper right) as for some

70. the auto-shelves when the room owner wants to work and receive information

people such pictures give a better atmosphere at moments when their room has to turn into a workshop. In the upper right-hand corner is a sculpture from a previous era which reminds him of the era of explosion (20th century) which is now in the past.

After working hard and receiving all sorts of information, he decides to forget the present situation and go back to the era of explosion in order to understand better how people broke the ancient and older cultures and started experimenting for a new type of synthesis. To achieve this he pushes five buttons (Fig. 71 lower right) twice and this means the following: the first column (left) turns and takes the books lower and brings forward the sculpture which was behind them, the second column repeats the same movement taking the slide projectors down to bring another sculpture in. The third column turns the television set off. The fourth one repeats the process of the second and the fifth closes the auto-table and turns the inner light off. All the lower parts of the columns simultaneously receive special covers which present a Picasso synthesis, and the light now comes from the ceiling so that everything will appear in the same atmosphere.

The auto-shelves have changed the whole situation, and such a method leads to many solutions, as everyone can select the parts that he prefers for any occasion.

71. the auto-shelves can change the whole situation by bringing forward works of art

When the study of the past is over and the owner wants to relax he pushes the buttons again, but in a different way, and thus the past is forgotten and the television turns on. News is transmitted about life in his city, beginning with a few minutes in his neighborhood's public square where people meet to hear the new committee for preservation of the old square and its enrichment with new sculpture. There is no light in the room except for the ceiling being slightly illuminated from inside (Fig. 72).

72. the auto-shelves illustrate the present and bring forward the television set

It is late and the owner decides to go to rest, read and sleep. He pushes his buttons again (he can do this even from a distance with the small "auto-leader" in his pocket) and arranges the book shelves to turn enough so that the big professional encyclopedias and books go up and behind, and the fiction and history books come up — from pocket books to hard cover ones. The light is limited to these shelves and the ceiling keeps the previous slight illumination (Fig. 73).

73. the auto-shelves turn to reveal the fiction and history books

This is the end of the day. The owner is fed up with all the information he has received during the day (too much information is noise, as they used to say) and pushes the buttons again. He does not want to see and remember anything, so that he can concentrate on the poems he likes. He pushes the buttons and everything is covered by a beautiful color photograph that he took years ago in the most beautiful landscape he ever visited. He can now dream and be creative or go to sleep (Fig. 74).

74. the walls are covered by a beautiful color photograph

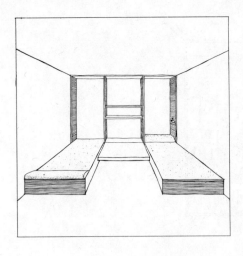

75. the auto-bedroom

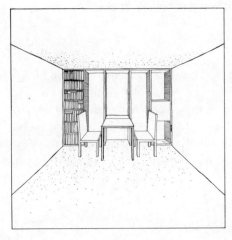

76. the auto-dining room

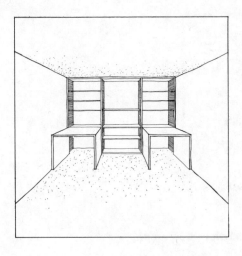

**77. the auto-room can be any synthe-
sis that you want**

The auto-shelves we have seen are normal ones with a depth of 60 cm (2 ft) in order to allow two of the 30 cm (1 ft) normal shelves to change places. There are cases, however, where people own much less space and cannot have special bedrooms or dining-rooms. In such cases they select the deep auto-shelves of 90 cm (3 ft) which can easily include the two beds we see here that come down by button pushing. This is the auto-bedroom. The beds come out with their cushions, as in the one at right, for normal lighting at reading time; or the cushions move (left) so as to allow one to see the special television programs where, by paying more, one can select high-quality programs at any time without any interruption. The small table comes out to serve dinner at night, and in the morning everything goes back and the wall can look like Figure 72 or 74. The quality is the same (Fig. 75).

In the same way, the dining-room is created with a table and sofas for four persons which come out, the central wall which opens with all its drinks, and boxes on the auto-shelves which move up and down to help people reach them.

Two more chairs can be added and the "dining-room" now serves six persons very comfortably or nine in case of need. This is the auto-dining-room which will be used for a maximum of two hours a day and then occupies only a small part of the total space. The economy of space is great (Fig. 76).

A similar wall with deep auto-shelves can hide a full office for two young students, who can have their tables, shelves, books, etc. in the wall opposite their auto-bedroom. In this way a room of 4.5 × 5.25 m (15 × 17.5 ft) can be both an ideal studyroom or bedroom without any conflict between the two, either in terms of space or of optical impressions. Or you can combine the auto-dining with the auto-bedroom or any other synthesis you need. You always need to be in a different environment depending on your goal of work or rest or anything else (Fig. 77).

The chairs will turn into auto-chairs for the same reasons that shelves turned into auto-shelves — for a better use of space and for one more reason. Anthropos needs stability and safety in his chairs and this is why he has so far developed them successfully; but he also needs flexibility because he cannot sit stiffly in one position. He has not been successful on this point and he has had to develop too many types for all his positions.

The chairs of the future will give Anthropos what he is missing, that is, changing furniture. Because of space availability and our needs, we cannot have all types for all our positions. So we will have the changing chair or auto-chair — adjusting to vertical standing, for eating, for breathing more easily, etc., to almost horizontal with arm rests to low, from soft to hard, from not moving to moving as in Figure 69; and all this will be achieved by pushing buttons.

The auto-chair shown here demonstrates how it can be used as a stiff chair for dinner (Fig. 78a), how it can be made softer by pushing a button which will increase the air in the cushions of the seat and backrest and extend a footrest for those who like it (Fig. 78b). When necessary the armrests can come up from below (Fig. 78c) and when a child joins the family at the table, it can use the same chair whose dimensions will be adjusted, both lifting it up and helping it to climb (Fig. 78d). In the same way small metal balls can come out and the chair will move where we guide it.

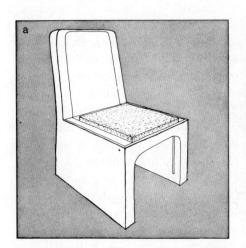
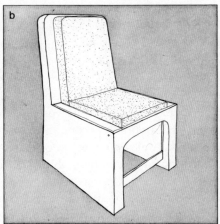
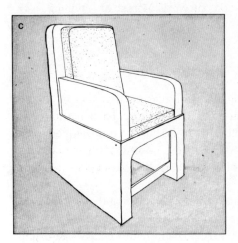
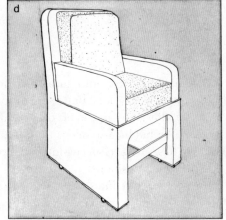

78. the auto-chair

The auto-armchair, which looks quite normal (Fig. 79a), can be given more opportunities for adjustment through button pushing to enable the legs to rest (Fig. 79b), a table to come out and the legs to go up (Fig. 79c); and finally can practically be turned into a bed (Fig. 79d). All these happen automatically through button pushing and in the same way as with the chair, this auto-armchair can have its metal balls out and run by simple muscular guidance.

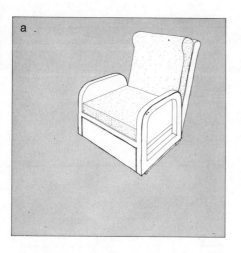
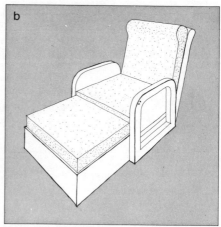
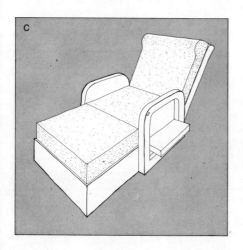
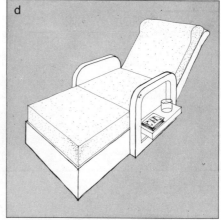

79. the auto-armchair

The auto-beds give people the chance to sleep in the traditional way (Fig. 80a) and have their bedside table (Fig. 80b) which can be filled with their books, etc. and with a top which can be lifted. They can also raise the mattress when they want to read or look out of the windows or receive others and communicate properly (Fig. 80c). In the same way, beds can lift the lower part of the body to allow the legs to change position for a better rest of the muscles or for massage (Fig. 80d). Another table can be brought out in a more suitable position.

In a way similar to that of the armchairs, the beds can also become softer (Fig. 80b, c) and thus be used in the most suitable way for any person lying on them, as some people like and need harder beds and others softer ones.

Some beds which lift the back and legs are already produced, but only for sick people. With a better development, everybody will use them.

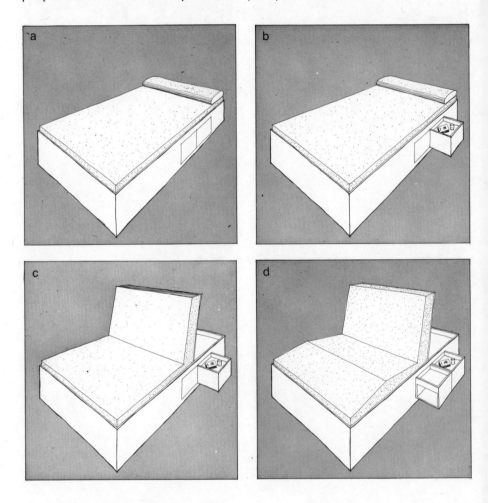

80. the auto-bed

The auto-tables will be of many kinds. They can be quite simple ones for dining, playing or working for four up to eight persons (Fig. 81a) (depending on the function) which by button pushing can expand to seat ten (Fig. 81b) or twelve persons. More complex auto-tables can include both refrigerators and heating units, which will be closed during the day (Fig. 81c) and will open during dinner, for everything, for working and playing hours for drinks or coffee (Fig. 81d) and can be enlarged to serve eight persons (Fig. 81e). The difference from the first table is that it cannot serve twelve persons, but it can help them enjoy sitting together. Exercise of muscles is very useful for Anthropos, but not necessarily when rest is needed. It should be confined to when exercise of the whole body is necessary, as in walking, as in sports, gardening, creating or dancing.

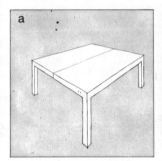
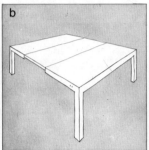
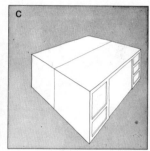

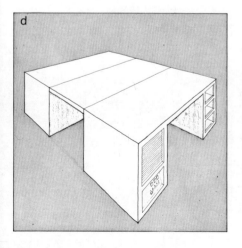
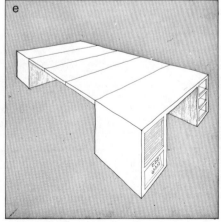

81. two kinds of auto-tables

Work desks will be very different from those of the present as they will serve all present and future needs in a much better way by turning into auto-desks. Their external appearance can be very simple or very artful like old Japanese chests (Fig. 82a) so that they do not remind anyone of work and its problems. When the moment comes they will open from one or both sides for one or two persons (Fig. 82b) and then during work time one or both sides can come out (Fig. 82c) and parts of them including files, telephones, telecommunications equipment can open or close (Fig. 82d).

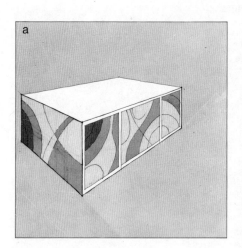
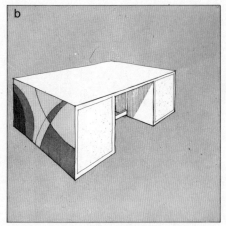
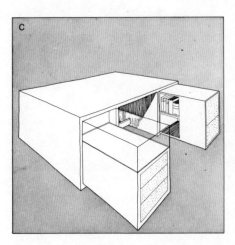
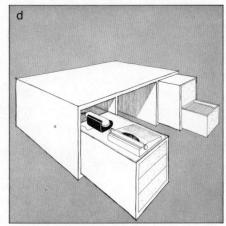

82. the auto-desk

The steps to the future

The change will not be revolutionary as everyone has his and her furniture; nor is industry prepared for the revolutionary change that we need. It will happen progressively, first probably with the most needed and more easily changed pieces, like the auto-chairs. This does not mean that the chairs of the past or present will not survive, especially those which have an esthetic or traditional value, but the new ones will be added by steps as will happen with all other pieces of furniture.

The change to the new type will not happen overnight as technology is not prepared for the new more flexible materials such as those required for the auto-shelves to turn around (Fig. 71). The first step though, in this direction will be by sliding panels which will allow the opening of several parts of the shelves (Fig. 83) or the closing of all and the formation of a wall covering the working and confusing image of so many objects and messages. The sliding panels will be on different lines (Fig. 84), but when they all close they can be automatically on the front level and appear as Figure 74.

83.   sliding panels

84.   the sliding panels can all be on the same level

7. The room

Ekistic Population Scale	Name of unit	Population range	Ekistic units covering this chapter	Kinetic field	Com. class	Ekistic unit
1	Furniture			a		1
2	Room			b		2
5	House	3 - 15		c		3
40	Housegroup	15 - 100		d	I	4
250	Small Neighborhood	100 - 750		e	II	5
1,500	Neighborhood	750 - 5,000		f	III	6
10,000	Small Polis	5,000 - 30,000		g	IV	7
75,000	Polis	30,000 -200,000		A	V	8
500,000	Small Metropolis	200,000 - 1.5 M		B	VI	9
4 M	Metropolis	1.5 M- 10 M		C	VII	10
25 M	Small Megalopolis	10 M- 75 M		D	VIII	11
150 M	Megalopolis	75 M- 500 M		E	IX	12
1,000 M	Small Eperopolis	500 M- 3,000 M		F	X	13
7,500 M	Eperopolis	3,000 M- 20,000 M		G	XI	14
50,000 M	Ecumenopolis	20,000 M and more		H	XII	15

The present situation

The general desire for a great change resulting from the explosion we are in at present also[1] has an influence on contemporary discussions and proposals about the room. People understand and feel the need for a change, but their proposals lack proper understanding of what the room is and how it has developed so far. Thus several people propose a dome-like room, forgetting that Anthropos has tried it in many cultures and always abandoned it as soon as he discovered the square room with a flat roof, and that he had many very important reasons for this choice[2], from physiological to structural.

Other proposals accept the basic flat roof, as they insert the room into a block of flats, but then they try to express a desire for change by altering the shapes of rooms or of windows. From square and oblong they change them into irregular pentagons, hexagons, etc., at irregular heights. If this is the correct shape for a window, it could also be correct for our books. It is crazy. This is completely wrong as it overlooks the basic physiological needs of the eye and body as well as structural realities. Inhabitants of such rooms are not convinced by such solutions; and it is interesting that they do sometimes rent them (certainly to experiment) but do not buy them[3]. Buildings with these rooms will be abandoned or in a few years will change their rooms to regular ones.

Other proposals do not change the basic shape of the room but experiment with the materials and the location of several of its parts. Many of these proposals move in the right direction as they bring in much better materials and equipment and find good solutions for their synthesis as a whole. There are also however, proposals and efforts made which prove that we do not have the proper understanding of the rational relationship between Anthropos and his room. Such are proposals for walls which reflect the light and create a confused image of space. Others place the fire in the middle of the room and armchairs and sofas around it disregarding the fact that such a situation, apart from the problems of smoke, harms the eyes of people who try to see across the fire and communicate with each other and disregarding that Anthropos started in this way and abandoned this alternative.

We also have people who insist on eliminating the doors so that Anthropos can move "freely" from room to room. I have a simple answer for this, as it destroys the need for retreat and isolation. One example from personal experience can help. An architect friend of mine invited me to see his new home without doors. We sat in beautiful armchairs and started talking, and then I heard his wife enter the bathroom, sit on the W.C., get rid of liquids and solids (three pieces), finish, wash her hands and other parts in the bidet, take a shower, go back to her bedroom, open the cupboards, dress, gossip with her friend over the telephone and then come to see me.

It is time we realized that the present-day room represents the experience of tens of thousands of years. Like everything else, it can still be improved but we should not go back to solutions that failed. Changes must be and will be made for its amelioration but not just for the sake of change. They have to respect the real needs of Anthropos and the long experience gained by him through trial and error.

In all our efforts concerning the room of the future we must start with its shape. We can find many truths about it by a proper analysis of its past[4], and the real alternatives for human space[5]. We then must clarify the dimensions as Anthropos cannot live happily in a very small room, as in a sleeping wagon which he accepts for a few nights only, any more than he can live in a cathedral. Anthropos's body, senses[6], mind and psyche define everything inside a room, from shape to dimensions, materials, colors, lights, etc. We must proceed on this basis and the room of the future can be definitely much better than the present one.

The room of the future

The room will be much more pleasant than it is now, not because of different shapes or dimensions, but because it will give its owner as many choices as he wants. As it will be an automatic room or auto-room it can be completely open or enclosed just by getting instructions through pushing buttons or oral instructions by its owner: "open front wall, open side wall, open roof!" The electronic system and the new materials will execute these orders in the best possible way.

In this way every person will have his own room in a society which will recognize this basic right for every citizen[7]. It is doubtful if many people will need more than one room because they will have everything available and no one will need to use more space and spend more energy to keep it clean, etc. This will be the big change: instead of trying to have different rooms for different purposes as we still try to do today, to have one room satisfying all needs in the best possible way.

The auto-room (Fig. 85) is only 4.50 × 4.50 m (15 × 15 ft) but it is open to the next room to the right and to the courtyard and the sky. By studying the human space we find that Anthropos likes all types of optical relationships with the space around him[8]. From careful studies we learn that Anthropos does not like to be in

85. the auto-room

a completely open space (with just one floor, which means for example a desert) except for short periods, and not as his home. Thus in the auto-room we can start with the maximum of open space possible in an urban home; that is three sides enclosed (floor and two walls) and finish with all six sides closed as we can see happening in this same room (Fig. 86).

We can see in the first possibility that Anthropos keeps his contact with Nature in the courtyard behind, which contains both water and plants attracting also certain types of birds. Anthropos serves his body allowing its movement (walking, swimming, lying down, naked in the sun as nobody can see him or her), his eyes by selecting the distance he wants to look at and his ears when he wants to hear the wind and the Society around him.

86.   the auto-room with all six sides closed

He can use his auto-room in many ways, as we have seen, by using the auto-shelves and auto-furniture (Chapter 6). For this reason I cannot call the room a bedroom or studyroom, etc., but only a room. There are also the auto-walls which make the room large or small, open or closed as we will see now.

The auto-room changes — the moment has come when the wife (I do not always speak of the husband and I prefer to think of the lady in her room) wants to concentrate on writing some letters on difficult family subjects. She does not want her attention to be distracted by anything, birds flying, late in the afternoon, or her husband exercising in the courtyard. She orders: "room close" and she is completely isolated in a very quiet and lightly colored room with auto-walls and auto-roof which close automatically.

In this way she does not receive any messages from outside through any of her senses. She has learned by now that external sounds are needed at times (we cannot grow in isolation), but also that they are dangerous if not under control. She is especially aware how many diseases are caused or strengthened by too much noise and how she can lose her sexual desires and abilities. Now she does not see outside, having instead pushed a button to receive her auto-wall with the painting which relaxes her. She only hears Bach and smells her own beloved flowers, as she has arranged the electronic equipment to bring a slight light on the ceiling, Cézanne on the wall and the scent she likes. This is also how she can sleep really quietly without any noise and wake healthy and happy.

When her work is done and she no longer needs complete isolation, she orders: "room open!" opening the ceiling and two walls. But next door is her husband with work to do, and the wife relaxing and reading on the bed prefers to be by herself. After talking to him she only says: "wall two close!" and the room gives her four sides enclosed: the floor and three walls (Fig. 87).

87.   the auto-room with four sides closed

When the sun bothers the lady sitting on her bed she pushes one button to be shaded by the roof. This roof is solid and not transparent, as this owner does not like to see the sky when it is cold or raining. Others have two auto-roofs, one transparent and one opaque (Fig. 88).

88.   the opaque auto-roof

The husband is visited by a friend and the wife prefers to remain inside and sunbathe by herself. She only says "front wall close!" "roof open!" and she is now enclosed on five sides, but enjoys the sun (Fig. 89).

89. the auto-roof opens to the sun

After half an hour she has enough of the sun, she asks the husband whether he is alone again, receives the answer "yes" and orders "front wall open, roof close!" Again she is enclosed on five sides but in a different way (Fig. 90).

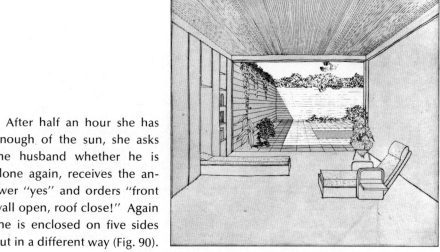

90. the front wall opens

In the afternoon it gets cold. It is time to close the room, and the wife orders "transparent front close!" and a new type of glass, a new invention, slides from behind the auto-shelves to the left and becomes the front "wall" as transparent as glass, but plastic so that it can bend 90° and thus turn. The straight line at 105 cm (3 ft 6 in.) separates the upper from the lower part of this transparent wall, so that the wife can leave her infant alone, and separate it from the swimming pool by calling for the lower part to close (Fig. 91).

91.   the transparent wall can be separated into an upper and lower part

Night comes and it is time to sleep. Neither one of the couple like to see out; they want to have a drink and to gossip and sit close together and therefore the lady owner orders: "color walls in wall two open!" In this way the room is enclosed on six sides by additional plastic walls full of color which change the image completely. "Door one" is where we stand and leads to the living-room behind us while "door three" is to our right and leads to the bath-room (Fig. 92).

92.   plastic walls of color change the image of the room completely

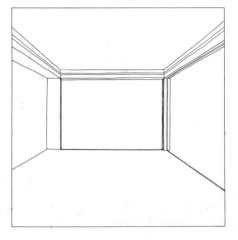

93. the frame of the auto-room

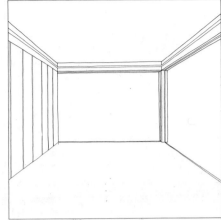

94. the auto-furniture usually covers one or two walls

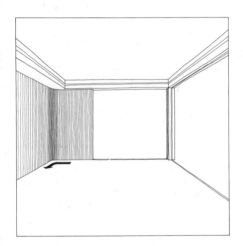

95. the auto-walls move behind the furniture

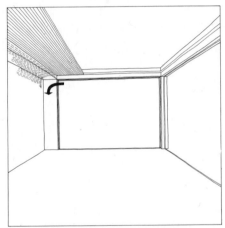

96. the auto-roof moves behind the furniture

The structure of the room is very simple and standardized. It consists of a frame (Fig. 93) existing in different sizes which are multiples of one of the two basic moduli of 75 and 90 cm (2 ft 6 in. and 3 ft) which are used by designers and industry. On this frame any type of auto-roofs, auto-walls and auto-furniture can be inserted.

The auto-furniture usually covers one or two walls and fits to the same moduli (Fig. 94). The auto-walls move behind the furniture (Fig. 95) as does the auto-roof (Fig. 96).

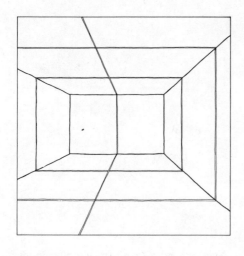

97.   a big auto-room

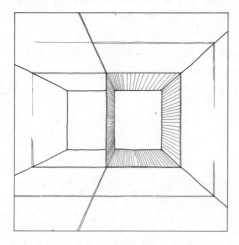

98.   the big auto-room can be sub-divided into "auto-cells" or "auto-tanks"

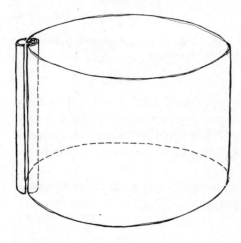

99.   cylindrical "auto-tanks"

In the same way we can use certain parts of walls as "fence walls" to keep children safe, as we have already seen in Figure 91, or to isolate grown-ups from the children.

In office buildings such auto-walls can have smaller distances between them in order to create all types of rooms, from very small ones for some people who need isolation at certain moments only, being in a wider room at other times, to larger "think tanks" where Anthropos can be enclosed on all six sides but completely free to walk or lie down in order to give his organism the proper rhythm that helps him to be creative. In such cases we have a big room (Fig. 97) which can be subdivided when necessary into "auto-cells" (Fig. 98), or "auto-tanks", which in very special cases can even be round ones (Fig. 99), opening their wall from small cylinders which normally exist as simple columns of the big room, etc.

Very special rooms requiring installations will be standardized. In this way we will have stan-bathrooms, stan-kitchens and stan-storerooms, including everything from deep freezers with adjustable temperature ranges to warmer places, for the storage of all sorts of items. There will be stan-supply rooms receiving all sorts of products coming automatically through pipes, and stan-wasterooms where we can place anything we want to get rid of from leftover food to equipment that has to be thrown away. Everything will be placed in a special part of this stan-wasteroom, because recycling of materials will have become very basic and the first classification will take place inside the house. Such rooms will be always placed in certain central locations so as to be properly connected with all sorts of pipes, and will be taken out by special machines, repaired, or replaced by new rooms.

The steps to the future

We cannot attain the auto-room tomorrow, particularly because we do not yet have materials that can bend and turn, enabling the outside walls to turn back behind the auto-shelves, and because our technology and incomes do not yet allow auto-roofs at reasonable cost. However, the effort to achieve this technology is already beginning to take place with the use of sliding external walls, not only small ones, which are quite common, but also big ones as in the Apollonion Symposion Hall (Fig. 100). This can be closed or open depending on the weather and it is very characteristic of this trend. Such sliding walls can be considered the first step to the future (Fig. 101).

It really started several decades ago, but the way it is done means losing a large part of the site to the frames moving out as the walls showing at the sides prove (Fig. 102).

100. the Apollonion Symposion Hall in Porto Rafti, Greece (1975)

101. the solution of the sliding walls in the Apollonion, Porto Rafti, Greece (1975)

102. the Apollonion sliding walls shown from the outside

The basic disadvantage of this first step is that only half of the wall can be opened because the other half is covered by the sliding frames if they do not move outside as in Figure 102. The second step is, therefore, the multi-panel wall, which reduces the non-opening part to one third, fourth, etc., depending on how many panels we create for the sliding doors (Fig. 103).

This effort has also already started, both with the total length of walls or windows divided into three sliding parts which give the opportunity of opening up to any two-thirds of the wall that you prefer (Fig. 104).

In such a way we can shift the opening to the preferred place (Fig. 105). Thus if you are at your desk or in bed, you have the chance to see either the modern city of Athens or the ancient Acropolis.

This step will be completed by the subdivision of the length of a wall into more than three panels so that the largest possible part opens. This will be done by lighter frames with a lesser thickness so that no problems will be created.

The third step will be the auto-wall made from new materials, turning inside the house in its solid part as in Figure 95; while the transparent wall will still be made from glass, and thus will remain a multi-panel wall covering a small part of the elevation. The last step will be reached when all parts of the wall are made from new materials which will bend properly and will be hidden when not wanted.

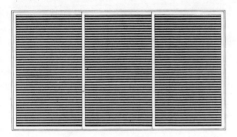

103. the multi-panel wall

104. any two-thirds of the wall can be opened

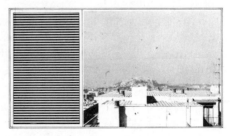

105.   the opening can be shifted to the preferred place

The auto-roofs will be more difficult; but they will happen in a few decades. In some way they are already beginning to be used in some Mediterranean theaters which open their roofs in the summer (Fig. 106). This may not be a contemporary invention, as it is quite probable that the ancient theater of Herodus Atticus in Athens had such a roof, open or closed with sails as on boats, although it was built in the 2nd century A.D. and was certainly not automatic.

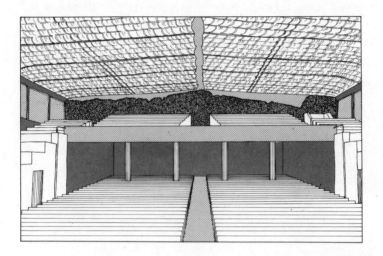

106. a contemporary auto-roof

Changing the existing rooms

The future room will not always be as I have described it, because many old houses will survive and will be inhabited if they represent some cultural values. We should never forget that values of the past are first overlooked when a change is necessary, but later they are understood and re-established. In this spirit we must expect to have two types of rooms in the future: those of the past will exist in a decreasing percentage; they will not change, but will get doors, windows, floor and walls of better materials but in the same dimensions. Those of the future will be increasing in numbers and percentage since Anthropos will be served much better inside them, especially when inside cities; while in the countryside he will save more of the older types which have a traditional value.

8. The house

Ekistic Population Scale	Name of unit	Population range	Ekistic units covering this chapter	Kinetic field	Com. class	Ekistic unit
1	Furniture			a		1
2	Room			b		2
5	House	3 - 15	▨	c		3
40	Housegroup	15 - 100		d	I	4
250	Small Neighborhood	100 - 750		e	II	5
1,500	Neighborhood	750 - 5,000		f	III	6
10,000	Small Polis	5,000 - 30,000		g	IV	7
75,000	Polis	30,000 -200,000		A	V	8
500,000	Small Metropolis	200,000 - 1.5 M		B	VI	9
4 M	Metropolis	1.5 M- 10 M		C	VII	10
25 M	Small Megalopolis	10 M- 75 M		D	VIII	11
150 M	Megalopolis	75 M- 500 M		E	IX	12
1,000 M	Small Eperopolis	500 M- 3,000 M		F	X	13
7,500 M	Eperopolis	3,000 M- 20,000 M		G	XI	14
50,000 M	Ecumenopolis	20,000 M and more		H	XII	15

The present situation

The house meant here is the structure serving as a dwelling or a household in general for the single family containing one to several people (usual average of four to five). It is the most important unit in Anthropos's life. By house, I mean here what is called home, flat, etc., irrespective of where it lies and how it is shaped. House is the residential unit where Anthropos spends 67% of his life, whether with his family or alone. It is true that 40% of the total time at home is spent inside his room, 1% inside his mother and only 26% in the other rooms[9], but out of that 40%, the greatest part is spent in sleep. What really matters is the unit "house", because the room by itself may be a prison or hospital room, whereas it is in the house that Anthropos is developed, which he uses as his base and although he moves far out into all sorts of larger units it is the house that shapes him more than anything else and leads to safety and happiness and sometimes becomes a paradise for children.

There are now some doubts about the importance of the family house versus a communal one and many experiments are under way in many countries by younger groups of people who try communal living in micro-societies. On this aspect we must be aware of two facts. First, this is not an invention of our times, as many believe, because Anthropos began by living only in such clans of several tens of people and later turned to patriarchal and single family life. He tried the same experiment again in different times and cultures. Second, we have not, as far as I know, any sign that this method was successful enough to continue forever and to spread to other people. All experiments which I have seen or learned about prove that communal living is at times worth trying, but never worth making permanent, or if so only for very few people. The fact that we like to drink very much at certain times and can enjoy it does not mean at all that this would be advisable as our permanent habit. The conclusion is clear: the family house has been for thousands of years and will continue to be the most important spatial unit for our life.

In spite of this truth, we are now in the phase of two great changes which are destroying the values of the house. The first one is that in the high-income societies people tend to change their houses very often and this does not help for their happiness and safety. A study recently announced by experts of the Washington School of Medicine on stress and physical illness[10] demonstrates that change in residence, school and related activities creates many problems of stress. How far should we allow this trend to continue at such a high rate? The second great change is that we have moved the house up onto the tall trees of the multi-story buildings, forgetting the human need for contacts with other people and the natural environment, as I have already explained.

Without question, if we speak of Anthropos and his interests we need a very radical change to avoid the stress of moving too often to another house and disassociating ourselves from our total natural environment.

The house of the future

When studying the room, we saw the backyard of the house and the swimming pool. Now we see the house from the front (Fig. 107). We enter from the hustreet through a gate that is three feet high so that preschool-age children[11] cannot leave by themselves. To the right is the early childhood garden inside which children can play safely. It is at the same level as their playroom, is surrounded by walls and has plants so that the contact with Nature can start early, and a small hill so that the training of the body can start as early as possible in a three-dimensional and safe place, since it has now been proved that the child has to start its muscular training very early[12]. The room is closed because it is morning and nobody is at home.

107.   the house of the future shown from the front

To the left is the garden connected with the livingroom, also closed so that the house is completely safe. In the upper floor, the middle section is closed, but the infant's room to the right is partly open to receive air and sun (the lower part covered with the plastic fence) and the older boy's room to the left is open to the sun but not to the air, being closed by the new plastic "glass". The horizontal line is always there to remind us where the "glass" is; but now the tall boy prefers it lower so that when sitting he can look out. This lower part of the wall is covered by a glass that allows people inside to look out, but not the opposite. The upper part allows the view both ways as a beautiful girl lives opposite.

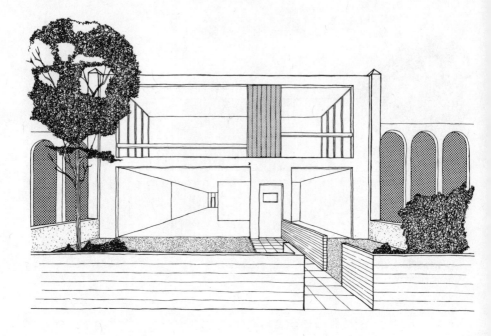

108.   the house in the afternoon

This house is completely different in the afternoon when the family is preparing it to receive their neighbors and other friends. Now the gate has been turned to the wall on the left and the neighbors enter into the livingroom either from the front door or directly from the garden, as the auto-wall has been absorbed by the wall to the left. The visitors who come by auto-mobile reach the livingroom from the door at the far end which leads to the corridor and to the livingroom. To the right of it, that is at the center of the house, we see the stan-kitchen and stan-WC (see Chapter 7). To the right the playroom is also open and so is the gate to it (Fig. 108).

On the upper floor everything is open except for a part of the daughter's room in the middle because she is still dressing and does not wish to be exposed. The family now communicates with all its neighbors, whereas this usually happens only with the child who sees and speaks to the neighbors and the passers-by.

It now becomes clear that this house can be completely open to the outside world (view, talk, entrance, etc.) or completely enclosed when the auto-walls are closed as in the major part of Figure 85 or open for the eyes but not for air or noise. This house gives people all opportunities, from complete enclosure and isolation and 100% safety (the auto-walls cannot open from outside) to completely open communication. The doors and windows are not limited to certain sizes but can be of any size we want.

The whole house can be seen from the air so that we see the front of it as in Figures 107 and 108, as well as its backyard as in Figure 85. We now see the natural garden in front where the inhabitants communicate with Society and the inner courtyard where the privacy is absolute as no one can look into it — there is no higher house or any other way of looking at it. The security is also complete as nobody can climb over the walls because of electronic warning systems (Fig. 109).

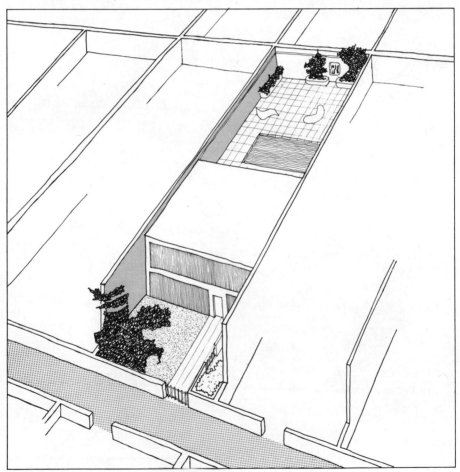

109. the house seen from the air

It is in such a house that Anthropos has the opportunity to serve and train his body by having three completely different types of space, a two-level house, a natural garden and an inner courtyard at a higher level and Anthropos can either walk up and down the stairs or in case of illness use the small stan-elevator at the core of the house.

What we tend to forget in many cities is the great opportunities that gardening gives people, not only to enjoy themselves but also to train their bodies. Horticulture can be a real therapy and development tool. This has been known, or at least felt, for centuries.

Here we can see clearly how many opportunities Anthropos has for his eyes, from the enclosed room (Fig. 86), to the inner house and courtyard (Fig. 85), to the garden, hustreet and some neighbors.

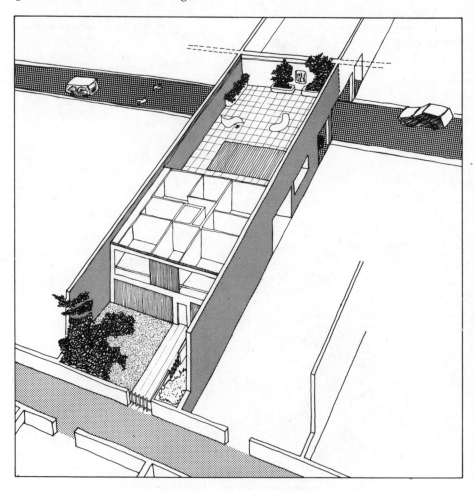

110.   the house with the auto-roofs open

When we open the auto-roofs we see that the upper floor consists of six main rooms (front and back) and auxiliary rooms with a core consisting entirely of stan-parts (bathrooms, WC, waste disposal, etc.) (see Chapter 7) which can easily be changed by a special crane which takes one stan-bathroom out and puts the other one in (Fig. 110). In the backyard we no longer see the swimming pool as in Figure 109 because its auto-cover is in place to facilitate the reception of a larger number of people.

In the lower floor we can see the mecstreet shown in cutaway (see Chapter 5) which cannot normally be seen unless we break the concrete that covers it. It allows auto-mobiles (they are now real ones and many) to come into it and then turn to the parking of every house, which can have just one place or up to five (in this case) or several more. In this way we understand that in front of the house we have the hustreet for people to communicate with each other and children to develop, and in the back the mecstreet serving different needs of humans for their mechanical movement and for all goods they may need.

It is winter now, very cold and windy, but a sunny day and we see the front with the opaque auto-walls withdrawn, but covered by the plastic auto-walls which allow all the sun's rays to pass through (Fig. 111).

The inner courtyard is covered by the transparent auto-roof which turns it into a summer climate and the swimming pool opens. By the use of this roof the whole courtyard becomes an ideal place for all sorts of life, for all seasons, for all purposes as it also offers complete protection from noise (which is becoming the great, even if unsuspected, enemy of Anthropos). In this way this house gives the opportunity to its inhabitants to have any type of quality of life they want, from complete isolation (back part), to complete participation in their community, from winter to summer conditions at any time of the year, from lying in bed to exercising in many ways for all types of humans, from prenatal phase to real old age, from healthy conditions to the opposite.

In the back we see the covered mecstreet which belongs to the neighborhood in the same way as the hustreet in front, and on the sides we can see the walls which, by regulation, divide all plots and houses.

111. the transparent auto-walls and the auto-roof over the courtyard allow the inhabitants to enjoy a sunny winter's day

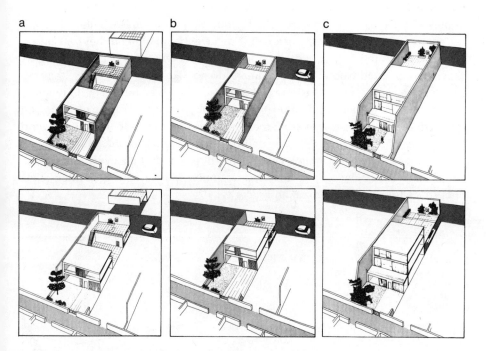

a   b   c

112.   variations of the house of the future

The house already seen is just one typical example of the future house, but it has many variations. The simplest one is the first house above, that is a small two-story, four-room house, a garden in front and a courtyard behind with a terrace, below which is the garage. The hustreet is as before, but the mecstreet is open in the first phase of its life (Fig. 112a).

Another variation is in a shorter plot where the auto-mobile comes under the courtyard which is, however, smaller, and the house can be either a three-room one (one living, two auto-rooms above) or much larger (Fig. 112b). The mecstreet is open again.

A third alternative, for high-density areas, is the three-story house (Fig. 112c) which can be very large and can have a very large ground floor for all needs and two upper floors, one at the level of the back courtyard as in Figure 109 and one even higher for greater isolation and complete privacy.

There is also a need for much greater variation either with houses not touching each other (lower densities) or at much higher densities. The first one is common in several countries with the Anglo-Saxon tradition, and other ones with a high bourgeois class or a "second home" tradition. Such houses will be more expensive in terms of energy and money for the city and this will be understood some day so they will decrease in numbers. The big question for them is whether they will be separated by walls or not. Personally I believe that in the end they will always be separated in the back and open in front, but as there are key anthropologists like Margaret Mead who think that humans do not like such walls unless they are Mediterraneans like myself[13], I present the case of such a house (Fig. 113) where the continuous garden is of importance and therefore the mecroad has gone underground and people walk from their underground garage to the underground floor of their home where they have all the stan-storerooms, etc. Such a house has many problems: the infants can escape, dogs can bother everyone, no privacy, etc. This is why I have included an inner courtyard to guarantee some inner space for privacy, intimacy and security.

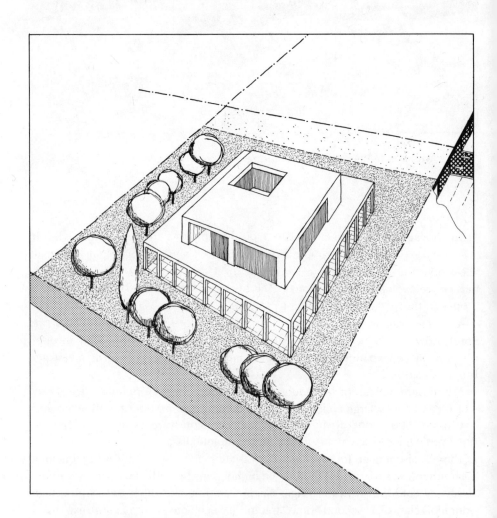

113.   the family house in the low density areas

The garden also may have to provide places for isolation and intimacy such as those that some people call the secret gardens, and there may be some hills formed from the soil to be excavated for the mecstreet; they can gradually be developed into gardens of Eden and include all sorts of elements as for example keeping fish in small ponds.

The opposite case is the family house in the highest density areas. This house is on a wider hustreet which people have decided to keep without plants, instead giving it an architectural character. It is mostly for families without children or for those whose children live with them only for a short period. It is meant to serve various couples, such as students, young couples experimenting with life, artists

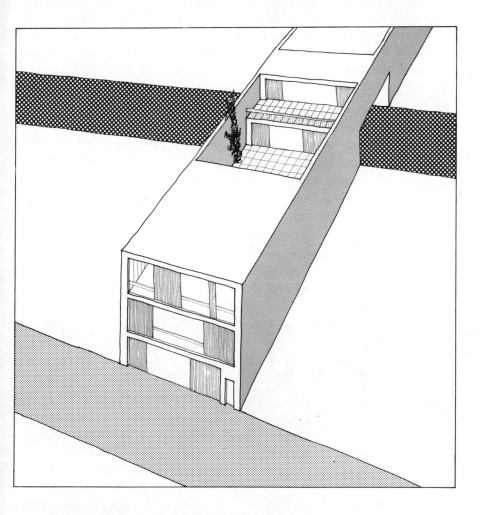

114. the family house in the highest density areas

who would like people to see them inside their atelier on the ground floor, or who might turn it into an artisan's workshop or a simple shop. It can be subdivided into a few flats (Fig. 114).

Thus we see the house for young adulthood or old age or very special groups like homosexuals living together (see Chapter 5), because it allows greater contacts with many more people or isolation without gardens which require manual effort, not easy after a certain age for many people.

The variations we have seen are related to the total structure of the house, but the appearance of each house will differ greatly from case to case and from spatial unit to spatial unit. Even the same units will change in accordance with the inhabitants and the phases of their lives. Thus a small inner courtyard which is a part of a whole backyard formulated for an infant, with some flowers to acquaint it with Nature, some sand to play with and a transparent auto-wall so that its mother can follow all its movements (Fig. 115), can change completely when this courtyard is inhabited by an old person liking his own symbols and forms (Fig. 116).

Similar variations can appear in homes incorporated into larger buildings as we will see in the next chapter.

115. the inner courtyard planned for an infant

116. the inner courtyard planned for an old person

The steps to the future

We cannot achieve this radical change of the structure of the house overnight; but all these changes do not need to happen overnight. I have already mentioned in Chapter 7 how the auto-walls can start right now using existing materials. In the same way we can create houses with the basic characteristics of the future house by introducing immediately the continuous system which has so many values (see Chapter 5) and by creating the front garden for social communications and the backyard for isolation and intimacy.

We have started to do this on many occasions, and the case I present here is from the Apollonion in Porto Rafti, Greece which is presented as a housegroup (Chapter 9) and as a neighborhood (Chapter 10) (Fig. 117).

117.   a house in the Apollonion, Porto Rafti, Greece

The present house changing in the future

If the house is in a high-density area it cannot change in any radical way. Only its rooms and furniture can change in ways already presented (Chapters 6 and 7). If the house has any esthetic, cultural and economic value, it can survive a long time and may have to be saved forever.

On the other hand, if the house is in a low density area it can gradually change and finally be replaced as we can see in Figure 118. The existing situation is controlled by the auto-mobile (Fig. 118a), but the mixed street can be turned into a hustreet, and the mecstreet and garage can be created in the backyard (Fig. 118b). In such a way the main house can be later replaced (when the time comes) but the garage will remain (Fig. 118c). When regulations allow, the house can be extended and the backyard can be reshaped (Fig. 118d). In the more distant future the garages and mecstreets can be saved but now the basic separating walls can be created (Fig. 118e) and thus the third house, some four or five generations from now, can be completely reshaped without any change of the basic structure of the mecstreet or hustreet (Fig. 118f), that is without any change that will affect the system of life. Such changes can take place more and more with the passing of time with prefabricated garages and rooms added when the need arises and the owner can pay for it.

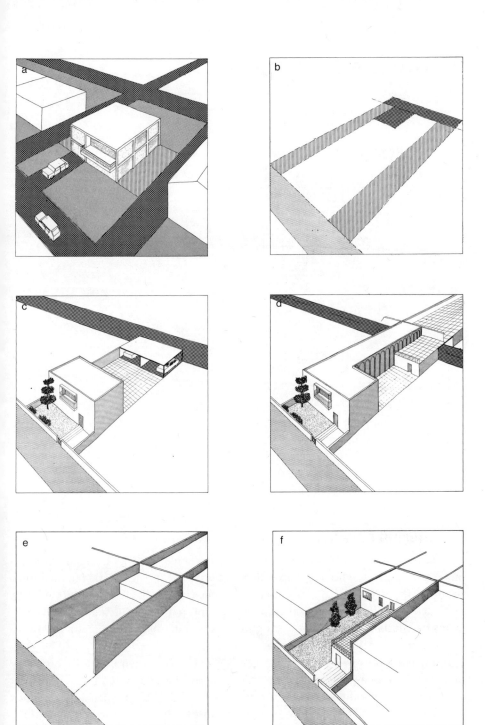

118. in a low density area the house may be gradually changed

9. The housegroup

Ekistic Population Scale	Name of unit	Population range	Ekistic units covering this chapter	Kinetic field	Com. class	Ekistic unit
1	Furniture			a		1
2	Room			b		2
5	House	3 - 15		c		3
40	Housegroup	15 - 100	░░░░░░	d	I	4
250	Small Neighborhood	100 - 750		e	II	5
1,500	Neighborhood	750 - 5,000		f	III	6
10,000	Small Polis	5,000 - 30,000		g	IV	7
75,000	Polis	30,000 -200,000		A	V	8
500,000	Small Metropolis	200,000 - 1.5 M		B	VI	9
4 M	Metropolis	1.5 M- 10 M		C	VII	10
25 M	Small Megalopolis	10 M- 75 M		D	VIII	11
150 M	Megalopolis	75 M- 500 M		E	IX	12
1,000 M	Small Eperopolis	500 M- 3,000 M		F	X	13
7,500 M	Eperopolis	3,000 M- 20,000 M		G	XI	14
50,000 M	Ecumenopolis	20,000 M and more		H	XII	15

The present situation

As the house is the building serving the single family with an average number of 4-5 people, so the housegroup is the next unit and serves several families and several tens of people. It corresponds to the clan or band of hunters which preceded the single family and later housed the patriarchal families in villages or towns and has gradually been forgotten as a unit, although in reality it exists in small streets or in blocks of houses.

Today we tend to forget its existence, or when we remember it we tend to think that it is an age-old notion which is disappearing in a natural way. But we are wrong. Do we think of clean air in the same way? Today machines pollute it — we recognize this and are trying to clean the air, and we will achieve this in the same way in which we dealt with pollution from sewers, etc. The fact that one ancient value disappears in the city of the present does not mean that this is desirable.

It is time that we considered this matter more seriously in several ways. First we must think in terms of values already existing in old buildings forming house-groups. We talk a great deal about saving them, but we do not manage to, either in the high-income capitalist countries like the U.S.A. or in the communist countries. We know that big parts of old Peking are disappearing and that in the U.S.A. out of the 1,500 buildings of real value (a very small number for such a big country) listed in 1933, almost half have since been torn down[14]. This is wrong, and we are losing the battle to save the old values.

Second we must remember that Anthropos does not only need a limited number of spaces to live in. From the house he must not be thrown directly into the big avenue or square as happens now. He needs all sorts of places in order to be happy, from the very small room for privacy, to the small street, square, etc. up to the open landscape[15]. In the past, Anthropos always managed to create the small units in a very natural way[16], but now he has forgotten this need.

Third, we forget that Anthropos needs a space for normal human contacts, which he had in the past in the small street or square. This opportunity has been completely lost because of the machines which have stepped in between people (see Chapter 5). At this moment we must remember that the problem is not only created by the motorcars (they are not yet auto-mobiles as we said in Chapter 5), but by all sorts of new forces and dimensions like the streetlights, advertisements, too many people in the streets, etc. Because of these forces we lose the normal human contacts which we had in the past near our house. We do have more contacts further out, but fewer near us[17]. It is a big mistake.

Fourth, we really forget the human scale and as an example we must look at two incorrect efforts made lately by artists in order to ameliorate the space we live in. On the one hand they create huge pieces of sculpture, forgetting that they can only please Anthropos, assuming he likes them, if he looks at them from an appropriate distance, which is very great. We forget that Anthropos — even as a child — is prepared even to kiss a human symbol[18]. On the other there is an attempt to paint huge walls[19] imagining that they embellish the environment and forgetting that Anthropos cannot be happy living in a jungle full of giants, or even worse, in a jungle where giants coexist with all sorts of small plants and animals. Why should we create jungles again since we know that Anthropos had to abandon them in order to be further developed?

Finally, we have to remember that we pretend to solve some of these problems by bringing people together in multi-story buildings. But this is not a solution as we have learned that neither proper contacts, nor safety and security nor human scale are in existence in such buildings. The problems of living very high create many bad conditions for mental health[20]. There are some people who advertise such solutions in both capitalist and socialist countries, but we have no sign of any such successful effort for Anthropos (Chapter 3, p. 32)[21].

115

If a multi-story building can serve as a good office or hospital this does not mean that it can replace a group of houses.

The above is valid for the majority of environmental and cultural conditions all over our globe, but not necessarily for every single case. As every rule, this one has exceptions also. In Siberia, for example, they have tried the solution of multi-story buildings and they report that the people are satisfied[22]. I cannot have an opinion on such a case. When the experiment has run long enough it may prove that for such a difficult climate this is the best solution. We need, however, time and experimentation to form an opinion on such special cases.

From such a description of the present situation it becomes clear that the housegroup is a natural unit which should not be eliminated. Its goals are to help people of all ages to have a broader area to move in where they can feel at home in a human scale and to help them all to interact if and when they like it.

If anyone doubts the value of such a unit in our city I will remind them that Anthropos has created this unit everywhere — after starting in different ways either with distant houses or with very compact ones where he jumped in from the roofs, he always finished by creating small streets for housegroups in all the civilizations we know and all the cities we admire. We can also study the existing neighborhoods which have survived and understand their values in allowing people to interact. This is very important if done in a natural and free way — not only in very specialized clubs, which are selective and distant from home and thus serve other needs, but do not serve Anthropos in the most natural way.

The housegroup of the future

The housegroup is a basic part of our city which gives us more space, various types of public spaces and becomes a very important element of the desirable city with quality. The proper housegroup, like Figure 119, demonstrates the case of a middle-income family. The frame is created by the city and the smaller communities within the city and every family is free to serve its own needs in its own way, keeping the rules of the game. This freedom means that houses will not be in exactly the same line, as one family may prefer to pull the house back and have a big garden open to the hustreet in front, while their neighbors may prefer an inside courtyard with a swimming pool for complete privacy.

These housegroups (we can also see a part of the next housegroup in the lower side) demonstrate the importance of Nature inside them from the courtyard where people prefer water, to the garden, with grass only, to the very green garden, to the green streets, etc. We can see that every group has the freedom to decide on the character of its hustreets. The lower one shown in the figure has a different regulation in terms of plantation than the upper one. In the housegroup we can develop our best feelings throughout our life, as home and

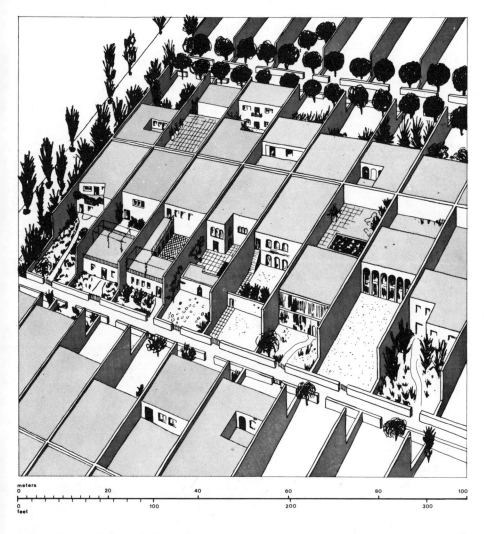

meters					
0	20	40	60	80	100

0	100	200	300
feet			

119. the middle-income family housegroup

neighborhood are "often the whole world to a child"[23] and "Our attachments last through life, but also prepare us to embrace alternate habitats of similar qualities"[24].

It is here that we can serve our natural contact with Nature and people in the best possible way because we have a hustreet. All this can be achieved only in a horizontal system of movement, because if we climb up one floor, that is 3 m (10 ft), we spend fifteen times more energy, equivalent to walking 45 m (150 ft) and thus we tend to avoid it. In this proposal we see how we solve our problems of conflicts between humans and machines.

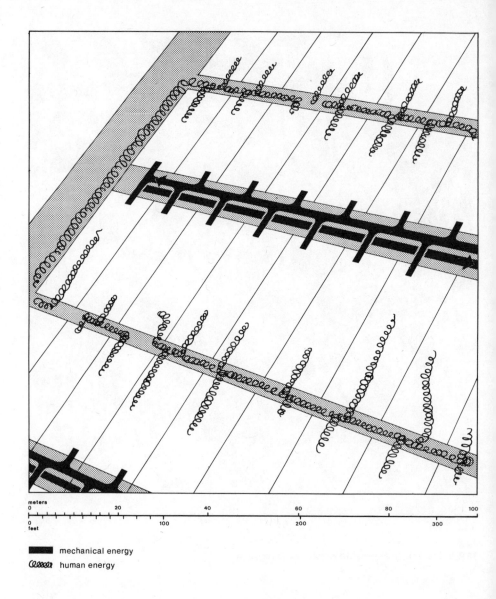

meters
0   20   40   60   80   100

0   100   200   300
feet

▬▬ mechanical energy

ᶜᵉᵉᵉᵉᵉᵉᵉ human energy

120. the housegroup as a system of movement

Looking at this same housegroup as a system of movement we can distinguish how the hustreets and mecstreets are separated (Fig. 120), and how all inhabitants feel at home to walk out and communicate. The hustreet becomes a real home-street and children can now develop properly.

118

It is a real group of equal people, because no one family can rise above the others; and even if one family prefers to build a one-story house, the neighbors do not seem to loom above it and cannot look into its courtyard.

The whole group is organized as a legal and administrative unit which can protect itself by not allowing outsiders to enter its streets, in the same way in which we can now forbid non-residents to enter our block of flats. We will gradually understand that about 10% of young boys enjoy acts of violence[25] of varying degrees and that there are criminals in our world who should not be given the chance to attack. This certainly does not mean that those who prefer complete "freedom" for movement anywhere should be forced to keep safety rules in their own group; but those who want safety will apply such rules in their housegroup which will serve some needs of what is called the extended family. In this way the group will feel, because of contacts, friends and safety, they are living in a happier place.

It is here that people remember and understand what S. Giedion said, that "No machine can replace physical nearness, neither telephone nor radio, home movies or television"[26]. People will feel once again what the human scale means, since they will not be menaced by machines. Even animals were a threat, as we can understand by reading Plato: "And likewise the horses and asses are wont to hold on their way with the utmost freedom and dignity, bumping into everyone who meets them and who does not step aside. And so all things everywhere are just bursting with the spirit of liberty"[27]. Anthropos needs real freedom and he cannot have it if he lives with machines.

It is only in the housegroup that our new human culture can be born again.

In this unit the husystem prevails (Fig. 67), as we can see how it looks and the mecstreet cannot even be seen (Fig. 119). We can see how large an area the hustreets cover in relation to the mecstreets (Fig. 120). In this way not only are contacts made possible, but the full training of the body takes place, as the child runs to meet friends, the adults train and old people move safely. The mecstreet serves other needs for longer distances, for movement of the sick or of goods or, if you prefer, for hiding your contacts when you receive friends (perhaps for a love affair or homosexuals, or for secret business) that you would not wish anyone to see.

The physical appearance (Fig. 119) and the Networks of hustreets and mec-streets (Fig. 120) do not sufficiently explain how in this housegroup we can better serve our eyes and ears. We can see this in Figure 121, where we have the same housegroup but the neighboring houses have been eliminated by very dark color. Inside this housegroup we have an area of 100% visual communication, another one with lower communication which is possible only when we are near, a third one where we can communicate only from a few houses opposite and the fourth one of no communication at all. We should not forget that the value of "seeing lies in the information capacity of vision. Its capacity is at least 100 times that of hearing, and over 1,000 times that of any other human sensory channel. Indeed, in our everyday activities, by far most of the information about the external world comes to our nervous systems and brains through the eyes"[28]. This is why we are obliged to create the proper system for our eyes which create most of our contacts. This is also true for our ears, which are served 100% in the hustreet and are completely isolated inside a home or courtyard, when its auto-roof is used, as the two houses to the right have done.

We understand now how every family can select the type of house that it likes, depending on the degree of communication that it wants. Such a system also gives more opportunities to select what type of exposure to currents of air we prefer.

In this case all houses are very close together for the reasons already explained (see Chapter 5, p. 59) but every house has a completely different character (see Chapter 8) and gives many different choices to its inhabitants both inside and outside.

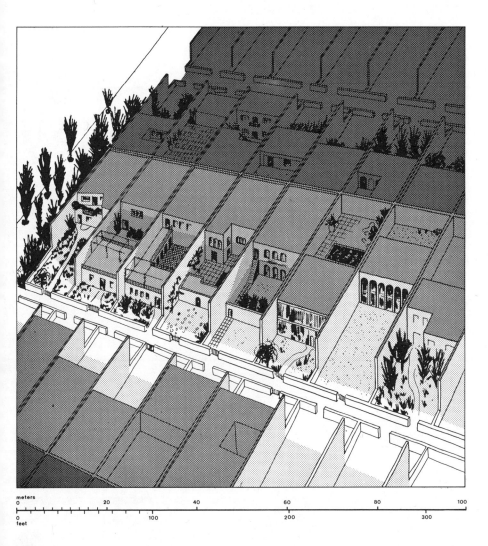

meters
0   20   40   60   80   100

0   100   200   300
feet

 shades ranging from white
to very dark indicate intensity and degree of visual communication

121.   areas of visual communication

121

Studying several hustreets, we can understand how they may differ depending on climate, topography, income, culture, tradition, desires, etc.

They may range from a hustreet closely resembling the old traditional streets in villages and small towns in many parts of our globe (Fig. 122a), to another resembling a traditional street from larger cities (Fig. 122b).

They may range from the one we have already seen in the housegroup in the three previous plans and which is shown here as a perspective as pedestrians see it (Fig. 122c) and to the very high-income (only those who can afford it) and very low-density hustreet (Fig. 122d).

The conclusion is clear that in the future we will have the greatest possible freedom for our system of houses and their groupings. A complete balance may be achieved by using similar types (Fig. 122b) or there may be a completely free but normal synthesis (Fig. 122c) or even the complete disappearance of "house" behind Nature.

People will grow up in all types of hustreets, and in the more distant future (six or more generations) science will know exactly which human needs are better served by which hustreet and thus people will be able to select them not by mere intention but also by proper information and guidance.

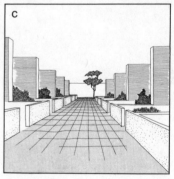

122. varying types of hustreets

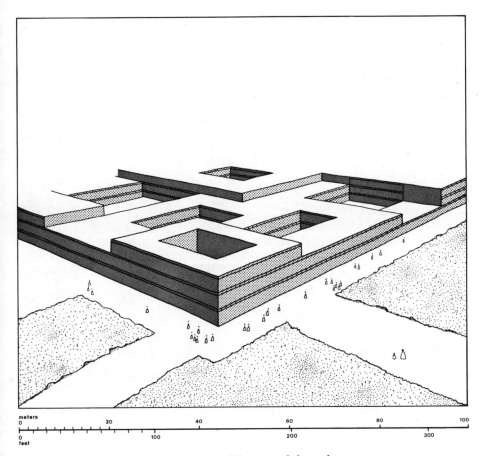

meters					
0	20	40	60	80	100

0	100	200	300
feet			

123. the housegroup as a block providing special services

The housegroups will not always have the hustreet as their axis, although most of them will have such a basic structure. There will be, however, other groups of different types, some of which are already developing as blocks of flats providing several services, from commerce to sports. Such blocks are not inhabited by regular families with children, but by special groups like divorced or separated mothers who need a more cohesive social group in order to be properly assisted.

The old and sick do not live in such small groups as they need better services which can be more easily provided for larger groups like a neighborhood as explained in Chapter 10. The inhabitants of housegroups are mostly young, like students, and there will always be a few communes existing to serve the need for human experimentation. Such blocks do not have the structure of a hustreet or multi-story building, but consists of several blocks with one, two or three stories in a synthesis allowing for the proper interplay of all types of open or closed spaces (Fig. 123).

The unit of the housegroup (that is the 50 or more people living in it) does not only need houses, hustreets, and mecstreets. The inhabitants also need assistance for more training of body and mind, for recreation and also for commerce, health, etc. These latter sectors, especially health, cannot be provided at this low level, but the others (training, recreation) can, and this leads to the formation of husquares belonging to the housegroups where children can find their playgrounds and which mothers and fathers can use as gossip squares. In special cases, when two or three groups agree to collaborate, even a small shop can exist as the ancient cornershop, especially when an old couple of the group is interested in keeping it, not so much for profit (which is very small) as for their own entertainment.

Such a husquare will exist mostly at the entrance to the group's hustreet (although it can also be inside it), and serves all needs from proper training to commercial services. Its form can therefore range (depending on the housegroup) from a real play and gossip square (Fig. 124a), to cornershop square (Fig. 124b) or playgarden (Fig. 124c).

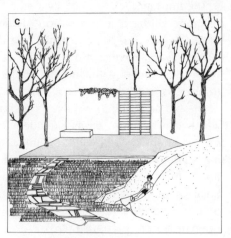

124. different types of husquares

These plans explain the structure and the phases for the creation of the house-group, starting by the clarification and definition of landownership and properties (Fig. 125) beginning with family ownership, to housegroup ownership of hustreets and squares and of mecstreets. The second phase explains the creation of all utility corridors (Fig. 126), the third one the creation of the mecstreets (which may have or be at a lower level also) and parking spaces (Fig. 127) and the fourth one the construction of the dividing walls (Fig. 128) inside which each family then creates the house that it prefers.

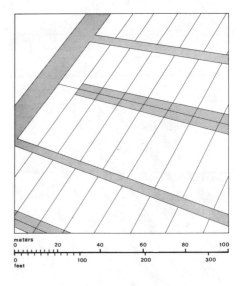

125. first phase: definition of land-ownership and properties

meters
0   20   40   60   80   100

0   100   200   300
feet

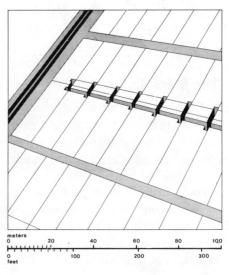

126. second phase: the communities (class one and two) build the utility corridors

meters
0   20   40   60   80   100

0   100   200   300
feet

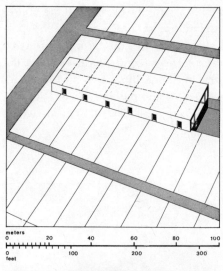

meters
0   20   40   60   80   100
0   100   200   300
feet

127. **third phase: community class one builds the mecstreet and garages**

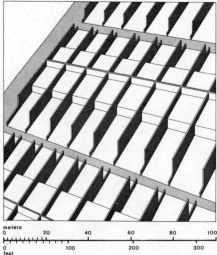

meters
0   20   40   60   80   100
0   100   200   300
feet

128. **fourth phase: community class two builds the dividing walls**

The steps to the future

We cannot create the future tomorrow, but we have already started the process by creating hustreets and husquares separated from the mecareas.

One example is from Eastwick, Philadelphia, Pa., and it demonstrates the hu-areas which connect many houses (Fig. 129). The other is from another continent and a much lower income group, that is from Islamabad, the new capital of Pakistan, where the government had the courage to create the basis for the human systems of contacts (Fig. 130). Similar efforts have been made in Africa where three countries so far, Ghana, Zambia and Nigeria have taken the initiative to create separate systems of hu- and mecstreets, as we can see in the new cities of Tema in Ghana (Fig. 131) and of Kafue in Zambia (Fig. 132).

126

129. the hu-areas in Eastwick, Philadelphia, Pa.

130. the husystems in Islamabad,
Pakistan

131. separation of hu- and mecstreets in Tema, Ghana

132. separation of hu- and mecstreets in Kafue, Zambia

Under different conditions, this new (or age-old) concept of housegroup with hu- and mecstreets has been very successful on the hillside where we built the Apollonion in Porto Rafti outside of Athens, Greece. We can see the hustreet in Figure 133, and the whole housegroup in Figure 134. It is a whole neighborhood for middle and high incomes, of which we saw a house in Chapter 8 and we see the total in Chapter 9.

133. the hustreet in the Apollonion, Porto Rafti, Greece

134. the housegroup in the Apollonion, Porto Rafti, Greece

The mecstreets of the Apollonion have not yet taken the underground location of the future, but many steps have been made in this direction as when we live or walk in the upper group of houses (Fig. 135) we do not suspect the existence of motorcars. But when we move at a lower level, we can see the parking from a terrace with an exhibition (Fig. 136), and when we are at the middle level we are in a mecstreet only (Fig. 137).

In this way the separation of Anthropos and machines is complete, no child ever needs to cross the mecstreet to go anywhere, and no one can see it from any house, either below or above it.

135. the upper level is a hustreet

136. the mecstreet is visually exposed to the lower level

137. the middle level is a mecstreet

In the same way we have already begun to create husquares for small house-groups as in Mosul, Iraq, in the tradition of local architecture but with modern technology (Fig. 138) and even for office buildings, like the headquarters of Doxiadis Associates International in Athens, Greece, where the parking is underground with the husquare above (Fig. 139), a few steps higher than the mecstreet level so that machines will never invade this husquare.

It becomes clear that many steps have already been successfully tried and can guarantee the entopian character of what is described on pp. 116-125.

138. husquare in Mosul, Iraq

139. husquare at Doxiadis Associates International, Athens, Greece

The present housegroup changing into the future

The housegroups of the present exist as blocks of flats with few dwellings or as small streets (most of them turned into mixed hu- and mecstreets), or as groups of trailers, and as isolated hamlets.

In the existing blocks of flats we cannot expect any radical change. They will survive as long as it is economically justified and then they will pass away, especially the taller ones for many reasons.

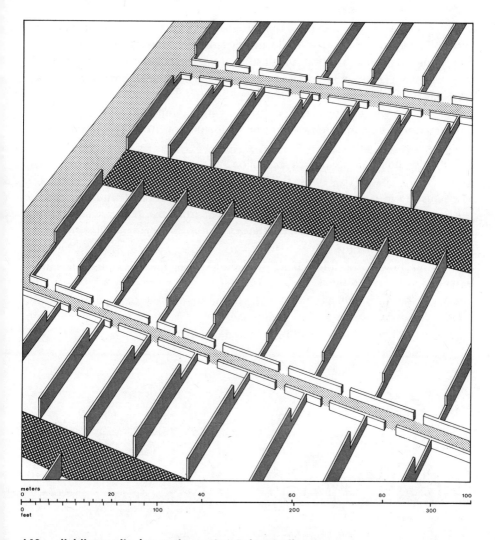

meters
0   20   40   60   80   100

0   100   200   300
feet

140. dividing walls, hu- and mecstreets in a trailer camp

The groups of trailers will survive only as long as we do not provide those people who cannot afford a big plot and house with the units they can afford to pay for. When this has been done the number of trailer camps will be reduced, except for young adults, married or not but without children who need to con-quer the world[29]. But even these camps will be much better organized than at present, so that Anthropos will not be exposed to the machine as at present. This may require the creation of a system of hu-and mecstreets and of separating walls (Fig. 140).

131

The hamlets, which are the housegroups isolated in the countryside, will survive if they are not very close to the dynamically growing cities (dynapolis), and if they represent cultural and historical values as they will very probably be selected as second homes or taken by groups to be used as temporary escapes, let us say part-time monasteries.

The existing housegroups along narrow streets can only survive if these streets are turned into hustreets for a length of up to 100 m (330 ft), and the machines will pass outside.

For those housegroups which exist along wide streets, there may be a possibility for a change by steps as shown in Figures 141-146. At present the machines are in control and no human values are respected. The first change will be the separation of the residential street from the traffic avenue, using fences to create courtyards for each house. The second change will be to create the home-street or hustreet for pedestrians, leaving the old street to be used only by machines. The third change will be to cover the machines where they enter the properties and to separate pedestrians from machines in the traffic artery. In the fourth change the mecstreet will be entirely covered and we will build terraces, thus eliminating about one half of traffic arteries. In the fifth change we will build the separating walls and feel free.

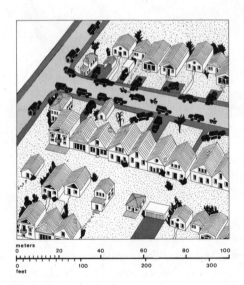

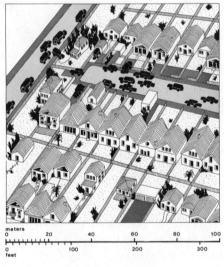

141. the present situation: who is in control? where is the human space? where is privacy?

142. from present to future first change: separate the residential street from the traffic avenue, use fences to create courtyards

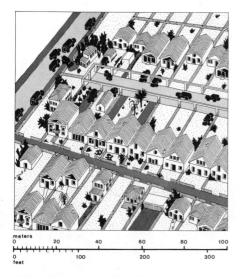

meters
0   20   40   60   80   100

0 feet   100   200   300

143.   from present to future
second change: create the hustreet for pedestrians, leave the
old street only for machines

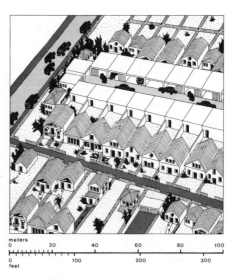

meters
0   20   40   60   80   100

0 feet   100   200   300

144.   from present to future
third change: cover the machines inside the properties,
separate pedestrians from machines in the traffic artery

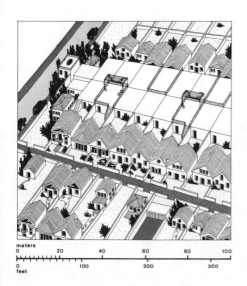

meters
0   20   40   60   80   100

0 feet   100   200   300

145.   from present to future
fourth change: cover the mecstreet and build terraces, eliminate one half of traffic arteries

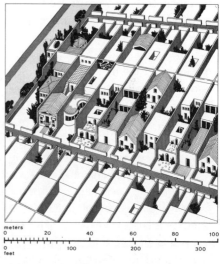

meters
0   20   40   60   80   100

0 feet   100   200   300

146.   from present to future
fifth change: build the separating walls and feel free

133

10. The neighborhood

Ekistic Population Scale	Name of unit	Population range	Ekistic units covering this chapter	Kinetic field	Com. class	Ekistic unit
1	Furniture			a		1
2	Room			b	·	2
5	House	3 - 15		c		3
40	Housegroup	15 - 100		d	I	4
250	Small Neighborhood	100 - 750	▓▓▓	e	II	5
1,500	Neighborhood	750 - 5,000	▓▓▓	f	III	6
10,000	Small Polis	5,000 - 30,000		g	IV	7
75,000	Polis	30,000 -200,000		A	V	8
500,000	Small Metropolis	200,000 - 1.5 M		B	VI	9
4 M	Metropolis	1.5 M- 10 M		C	VII	10
25 M	Small Megalopolis	10 M- 75 M		D	VIII	11
150 M	Megalopolis	75 M- 500 M		E	IX	12
1,000 M	Small Eperopolis	500 M- 3,000 M		F	X	13
7,500 M	Eperopolis	3,000 M- 20,000 M		G	XI	14
50,000 M	Ecumenopolis	20,000 M and more		H	XII	15

The present situation

The neighborhoods are those units, both in rural and urban areas, which house from over one hundred people up to a few thousand. They are not as old as the housegroup, which existed much earlier, but are about ten thousand years old as they developed in the first farmers' and cattle-breeders' villages and became very important in towns and cities. Their importance was also quite often officially recognized and we can mention many cases, such as Hippodamus who in the fifth century B.C. "invented the division of cities into blocks and cut up Piraeus" as Aristotle mentions[30]. What he really did was to organize cities by communities corresponding to neighborhoods, as we can see in Miletus which was well organized into three neighborhoods[31]. In a similar way the Chinese organized their first big capital, Chang'an[32] in the 6th century A.D. by communities; and later the Arabs gave each neighborhood the opportunity to have its own local leader.

Today we have completely forgotten the existence of the neighborhood and no longer build cities consisting of neighborhoods; but the very interesting phenomenon is that people tend to form neighborhoods in a very natural way by creating shops, churches, mosques or temples and other facilities which bring people together within certain territories. We studied (at the Athens Center of Ekistics) this phenomenon very carefully in Athens which is nowadays a metropolis with 2.7 million inhabitants, where not a single neighborhood was planned or foreseen and we found that the whole population actually lived in 1965 in 286 neighborhoods of an average population of approximately 6,500[33].

We must remember that the neighborhoods have various types of needs which must be properly served at this level, I will mention a few of them. First, the neighborhood units must be very clearly defined so that everyone knows where he belongs and can participate in solving the problems of his area, and also be properly served by corresponding services. Every neighborhood should have very clear physical boundaries, like green areas or mecstreets (the hustreets are the connecting links, not barriers), or walls separating rows of houses, and form its own simple administrative unit.

Second, the neighborhoods should serve all local social needs. One example is children's needs. When we study children and their development, we will find that they need their neighborhood which should contain a kindergarten or small school. Children should not be taken to their first natural unit of contact by motor cars or buses. This is one of the greatest weaknesses of our cities: not allowing children to make their contacts with their closest neighbors in a natural way. This leads to great confusion.

During the last few years people have begun to be aware of several such dangers, and some research work, like that of Professor T.R. Lee of the University of Surrey, England[34] leads to conclusions strengthening these views. However, much more systematic research is needed to prove everything in detail. In the meantime we can be sure of one thing — that we have to re-create the neighborhoods for all our local needs.

Third, there is an imperative need to serve certain economic needs locally. The fact that the super-markets and super-shops have developed and serve wider areas of tens of thousands of people does not mean that we do not need smaller ones. A highway is needed to serve a city of half a million people, but this does not mean that we have to eliminate the smaller city streets. We are in the phase where we pay attention to new inventions and overlook the eternal needs of Anthropos. In some countries, as lately in France, a big battle is under way to save the smaller shops which are being eliminated by the big commercial chains. It is quite clear that the large chains can provide many better services, and this is why they succeed, and this means that we do not need as many smaller shops as in the past, but in fact we do need them, and we must understand how to find the balance between the large and small shops.

Fourth, we turn to technology which, by developing more and more, solves many of our problems, but at the same time creates others. One is the congestion and pollution of streets by machines (much more complex than usually understood) already mentioned. These problems and many others dissolve the neighborhood because they help people to go far out, but not to meet each other in the streets. Such observations strengthen the need to develop further technology without allowing it to break any of the human values. It is clear that technology can solve many problems and provide for the proper operation of neighborhoods in the human scale.

Fifth, is the cultural aspect which has already been mentioned in the elimination of the housegroup (Chapter 9, p. 114). I turn back to it in order to emphasize that there are people insisting on creating art on a huge scale within neighborhoods, and thus eliminating any relation of sculpture to Anthropos. There are even corporations which insist on creating huge buildings and turning them into completely confusing mirrors. One of them advertises "if you want to be a good neighbor put a landscape in the sky" and presents a tower which turns into a mirror where you can see the worst type of urban landscape, becoming even worse in the huge mirror-wall. Humans need to express themselves in open spaces, but they cannot achieve this when even their dancing is in an inhuman landscape, as happens with dancing at the center of Chicago (Fig. 147). What is the relation of Anthropos to the city? Where is culture?

147. what is the relationship of Anthropos to the city when we dance in front of skyscrapers?

The neighborhood of the future

This neighborhood (Fig. 148) contains eight housegroups, including the one we have already studied (Fig. 119) which is the second one from the lower right, and several other facilities. The eight housegroups are not at all similar, either in dimensions or in structure, and they serve several middle-class families of varying incomes and characteristics. The one at the lower right has smaller plots, but is a very high-income housegroup where several old people prefer to live. The next one is quite average and has already been described. The third housegroup took the decision to include all sizes of separating walls (from the shortest, left, to the

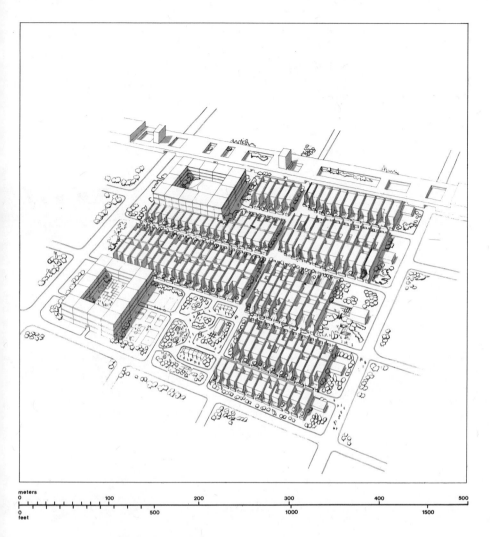

meters
0 ⊢ ┴ ┴ ┴ ┴ ┴ ┴ ┴ ┴ ┴ ┴ 100   200   300   400   500
0 feet   500   1000   1500

148. the neighborhood of the future

longest ones). The fourth is in favor of larger plots. On the left hand side of our figure, the lower housegroup is in favor of facing the park, the next one prefers many more families than all the others, the seventh is like the fourth, and the eighth one (upper left) is for very old people who need medical care.

Next to the three upper housegroups we see the center including all sorts of facilities and this is why old people who cannot walk very far, live next to it, while the others with high incomes live in their own homes (lower right).

On the extreme left is the educational center (and we will see why it is not called a school) and sports ground.

137

The same neighborhood is now examined (Fig. 149) as a movement system. It is not a transportation system, as we usually say, because the most important of all is Anthropos's natural movement, which is later supplemented by transportation. We have already discussed (Chapter 5, p. 66) hustreets forming a husystem and mecstreets forming a mecsystem, and here we can see both.

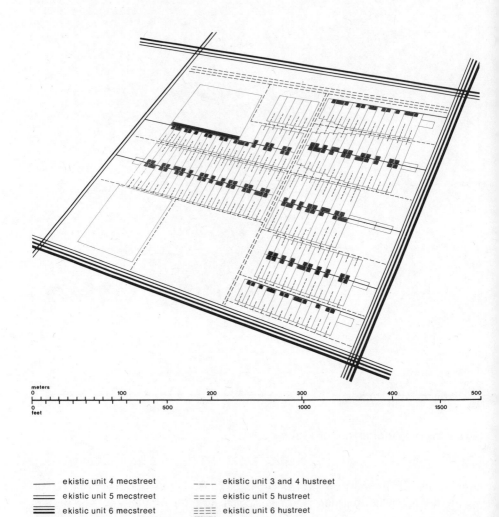

———— ekistic unit 4 mecstreet	_ _ _ _ ekistic unit 3 and 4 hustreet
════ ekistic unit 5 mecstreet	═ ═ ═ ═ ekistic unit 5 hustreet
════ ekistic unit 6 mecstreet	══ ══ ekistic unit 6 hustreet
════ ekistic unit 8 mecstreet	██ parking lots

149. the neighborhood as a movement system

The husystem is represented by the dotted lines, because Anthropos does not slide, but walks, and we see that it is really an internal system helping people to walk from inside their homes along the housegroup streets (class four) to the neighborhood street (class five) and the larger neighborhood street (class six). The mecsystem starts at the limit of the home (parking area — shown in light grey) and moves to the mecstreet (class four) and from it to class five (still inside the neighborhood) to connect with the outside mecstreets of class six inside the larger neighborhood in order to visit its center or to class eight, moving out and around it.

As we see in Figure 148 the hustreets are all on the surface and the mecstreets can either be on the surface and covered (Chapter 9, Fig. 119) or on the surface but, in earlier phases, not yet covered. In our case they are all covered in the housegroups, but then they go underground and (classes five to eight) in corridors which are covered with grass and flowers because the mecstreet is just under the surface (class five) or with trees also when they are deeper (class eight). In the case of class six the mecstreet is also below the surface, but covered by the continuous Shells of shops, etc.

One type of street that is not illustrated here is the bicycle street which is used a lot in countries like The Netherlands (no hills) and will be used more and more in countries like India, where it will take quite some time for many citizens to acquire motorcars. This street is a mixture of hustreet (in terms of energy used) and mecstreet (in terms of very different speed and dangers for the humans) and has to be very carefully designed, on the surface to please people, but in a way not creating dangers for the hustreets.

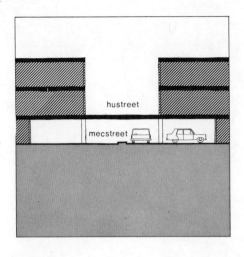

150. the mecstreet is on the surface but is covered by the hustreet

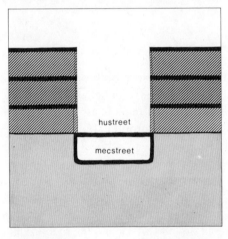

151. the mecstreet is below the ground

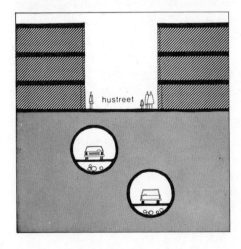

152. for mecstreets of higher classes, tunnels will have to be built

The structure of the different parts of the mecsystem is simple. We have seen how it works in houses and housegroups in Figures 110 and 120. A corresponding solution is valid for auto-mobiles entering those buildings serving larger groups as in the corners of the neighborhood (Fig. 148). They can either remain underground or, when it is preferred that people, like old and crippled ones, do not have to use elevators, the auto-mobiles can come up on the surface and be covered by terraces so that they will not be seen and spoil the total environment (Fig. 150).

In other cases, when the mecstreet goes below surface but to a shallow depth (class five in Fig. 149), there is a wide ditch dug first which can remain open at the beginning and be covered later (Fig. 151).

For mecstreets of higher classes the depth may have to be increased, and then tunnels will have to be built because we may wish to use the surface for buildings or for mecstreets of lower classes or because we may wish to increase the speed by using the force of gravity (Fig. 152).

In dealing with this problem we have to remember that the natural solution is (as we can also see in biological organisms) the higher the speed the deeper we go, as for example in the greatest part of our body with blood circulation.

meters
0   100   200   300   400   500

0   500   1000   1500
feet

grass and flowers

trees

153.   Nature as a system infiltrating the human settlement

In Figure 153 Nature is quite apparent as a system, starting with small or larger patches inside houses, and continuing as a hustreet without Nature (see Fig. 122c) or as a freely and naturally designed green street (Fig. 119 lower part), or a regulated natural system (Fig. 119 upper part). Thus we can understand the differences between all hustreets class four which gradually reach the hustreets of class five, six, etc., some of which are planted only with grass and flowers and others with small or very large trees.

This system gradually changes from a husystem which can even have hu-avenues with Anthropos being the main element and controlling most of the space (class four and sometimes five), into a Naturarea (see Chapter 4) where Nature is in control and Anthropos is a visitor.

In this whole natural system or Nasystem we see the reservation of spaces for sports (lower left), where again we deal with an Anthroparea inside the Naturarea or for some buildings like coffee houses, etc., which are Anthropareas. It now becomes clear that inside the whole husystem of the neighborhood we may have Nasystems inside which will be husystems. Thus we understand that both systems have to marry in a harmonic way. Of course, some of the hu and Na parts will be visited by machines bringing in or taking away plants or other plants or other parts. Again the balance and the harmony are the important solutions.

Inside this Nasystem Anthropos will be properly trained in many ways. First, his body will have all opportunities for walking, running or climbing hills, because even when we deal with a horizontal level plan, the opening of tunnels for mecsystems will leave soil or rocks which can be used to create a natural land-scape, instead of taking it away. Second, his eyes which from inside the home can see up to a few tens of meters and up to a few hundreds inside the house-groups (Fig. 121) can now see much further and many more variations and can recognize their symbols, a church or temple or mosque for some humans or the stadium for others. The same is valid for smelling all sorts of flowers, etc.

Inside the neighborhood people have natural contacts (non-organized) as they do inside the housegroups; but they also have organized contacts which help them to lose the feeling of isolation and separation from other human beings. This happens in all sorts of hustreets and husquares, and especially inside the organized buildings and services.

Such solutions can be seen first in the special housegroups for the very old people and for others, let us say homosexuals. Such people sometimes need to be mixed with other groups and sometimes need to be by themselves. These people will live in specialized housegroups consisting of three parts, the built-up part, the inner or isolated part and the outer or external one for communication with others (Fig. 154). Thus they can keep their own rules inside (nudists can remain nude in their courtyard) and the city's rules in the outside garden. In this way a neighborhood can contain many groups and allow for a great diversity.

The needs for health services can be satisfied either inside a specialized house-group, like the previous one, especially if it is for old people in which case it can be a first-aid station also, or by the creation of a special health station inside the elongated neighborhood backbone (upper part in Fig. 148).

Educational facilities in the neighborhood are served by the educational center (Fig. 155) as shown also in Figure 148 (left corner) which is no longer only a school but offers educational facilities for all age-groups and all needs because it incorporates special parts for nurseries, for classes, courtyards, sports grounds, etc. Instead of being used 40 hours a week, it can be used over 100 hours, from early morning to midnight.

Recreation and entertainment is provided for both in the Nasystem and inside the neighborhood backbone, which contains all sorts of facilities from clubs to restaurants and nightclubs, etc.

Commerce is the main function of the backbone, though it incorporates many other functions, as already described. It has all shops and workshops extending along hustreets with their auto-roofs (Fig. 156), as well as in husquares of various types for different uses, with a different character for every group of work places. It can be two or three stories high, or two inside and three outside if the ground floor is turned into a mecstreet. The best solution is for the mecstreet to be underground, because only then can we have the best interaction on the ground floor, as in the ancient Greek agora or marketplace.

154. specialized housegroups

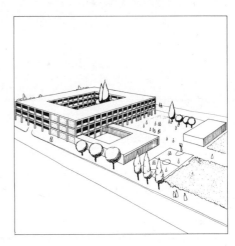

155. the neighborhood educational center

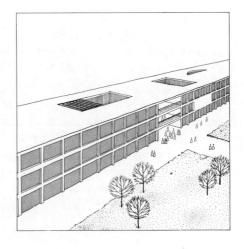

156. shops and workshops with auto-roofs extending along hustreets inside the neighborhood

145

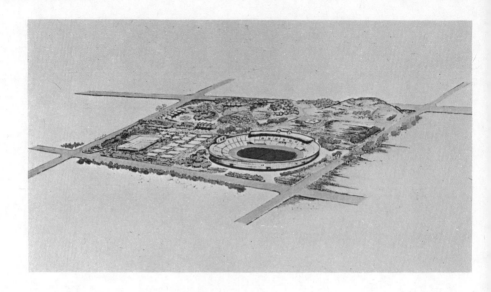

157.   the neighborhood sports ground

In the unit of the neighborhood, especially the larger one, there are also other types of installations, like sports grounds (Fig. 157), which may contain a stadium, a beautiful park, hills created by the soil from the excavations, etc.

In such a park, we can see how all the human needs for higher ground giving a view of the landscape or the city are again satisfied. In the past, several cultures and civilizations always tried to provide this, beginning probably with the ziggurats and the tower of Babel, continuing in ancient Greece with temples like Poseidon's in Sounion, in Peking, China with Coal Hill and again in the Mediterranean with the churches dedicated to St. Elias.

Figure 157 also shows one of the factories of the city!

This is not a mistake — it is the factory! Here we can only see its roof, because the factory is underground.

146

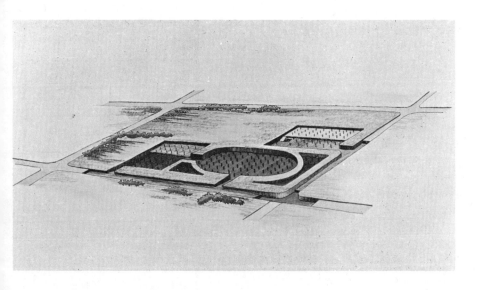

158.   the factory without its grass-covered roof

This is the only natural solution because:

1. Most of the production is automatic and very few people work underground — the controls and offices are above.
2. In any case factories have to be lighted by electricity and properly air-conditioned for the benefit of the few workers and products.
3. Airconditioning and better climate (heating-cooling) will be cheaper underground.
4. No space on the surface will be lost for automatic production. Even a polis (Chapter 11) can have four or many more such factories providing over 1,000 jobs.
5. No citizen will be disturbed by the noise or the appearance of the factory.
6. There will be no pollution — everything will go far away through underground pipes.

Now that we have taken the roof covered with grass, the sports grounds, the stadium and the offices away, we can see the factory in operation (Fig. 158). The materials come into it from the mecstreet and they move automatically into the production line. The products move out into the mecstreet without disturbing any one inside the city.

The steps to the future

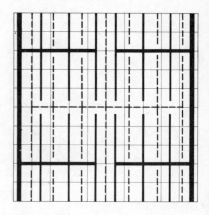

We do not need to wait for the mec-streets to go underground in order to ameliorate our neighborhood. We can move towards the future by steps, the first of which is to separate the hu-streets and mecstreets on the surface (Fig. 159).

The second step is to cover the mec-streets class four with concrete inside the housegroups (Fig. 160).

The third step is also to cover the mecstreets class five and create shopping centers, and the fourth one is to add auto-roofs, etc. (Fig. 161).

In this way we begin to separate Anthropos from machine in the most feasible way, because the initial cost is the same as the present-day solution of mixed hustreets and mecstreets, and later we can begin to add facilities by steps.

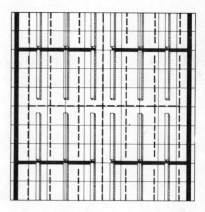

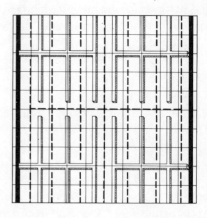

159. first step: separate hustreets and mecstreets

160. second step: mecstreets class four covered by concrete

161. third and fourth steps: cover mecstreets class five and add auto-roofs

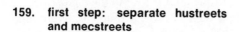

148

162. aerial view of neighborhood, Tema, Ghana

163. the university of the Panjab, Pakistan

We have already moved ahead and tried out the system of progressing by steps in many types of neighborhoods, both for normal housing and for colleges, universities, etc.

In the case of Tema, Ghana, we examine such a neighborhood from the air (Fig. 162), and in the new campus of the university of the Panjab (Fig. 163) the main hustreet already serves thousands of students in a system of courtyards and buildings, without any direct contact with machines.

An example of how this system of moving by steps can be implemented has already been shown in Figures 131, 132 with separated hustreets and mecstreets. We can now see how this system has been incorporated inside the whole neighborhood of Apollonion (Fig. 164) which completely serves 150 families, that is over 600 persons. This neighborhood, which also includes a special center for symposia, is served by only three mecstreets, one of which is only for the symposia. That is, 150 families are served by only two mecstreets, one of which has been seen in Figure 137 and about fifteen hustreets.

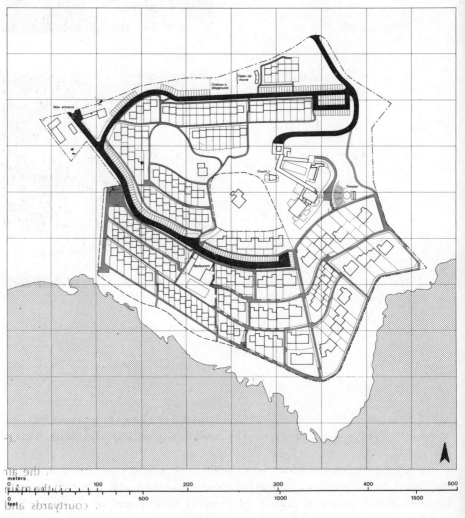

164. the Apollonion, Porto Rafti, Greece

The present neighborhood changing into the future

Present-day neighborhoods are of two basic types, rural (that is villages) and urban. Their future depends on the category to which they belong, and I deal here with the two basic ones.

We will not have many new villages in the old sense of farming, cattle-breeding and fishermen's settlements, with the exception of some very low-income countries whose farmers and hunters still live in isolated houses and housegroups and will have to come closer together in villages for a few generations, until their income provides them with machines.

What we will have is new "villages" or neighborhoods mostly used as second homes or for retirement, with part-time farming mostly for pleasure. These will be created, either in new locations, or in combination with existing hamlets and villages.

The existing villages, especially those with cultural values, representing a continuity of tradition and giving occasion for escape, will have a great future as second homes or as an escape, as we said for hamlets also. The reason for their gradual transformation into really almost urban neighborhoods is a two-fold one. The first is that some of them are so close to the expanding urban areas that they will be absorbed by them and will either keep their character (in cases where mankind is aware of their value) or lose it. The second reason that they will be gradually abandoned by their inhabitants is because once machines come in, all people will achieve great mobility — an income of $1,000 per capita will be sufficient. Thus the kinetic fields will allow people to use the maximum of one hour to cover easily 30 km instead of five. This means the strengthening of new human settlements or a new type of city because the new area will be of the order of 360 sq. km versus the average of 25 sq. km in the past, that is several decades larger, which means as large as ekistic unit eight.

The urban neighborhoods will gradually be transformed. Following present trends they will lose their values and character, but when these losses have been understood, the trends will change. The main way will be through the recognition of the need for territorial organization, which we have already lost especially inside cities. A system of neighborhoods will have to be created for better cohesion and provision of local, organized services.

The physical expression will be in terms of hustreets and mecstreets and the gradual creation of husquares and infiltration of green areas. In terms of buildings, the older notion of urban renewal will be replaced by a better understanding of what therapy means[35], which may be an amelioration of existing buildings or the replacement of some or, very seldom, of all.

What is of importance in all these cases is the separation of hustreets and mecstreets. This is beginning to happen even in central cities like Detroit through elevating the pedestrians one level[36] as we see in the case of the Edison Plaza already under development[37] (Fig. 165).

165.   the Edison Plaza project, Detroit, U.S.A.

11. The polis

Ekistic Population Scale	Name of unit	Population range	Ekistic units covering this chapter	Kinetic field	Com. class	Ekistic unit
1	Furniture			a		1
2	Room			b		2
5	House	3 - 15		c		3
40	Housegroup	15 - 100		d	I	4
250	Small Neighborhood	100 - 750		e	II	5
1,500	Neighborhood	750 - 5,000		f	III	6
10,000	Small Polis	5,000 - 30,000		g	IV	7
75,000	Polis	30,000 -200,000		A	V	8
500,000	Small Metropolis	200,000 - 1.5 M		B	VI	9
4 M	Metropolis	1.5 M- 10 M		C	VII	10
25 M	Small Megalopolis	10 M- 75 M		D	VIII	11
150 M	Megalopolis	75 M- 500 M		E	IX	12
1,000 M	Small Eperopolis	500 M- 3,000 M		F	X	13
7,500 M	Eperopolis	3,000 M- 20,000 M		G	XI	14
50,000 M	Ecumenopolis	20,000 M and more		H	XII	15

The present situation

I have already explained that the small towns and cities from 5,000 people up to about 200,000 are classified as polis. They are the traditional urban settlements which used to house from about 4-5,000 people up to 100,000 or sometimes more. They are younger than villages and neighborhoods, but are nonetheless about 8,000 years old and they were the largest human settlements until 1825, with very few exceptions, which we call metropolises, which I will discuss in Chapter 12. The long urban tradition of many humans is based on this type of city because although their character started changing in 1825 there are still many thousands of them all over the globe.

When we speak today about a City of Anthropos, we very often think of this size of city and refer back to the ancient traditions, the practical and successful achievements like classical Athens, Jerusalem or Renaissance Florence, or to the theoretical concepts like Plato's ideal optimum polis of about 50,000 people, or Thomas More's ideal Utopia of 90,000 people. This is really why people in new town movements tend to create such a polis corresponding to the traditional notion of their size. But theories that new cities should have a size of only 50,000 people and be static and isolated cannot be justified. Even in England, where the post-war new town movement was based on certain sizes, they are now taking decisions for greatly increased growth of the towns created in the last twenty years. The notion of the static polis has its advantages, but no more than Plato could influence the dynamic growth of Athens, can the modern theoreticians stop the growth of cities which remain dynamic in an era of great explosion of all forces: from polis they turn into dynapolis[38].

There are many thousands of polises existing from the past, many of which grow larger with every day that passes and turn into metropolises, while others are being absorbed by other expanding metropolises or megalopolises and becoming parts of them; and others, serving some isolated and not developing areas, remain static and quite often decline. In reality there are many polises, but many have turned into sectors or districts of major settlements, and in such cases we tend to forget their individuality and character as we do for neighborhoods with which we deal in the previous chapter.

We only recognize as polises those which are isolated from other urban areas and those very few which are being created now and which we call "towns" or "cities". What we need is to remember that the notion of "town" and "city", that is polis in a more specific way, is a very old and natural human settlement where civilization was created. No matter whether it is isolated as a built-up area or a part of a major settlement, it has to be recognized as a unit with its own characteristics and its own values. If we enter into detailed views, such as their economic and social structure or their physical and cultural aspects etc., we will find that we repeat the same mistakes we make for neighborhoods. That is, we forget that the polis, no matter whether old or new, has its own dimensions and its own scale; and if we impose on it solutions corresponding to larger scales, we do it a lot of harm and we destroy all its values.

The polis of the future

The polis of the future corresponds in size and territory to the polis of the past, as it contains from 5,000 to 200,000 people and can be seen as a built-up or Anthroparea with a surface of 2,000 by 2,000 or 5,000 by 5,000 m. I present here the smaller polis because it is the frame within which such cities as classical Athens or Renaissance Florence were included and is the unit which we expect the school-age child (six to twelve years) to grow in and become acquainted with[39]. This polis (Fig. 166) is either independent or a sector of a major city and consists of several neighborhoods including the one we have already studied (Fig. 148) in its lower part.

Such a polis continues to be really a system developing horizontally and rising vertically only up to a few stories with one exception only, the existence of some towers as symbols of religion, administration or education and development. The difference from the neighborhood is that it is on a larger scale and becomes necessarily more natural through greater adjustment to topography and reaching some stories higher in its larger center.

In the center of this polis we can see all central functions and how they are connected with the different neighborhoods by service corridors. In this way we

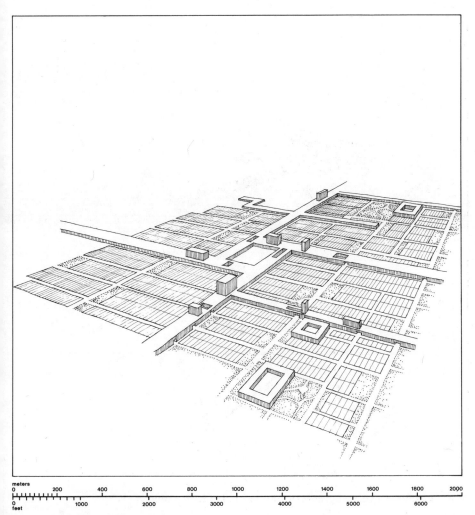

meters
0   200   400   600   800   1000   1200   1400   1600   1800   2000
0
feet   1000   2000   3000   4000   5000   6000

166.   the polis of the future

can see how people can move inside the polis, either by following the quiet and
green hustreets or, if they need contacts and services, by using their service corridors, from lower order ones to higher and higher and in this way they serve their
body, senses, (especially eyes) in the best way they prefer as they are given many
possible choices.

As we speak of the dimensions of polis (2,000 by 2,000 m in this case), we see the
center of the metropolis which is ot similar dimensions with the whole polis.
When we study such metropolises as Detroit, Michigan, we see that even today
their downtown or Central Business Districts (CBD) cover the same area as the
polis of the past[40]. In the future such areas will be organized service centers
instead of just happening as they have so far.

155

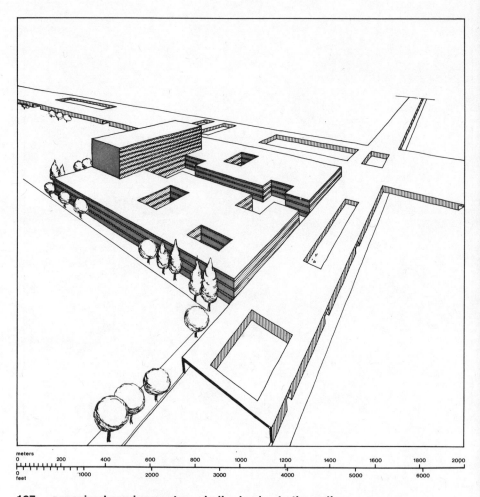

167. organized service centers similar in size to the polis

Centers such as that shown in Figure 167 comprise the administration of the metropolis, the central financial and commercial functions (headquarters of corporations) as well as special colleges, centers of health, entertainment, etc.

They are built so as to comprise the physical structure that Anthropos needs as proved by history, that is hu-avenues, husquares (open or closed by auto-roofs) and higher towers which are the symbols of the metropolis.

Such a compact system makes possible the utmost saving of human efforts and energy (second principle) as well as the most efficient use of mechanical forms of energy, as we do not deal with towers where we lose the maximum possible energy[41], but with compact systems. When the weather is very bad they can even close their hustreets and husquares and not only save energy, but also create human conditions for the best type of life in such a center.

By the creation of such a central service polis with four types of areas we achieve the best possible system for all central functions ranging from commerce, to natural social contacts, to democracy (which is really created by free human contacts). These areas are as follows:

— the mecsurfaces below ground (Fig. 168a) where machines are in control
— the public husurfaces such as avenues and squares (Fig. 168b) for all types of contacts
— the semi-public husurfaces such as inner courtyards for those using the surrounding buildings and their visitors, for exhibitions, etc. (Fig. 168c)
— the private hubuildings (Fig. 168d).

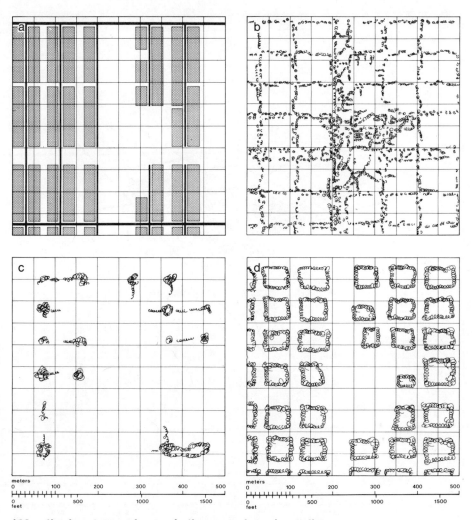

168. the four types of areas in the central service polis

The steps to the future

Most of the new polises which will be created from now on will become parts of metropolises. Therefore they must be conceived not as isolated settlements, but as parts of larger ones; as sectors of larger settlements or ekistic unit seven and eight inside ekistic unit nine, ten, and of higher order.

There will be some new isolated polises, which will be created as centers, to replace many villages as already explained and there will be others for special scientific purposes or for special types of production, of tourism, etc. Many of them may even grow more than was expected. Thus, they must always be conceived both as separate units and as parts of larger ones.

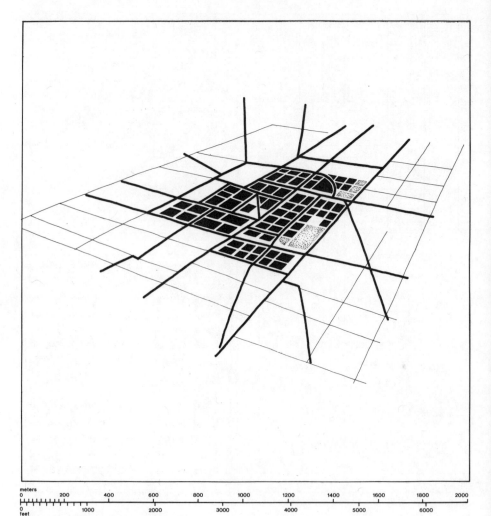

meters
0   200   400   600   800   1000   1200   1400   1600   1800   2000

0   1000   2000   3000   4000   5000   6000
feet

169.   the final static polis

As no polis will become static tomorrow morning, both because of population growth and the other explosions (income, energy, mobility)[42] there is an imperative need to conceive each one as a dynapolis which will some day become a static polis, both because of finalized boundaries and later because of finalized growth of all sorts. The plans already shown demonstrate the phase of the final static polis, and we can see how a dynapolis can reach this final phase. The proper road is when we conceive the future of a dynapolis in its early development phase (Fig. 169) and then guide towards its growth through plans covering several phases for certain periods (Fig. 170). This does not mean that such plans will not be flexible to serve new rising and unexpected needs or to use unpredicted technological solutions.

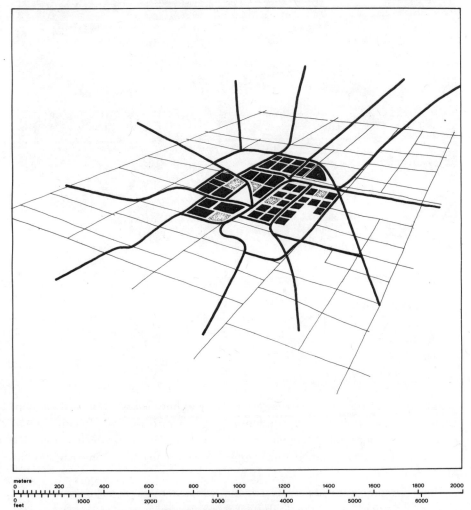

170. a dynapolis in its early development phase

171. Kafue, Zambia

Such types of polis have started to appear and here we see two of them conceived as "new" polises such as Kafue (Fig. 171) which will later become a part of the Lusaka metropolis, Zambia and Tema, Ghana (Fig. 172) which started as a small polis, has already turned into a large one and is going to become a part of the Accra metropolis.

There are some efforts to create a "polis" with pyramids only, like the ones they now try in France[43]. It is very doubtful if they can survive.

172.   Tema, Ghana

The unit of polis was the basic element for Islamabad, the new capital of Pakistan, and here we see the first two polises (Figs. 173, 174) already built out of the several tens that will form the metropolis as we will see in Chapter 12.

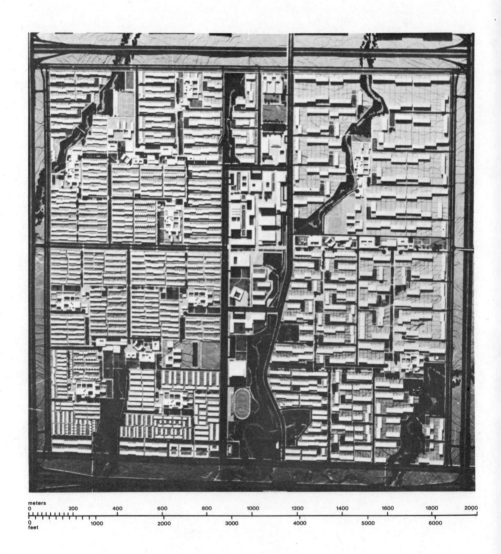

meters
0   200   400   600   800   1000   1200   1400   1600   1800   2000
0 feet   1000   2000   3000   4000   5000   6000

173.   Islamabad, Pakistan

In these two cases we can see how two polises which are built next to each other can be based on the same principles and, by respecting Nature and a variety of needs, become very different in appearance.

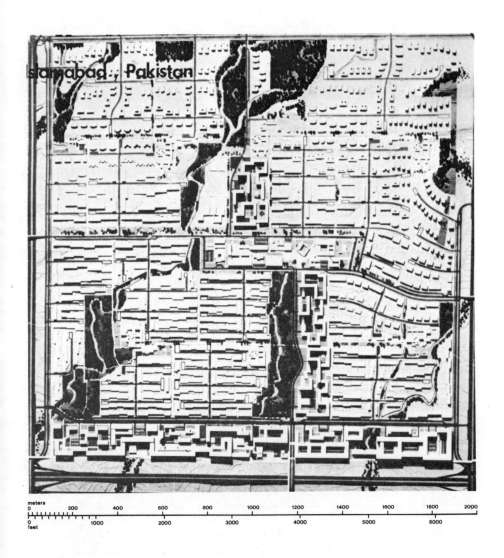

174. Islamabad, Pakistan

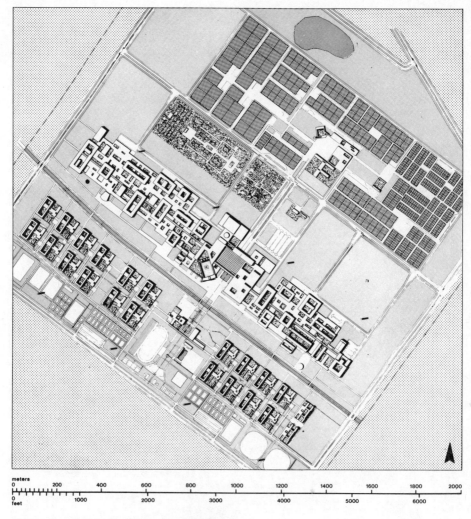

meters
0   200   400   600   800   1000   1200   1400   1600   1800   2000
0
feet   1000   2000   3000   4000   5000   6000

175. the university of the Panjab, Pakistan

A different kind of polis of the same size (2 × 2 km), housing and serving other types of specialized needs, is the university campus. We have already created several of them which follow the basic rules of separated husystems and mec-systems.

The first one is the University of the Panjab (Fig. 175) which started in 1960 and is in operation (we have already seen some aspects of it in Figure 163) and is nearing completion. It contains the residential sector (lower part), the academic one on the other side of the canal, a special neighborhood for the staff (upper part), and all sorts of parks and gardens both for the school of agriculture and for entertainment and all types of sports facilities.

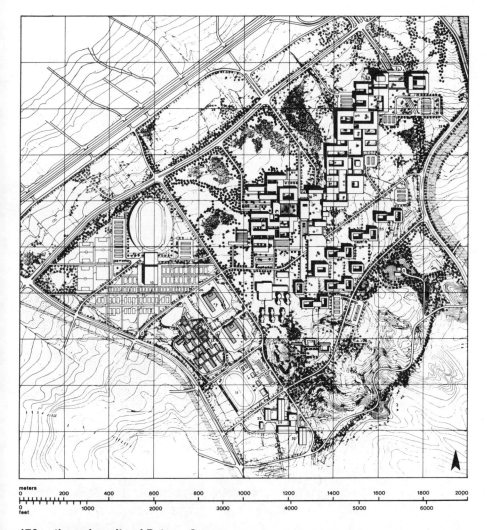

meters									
0	200	400	600	800	1000	1200	1400	1600	1800	2000

0	1000	2000	3000	4000	5000	6000
feet						

176.   the university of Patras, Greece

The other University is in Patras, Greece (Fig. 176). It has an older part (upper right), and the complete campus consists of the residential area (upper part), the academic (middle) and all sorts of gardens and parks, sports grounds etc.

What is characteristic of this campus, conceived as a husystem of both past and future, is that, like the other campuses created by our office, it consists of one, two and three-story buildings with the exception of one tower, housing the faculties of humanities and health, which has been named the Tower of Anthropos (left side). This has been created to become a symbol not only of the University, but of the polis and future metropolis of Patras, where no towers have been allowed up to now and hopefully this will last.

The present polis changing in the future

As we will not reach the future by eliminating the existing polis, we must prepare exact programs and plans for its evolution. In many cases the old polis will become a sector of a dynapolis turning into a metropolis etc. In the same way as the neighborhoods (Chapter 10, pp. 134-136), the polises can either save their existing values, or re-establish the lost values or change, if there are no values. In all cases there will be a technological modernization.

177. Athens, Greece

The solutions of problems will differ as in Chapter 10. One case I present here is indicative of how quickly we can achieve a radical change in a normal way. In 1937, as city planner of the metropolis of Athens, I proposed the creation of arcades and stoas along many central roads. The reaction of the services and especially of the city planner of the polis of Athens led to a decision only for three central commercial streets, as an experiment, one of which we see in Figure 177. The success was such that now it has been implemented in hundreds of streets, one of which is seen in Figure 178.

178. Athens, Greece

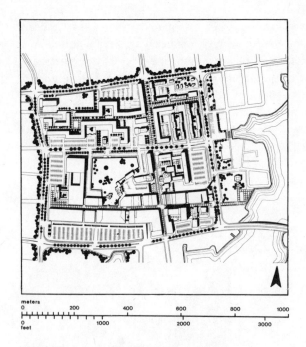

meters
0   200   400   600   800   1000
0   1000   2000   3000
feet

179. Hampton, Va., U.S.A.

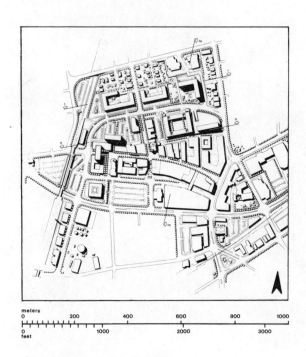

meters
0   200   400   600   800   1000
0   1000   2000   3000
feet

180. Malden, Mass., U.S.A.

In several cases we have made a major effort in small polises. Here is the case of Hampton, Va., U.S.A. (Fig. 179), where the goal was to re-establish lost values (it is an old polis, created in 1610) and of Malden, Mass., U.S.A. (Fig. 180), where the goal was to create new values in a huscale, which had been lost in both polises, whose centers were declining. Both plans are in the phase of implementation and lead towards the entopian polis as a part of metropolis.

In the same way in which we create new campuses equal to a polis (Figs. 175, 176), we can turn existing campuses into more human and entopian ones. An example is the Rensselaer Polytechnic Institute, Troy, New York (Fig. 181) which has been operating since 1824, has 5,000 students and prepares itself for the future[44].

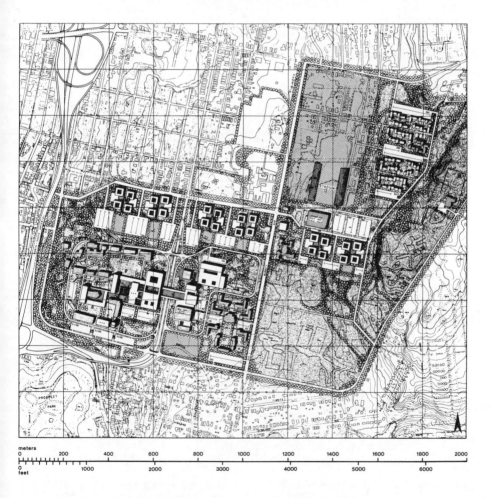

meters
0   200   400   600   800   1000   1200   1400   1600   1800   2000
0   1000   2000   3000   4000   5000   6000
feet

181.   the Rensselaer Polytechnic Institute, Troy, New York, U.S.A.

12. Metropolis

Ekistic Population Scale	Name of unit	Population range	Ekistic units covering this chapter	Kinetic field	Com. class	Ekistic unit
1	Furniture			a		1
2	Room			b		2
5	House	3 - 15		c		3
40	Housegroup	15 - 100		d	I	4
250	Small Neighborhood	100 - 750		e	II	5
1,500	Neighborhood	750 - 5,000		f	III	6
10,000	Small Polis	5,000 - 30,000		g	IV	7
75,000	Polis	30,000 -200,000		A	V	8
500,000	Small Metropolis	200,000 - 1.5 M	▓▓▓▓	B	VI	9
4 M	Metropolis	1.5 M- 10 M	▓▓▓▓	C	VII	10
25 M	Small Megalopolis	10 M- 75 M		D	VIII	11
150 M	Megalopolis	75 M- 500 M		E	IX	12
1,000 M	Small Eperopolis	500 M- 3,000 M		F	X	13
7,500 M	Eperopolis	3,000 M- 20,000 M		G	XI	14
50,000 M	Ecumenopolis	20,000 M and more		H	XII	15

The present situation

When we move beyond the traditional polis which reaches up to 200,000 people, we deal with small metropolises reaching up to 1.5 million people and metropolises which reach up to ten million. These settlements are really the achievement of our era. They began in 1825 (see Chapter 1) because until that date only the capitals of some empires surpassed 100,000 inhabitants and only those of great empires like the Roman (Rome), Byzantine (Constantinople), Mexican (Teotihuacan) and the Tartar and Chinese (Peking) reached the limit of one million. Such cities were usually due to the natural growth of the empire; their great size was not foreseen and they suffered very much, an example being Rome. We know of only three metropolises which were conceived as big capitals with more than 500,000 people and these were Teotihuacan (2nd to 6th century A.D.), Chang'an (A.D. 583-904) and Peking (14th and 15th centuries). From history we learn that Anthropos did not really know how to build metropolises because they happened very seldom.

All these metropolises of the past never covered an area larger than 10 × 10 km (6 × 6 mi.) which is the size of a typical American township[45]. Today the metropolises with a few million inhabitants cover areas which are tens of times larger. We can understand this huge change if we study cities like classical Athens (5th century B.C.) or 18th century London which have blown up to completely different dimensions[46]. In ancient times, metropolis meant mother-city; but its children were far away as colonies or within the empires. Today the mother-city keeps its children near by and grows by absorbing them and swallowing them into its own body. We now have several hundred metropolises and they all suffer in many ways from many problems because they have not been foreseen and properly conceived.

We do not need to expand on the character of their sufferings because everyone has experienced them and we have described them in general terms in Chapter 2 and more so in *Anthropopolis: City for Human Development*[47]. What we have to remember is that the suffering is of many types, although now the fashionable aspect for discussion is environment, and we do not solve the problems at all. Or if we do try, we do it in an uncoordinated way (like cutting through metropolises with highways). The result is that metropolises quite often suffer more from the "solutions". People continue to abandon their central areas; higher income people move out first and create economic and social problems[48], and the result is that our present-day metropolises are out of control. There are some proposals for the solution of these problems, but they are not realistic at all or even serious. The only seriously studied proposal is by Le Corbusier for Chandigarh. It is a useful contribution for the revolution that we badly needed, but even this proposal is utopian and does not lead to a desirable city. The reason is that Le Corbusier overlooks all pre-existing values and does not take into consideration the real human needs.

My conclusion is that today we are in chaos as far as the metropolis is concerned and do not do anything in the right direction.

The metropolis of the future

The scale of the metropolis is much larger in terms of population as it ranges from 200,000 to ten million people and a great deal larger in terms of area (see Chapter 4, Fig. 52). In order to understand it we must study the scales of 10, 20 and 100 km. A full analysis is given for the scale of 20 km as it is a quite representative one. But in order to connect with what we have seen so far, starting with furniture at the 5 meter scale (16 ft) (Chapter 6) and leading to polis at the 2,000 meter scale (6,400 ft) (Chapter 11), we will start with 10 km. We can thus get an idea of scale and then move to the analysis of 20 km.

The metropolis (Fig. 182) incorporates the residential polis we have already seen (Fig. 166), and the service-center polis (Fig. 167) in its lower and upper middle part. At this scale we can now see for the first time all four basic types of areas (see Chapter 4) as so far we have seen mainly the Anthropareas. In the upper left hand corner there is the Naturarea with a Cultivarea inside it. The main area is the Anthroparea, but to the lower right we can partially see the grass covering the Industrarea and even a park with small trees covering a part of it. This was the Industrarea outside the polis which has now become a part of the metropolis.

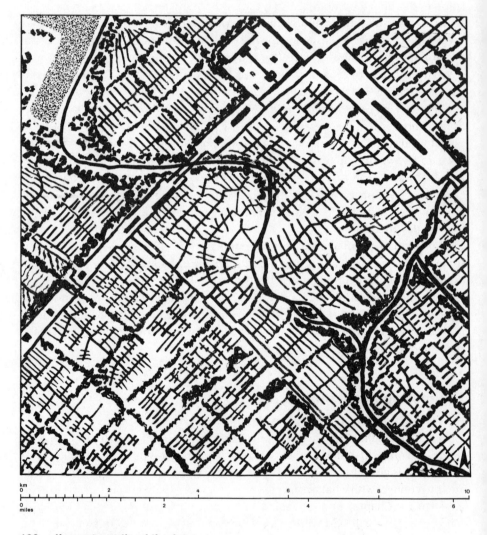

182.   the metropolis of the future

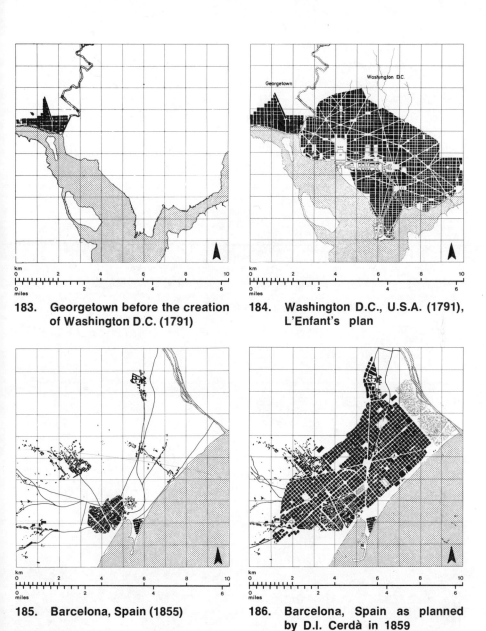

183. Georgetown before the creation of Washington D.C. (1791)

184. Washington D.C., U.S.A. (1791), L'Enfant's plan

185. Barcelona, Spain (1855)

186. Barcelona, Spain as planned by D.I. Cerdà in 1859

To understand how Anthropos has moved from polis to metropolis without taking the necessary measures (and thus the inhabitants suffer) and how in a few cases he took the necessary steps, we can study two cases of action with courage. The first one, in Washington, D.C., was the small polis of Georgetown (Fig. 183) which was planned as a metropolis in 1791 (Fig. 184). The second one is Barcelona, which was a polis (Fig. 185) and in 1859 was conceived as a metropolis (Fig. 186).

173

Most of the present-day metropolises are the cores of future systems and many more are new systems, either created afresh like Islamabad, the new capital of Pakistan, or as larger settlements related to present-day cities. Their main difference from present-day metropolises is that they are well-organized as systems of human life, consisting of polises both old and new, helping Anthropos to know where he lives and to develop more and better. When we look at them from the air in their real scale (Fig. 187), we do not easily understand them. How can we achieve this understanding using a scale of 20×20 km (12×12 mi.)? If we are experts though and look at the different elements of the metropolis we will understand how human and how helpful this metropolis is.

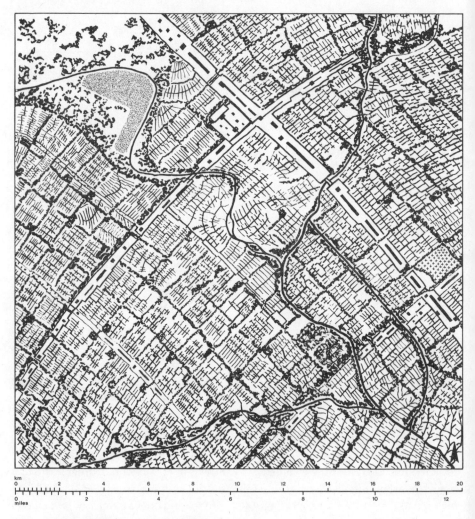

187. the metropolis seen from the air

The element of Nature, rivers and flora, that is the Naturarea, follows the original natural structure of the whole area (Fig. 188). Rivers are saved and their system is supplemented by canals where this is feasible (lower right in this figure). Plantations of value are saved and others are added where the soil is best for them and not so suitable for buildings. The result is a very natural system supplemented by green corridors and parks dividing the metropolis into polises (smaller units), and covering many underground or surface corridors. Thus, Anthropos can walk out of his small polis into a green corridor and walk to the park, the sports area and the river through hustreets. Or he can drive for leisure on special low-speed mecstreets or mecroads, as we will see. In this way Nature is married to the Anthroparea (Naturareas do not

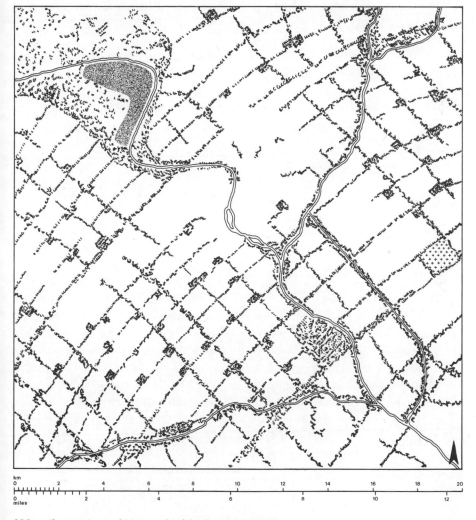

188.   the system of Nature inside the metropolis

form any belts and the Anthroparea does not rape them) and together they form the proper metropolis.

The whole system of the Naturarea consists of green hustreets, parks, hills, and is either a real Naturarea or absorbs the Cultivareas and covers also the Industrareas as we have seen in Figure 182 and we now see in Figure 188.

What we have overlooked so far is that this Naturarea should also cover Anthropos in his cemeteries, which today are being pushed out of the polis and thus are becoming inhuman because of the distance from the natural hu-area. In the future there will be cemeteries of all sizes belonging to the polis and the metropolis, forming parks or buried inside artificial hills repeating age-old traditions of catacombs. In this way the child will learn about death in time and will be adjusted to the reality of life[49]. With such cemeteries Anthropos keeps his contacts with the past and opens his eyes to the future.

The whole Society living in the metropolis is organized in a very systematic and rational way. Otherwise there is no hope for the freedom of Anthropos or of any social group. This is true both for the individuals and for corporations creating shops and facilities as well as for governments creating all necessary services from health to education and sports to entertainment. This means a coordination of social and administrative boundaries.

In this case (Fig. 189), we see the polis of several small sizes (ekistic units 7 and 8) and then the metropolis (ekistic unit 9), the large metropolis (ekistic unit 10) as well as the center serving a much wider area, that is a megalopolis (ekistic unit 11).

Such organization is expressed in very clear physical boundaries so that everyone knows how far his or her territory reaches, though of course this does not mean that she cannot move into any other territory that she may prefer.

The boundaries are formed by natural corridors or by physical structures of buildings of all sorts, as we understand by comparing Figures 187 and 189.

Only such a system helps Anthropos to be free to have all the contacts that he may prefer in a natural or organized way, that is to have the maximum of potential contacts (first principle) and achieve them with the minimum of energy (second principle). This is the deeper meaning of physical and social organization: the greatest and easiest possible choices for Anthropos.

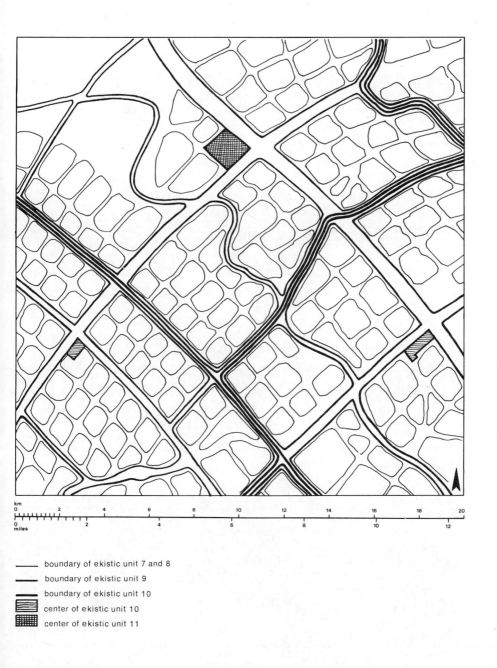

km
0 | | | 2 | | 4 | | 6 | | 8 | | 10 | | 12 | | 14 | | 16 | | 18 | | 20

0 | 2 | 4 | 6 | 8 | 10 | 12
miles

——— boundary of ekistic unit 7 and 8

——— boundary of ekistic unit 9

═══ boundary of ekistic unit 10

▤ center of ekistic unit 10

▦ center of ekistic unit 11

189. the social and administrative organization

177

All buildings, from the single house to neighborhood centers and polis centers, up to metropolis buildings of all sorts, are organized in a way helping people to locate them and approach them in the easiest possible way by walking or by using machines. The machines follow their own network; but here we show the systems of hustreets and buildings (Fig. 190). We see a clearly hierarchical system, but without any visual repetition of the same patterns, unless, of course, people prefer this repetition. We start with the small hustreets running between one, two, or three-story houses and we reach the big center of the large metropolis (ekistic unit 10) whose buildings may be up to 17 stories high and the megalopolis (ekistic units 11, 12) which goes up to 21 stories. Even the heights of the buildings alone transmit the message of what type of services can be found.

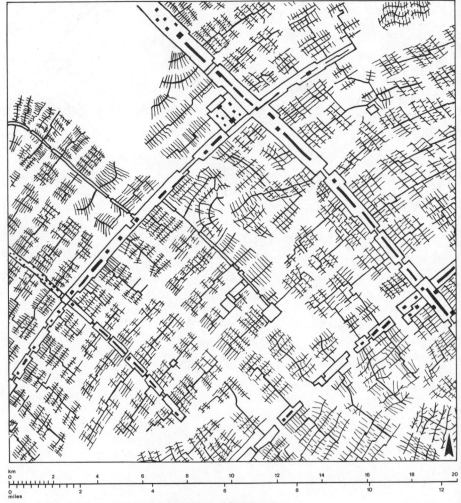

190.   the system of main buildings and hustreets

As we have already seen, the metropolis has service corridors and service centers of several orders, from ekistic unit 5 (quite seldom) to ekistic units 6, 7, 8, 9 and 10; and if it happens to be the central metropolis of a megalopolis then it has service centers of ekistic units 11 and 12. In the case of megalopolis, the corridors we see have many hustreets and squares and even hu-avenues, up to a length of two kilometers because this is the maximum distance that the human eye needs and is pleased to see and which most humans like to walk.

These service corridors contain all kinds of Shells from residence to health and welfare, education, entertainment, light industry and administration.

The simplest element of all (visually) is the system of movement in the Networks (Fig. 191) definitely including all the Networks, from natural humovement to trans-

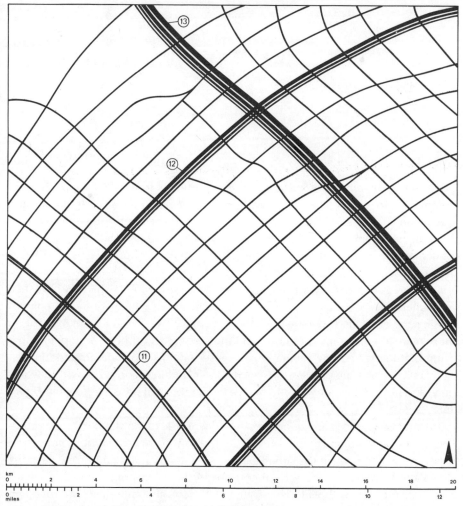

191.   the basic underground system of Networks

portation of people and goods, to all sorts of utilities from water supply to tele-communications. With the exception of the husystem they are all underground and operate in channels and pipes in the same corridors, belonging to certain classes, from the megalopolitan corridors (ekistic units 11 and 12) which serve much wider settlements than the metropolis, to the metropolitan corridors (ekistic units 9 and 10), to the polis corridors (ekistic units 7 and 8), etc.

Only three kinds of Networks are above ground: the hustreets which we have seen in smaller units (Chapters 7, 8, 9, 10, 11), the hustreets which are meant only for visiting and enjoying wider areas where only special auto-mobiles can move at no more than 40 km (25 mi.) per hour, and the mecstreets for heavy equipment that cannot (at least for a few generations) be inserted into the underground tunnels. At this stage and scale (Fig. 191) we see the basic underground system of Networks only, and not the husystem or the mecsystem in its small parts as shown in Figure 168.

The creation of so many underground Networks leads to the need for a multi-level metropolis and in Figures 192 and 193 we can see how it has been conceived for the new center which the Urban Detroit Area needs in the future[50]. Figure 192 shows the husystem in the service corridor of the metropolis, ending at an ad-ministrative center with its tower. Figure 193 shows the multi-level metropolitan service center and the three towers belonging to three different religious centers.

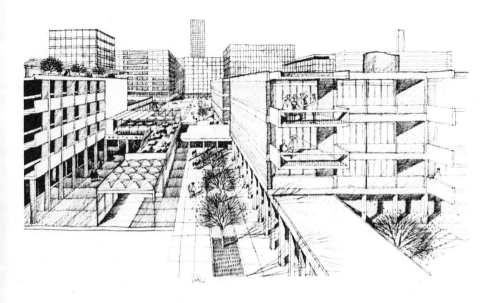

192. central business district proposed for the new urban center of Detroit, Michigan: the service corridor

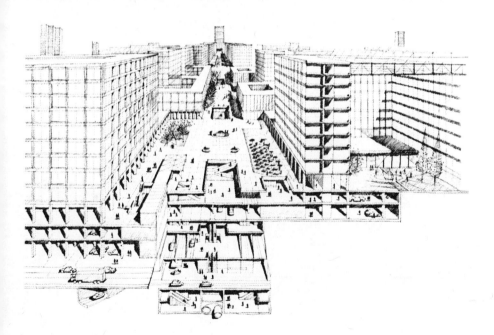

193. the multi-level view of the central business district proposed for the new urban center of Detroit, Michigan

The steps to the future metropolis

To prepare ourselves for the future metropolis we must be sure whether anything created as a "new town" that is a polis, will allow for the gradual transformation of its parts — as for example the transformation of its surface highways into deepways, separating Anthropos (who remains on the surface) from the machines forever. We must create in the same way those new metropolises that will be built from scratch, like some new capitals.

At this stage we must remember as in Chapter 11, p. 159 that the metropolis and large metropolis are not created overnight. And whether they are new or grow

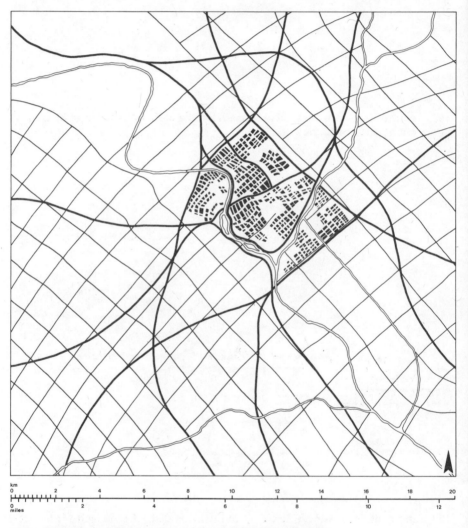

km
0   2   4   6   8   10   12   14   16   18   20

0   2   4   6   8   10   12
miles

194.   the existing metropolis and the dynametropolis plan

182

out of existing settlements they remain dynametropolises for a long time and end up as static metropolises. We can follow this process in Figure 194 where we see the frame of the metropolis and its first concept as the dynametropolis, in a plan only.

We then see in Figure 195 how the plan was realized and another one was prepared for another phase of the dynametropolis (it is unrealistic to believe that the notion of the final phase can be everywhere conceived early enough) which will help it to turn into the final and static metropolis.

km
0   2   4   6   8   10   12   14   16   18   20

0   2   4   6   8   10   12
miles

195.   realization of the plan, another phase of the dynametropolis

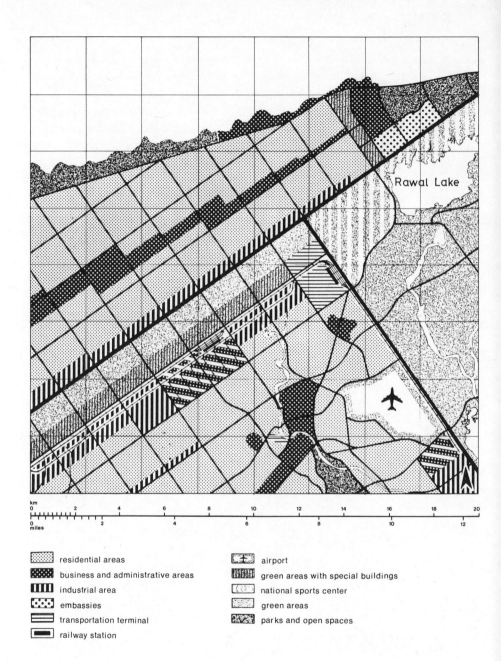

Rawal Lake

```
km
0        2        4        6        8        10       12       14       16       18       20
|‖‖‖‖‖‖‖‖|‖‖‖‖‖‖‖‖|‖‖‖‖‖‖‖‖|        |        |        |        |        |        |
0                 2                 4                 6                 8                 10               12
miles
```

⬚ residential areas		✈ airport
⬛ business and administrative areas		▦ green areas with special buildings
▥ industrial area		▨ national sports center
⬚ embassies		▧ green areas
▤ transportation terminal		▨ parks and open spaces
▬ railway station		

196.   Islamabad, Pakistan

184

The best example that I can present is Islamabad. We have already seen a housegroup (Fig. 130) and a polis (Figs. 173, 174). It has been conceived as a completely new metropolis connected to an existing polis. We see it here (Fig. 196) shown at the scale of 20 km which does not yet contain the whole, but clearly demonstrates how it consists of many polises and how it starts as a dynametropolis and ends up as a large metropolis or perhaps some day as part of a megalopolis.

In a few generations Islamabad, which is already a city of the present, will be a completely satisfactory City of the Future of the size of the large metropolis.

The present settlements changing into the future metropolis

Most of the metropolises of the future will arise from existing polises or metropolises, and from now on we will study several cases at scales ranging from 20 to 50 and 100 km.

The smallest cases are such polises as Rhodes, Greece (Fig. 197) and Kafue, Zambia (Fig. 198) which were very small and are now turning into larger and larger settlements; and Tema, Ghana (Fig. 199) which started in 1961 with the concept of a small polis, was soon afterwards conceived as a metropolis and is already attaining its size. We have already seen parts of it in Chapter 11, and photographs of its hustreets in Chapter 9, Fig. 131.

We can see how these changes will happen in the case of Detroit, Michigan (U.S.A.), where an existing "highway" (Fig. 200) will be covered and turned into an isolated mechanical deepway with the whole surface turning into a huspace[51]. This is the only normal evolution, since the so-called "horizontal elevator"[52] which runs above Anthropos must be excluded, and it certainly will. For those who doubt it, I recommend a visit to the avenue in Seattle, Washington (U.S.A.), where such a solution already exists.

Detroit, Michigan (U.S.A.), is also an example of a similar hu- and mecsystem in the process of being created inside built-up areas with many buildings as in the case of Woodward Avenue (Fig. 201). Here one or two levels will be added, either reserved for pedestrians, or also for some special auto-mobiles serving the service center only, for those who have to move inside it many times a day.

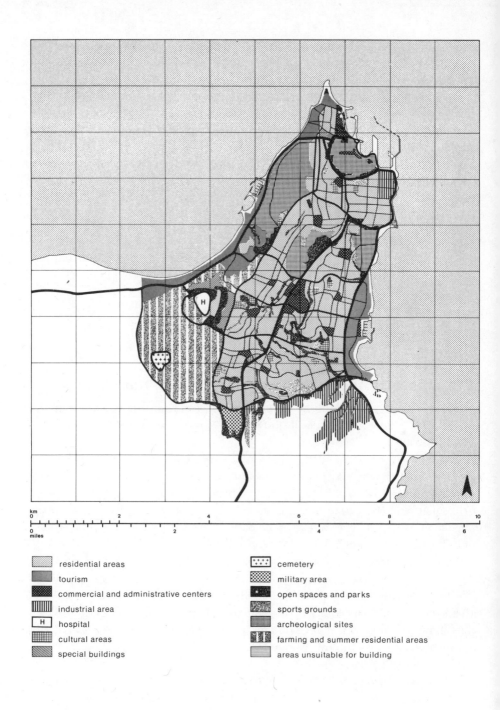

▨ residential areas	⊡ cemetery
▨ tourism	▨ military area
▨ commercial and administrative centers	▨ open spaces and parks
▥ industrial area	▨ sports grounds
H hospital	▦ archeological sites
▦ cultural areas	▧ farming and summer residential areas
▨ special buildings	▤ areas unsuitable for building

197.   Rhodes, Greece: master plan

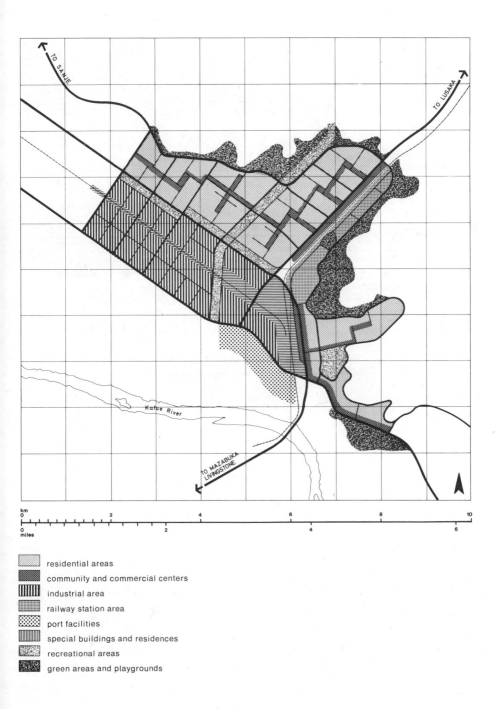

km
0   2   4   6   8   10

0   2   4   6
miles

residential areas
community and commercial centers
industrial area
railway station area
port facilities
special buildings and residences
recreational areas
green areas and playgrounds

198. Kafue, Zambia: master plan

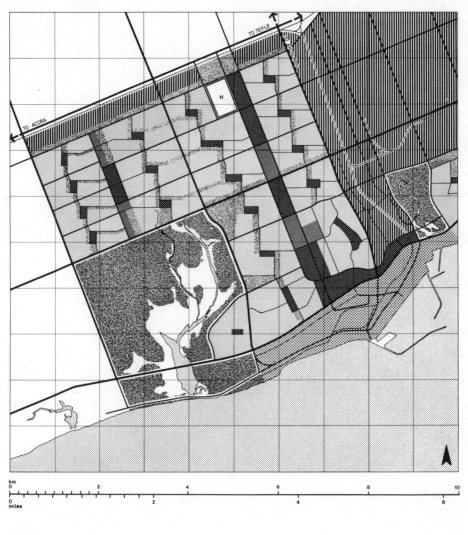

residential areas

civic, commercial, business areas

H hospital

institutional areas

industrial area

port and port facilities

green and recreational areas

open spaces and parks

199. Tema, Ghana: master plan

200. Detroit, Michigan, U.S.A.: creation of an isolated mechanical deepway; the existing open mecroad now turns into a covered one

201.　Woodward Avenue, Detroit, Michigan, U.S.A.:　creation of a multi-level avenue

Examples of a larger polis turning into a metropolis are Skopje, Yugoslavia (Fig. 202) which had to be conceived afresh after the earthquake disaster of 1963, and Riyadh, Saudi Arabia (Fig. 203) which has blown up from a small traditional polis into a huge capital city with all the contemporary problems.

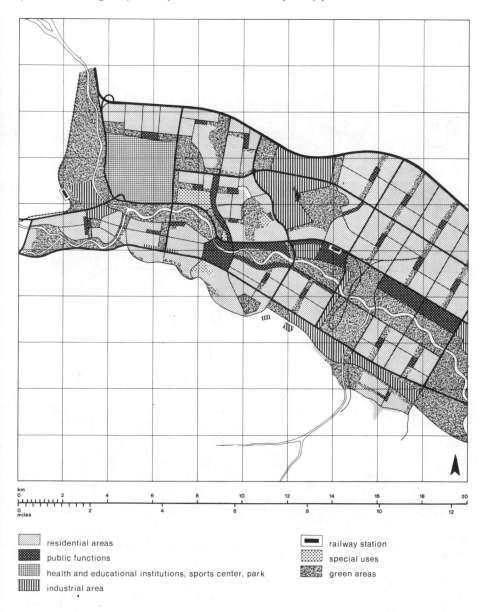

km
0   2   4   6   8   10   12   14   16   18   20
0   2   4   6   8   10   12
miles

residential areas   railway station
public functions   special uses
health and educational institutions, sports center, park   green areas
industrial area

202. Skopje, Yugoslavia: master plan

In both these cases, the really very old polis is now preparing itself for the future step by step. In both plans the difference between the old and future parts is quite clear as well as the very concrete structure of metropolis out of the units of polis.

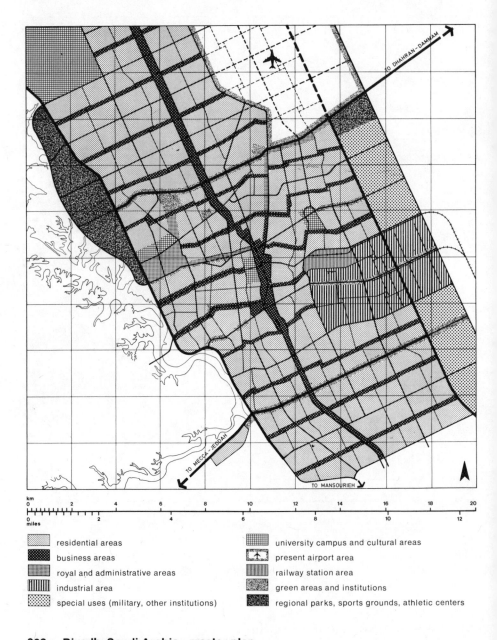

203. Riyadh, Saudi Arabia: master plan

After looking at the ten and twenty kilometer sizes of metropolises we now look at the fifty kilometer sizes and see three cases. First is Islamabad as a whole system (Fig. 204), also incorporating the existing polis of Rawalpindi. Second is Lusaka,

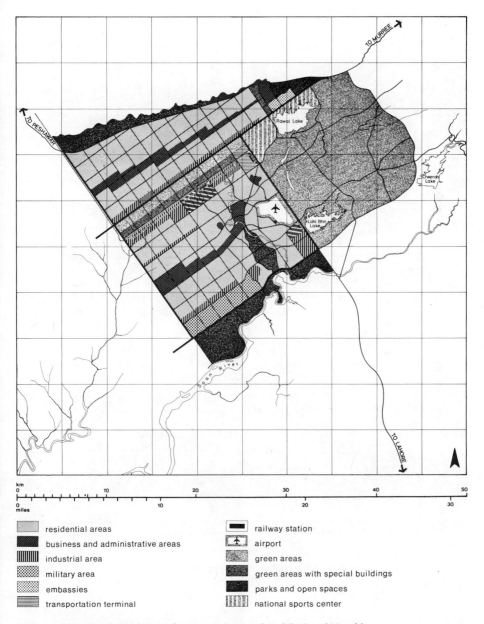

residential areas	railway station
business and administrative areas	airport
industrial area	green areas
military area	green areas with special buildings
embassies	parks and open spaces
transportation terminal	national sports center

204. Islamabad, Pakistan shown at the scale of 50 km (30 mi.)

(Fig. 205) the capital of Zambia, which was a small railway station and is now turning into a big metropolis. The third is Baghdad, Iraq (Fig. 206)which has already implemented a basic idea for proper canals connecting rivers, not only for irrigation as in ancient times, but also for the benefit of the Anthropopolis. This action has been overlooked for its further extensions, but will be understood and properly used in many cases.

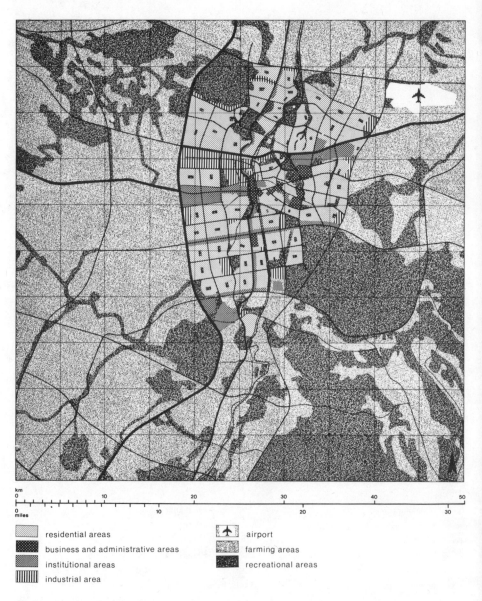

km
0   10   20   30   40   50

0
miles   10   20   30

residential areas

business and administrative areas

institutional areas

industrial area

airport

farming areas

recreational areas

205. Lusaka, Zambia: master plan

194

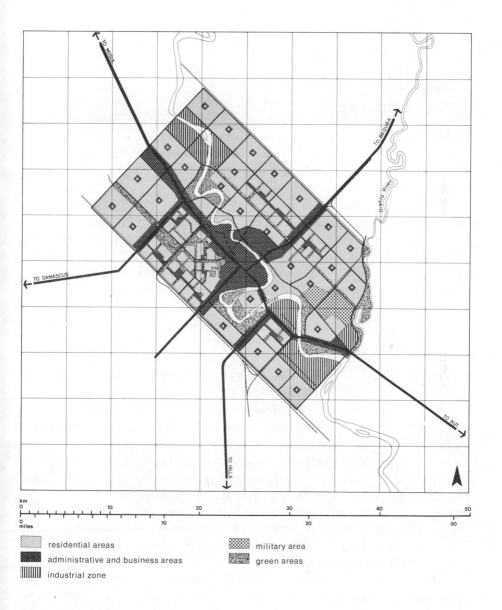

km
0   10   20   30   40   50
0 miles   10   20   30

- residential areas
- administrative and business areas
- industrial zone
- military area
- green areas

206. Baghdad, Iraq: master plan

195

The complete understanding of the metropolis cannot be limited to the size of 10, 20 and 50 km, because many metropolises are much larger and reach dimensions of the order of 100 km (60 mi.). Figure 207 shows the larger metropolis which comprises the previous part (Fig. 187) (lower left), and also the way in which its system of Nature is married with the city — that is the marriage of Nature and the human scale or non-human scale units of the Anthropareas. We can now clearly see that the geometric patterns which start with the house (Chapter 8), the housegroup (Chapter 9) and the neighborhood (Chapter 10), and which can still be understood in the smaller metropolis (Fig. 182) are now of minor importance. The larger the unit we look at, the greater is the influence of geography and topography.

This metropolis is a full system, but as can be expected, it is no longer as geometric as its parts. It is quite clear that a smaller percentage is Anthroparea and a much larger and more natural percentage is Naturarea. Here we can see Nature in full control of the basic structure as a system and its different parts, that is the Naturareas themselves and the Cultivareas, small parts of which we saw in the previous unit (Fig. 188).

Anthropos does not control this area by walking. He can move from one polis unit to another through the hustreets, but even this is a hard effort on such a larger scale. He can probably cover up to 10 km (6 mi.) when training himself, by visiting his neighboring polis and walking on some hu-avenues and sitting in some hu-squares in order to satisfy his desire for orderly Anthropareas. On the other hand he is interested in seeing the big hills and some mountains in the northwest. This is how far he is connected with such a huge scale through his eyes.

Society is organized and has its centers of different classes. Those ranging from ekistic unit 10 to ekistic unit 13 can be seen either as linear centers or as square centers, depending on the type of social functions they serve and the density and numbers of people served by them. They are all organized, because natural contacts do not work at such a huge scale.

What becomes more physically apparent at such a scale than social organization is the type of Shells. In some cases they are continuous systems, as large service corridors with avenues and squares inside them, and in some others they are not, depending on the local needs. These can be explained in terms of social organization as well as in terms of desires for esthetic satisfaction of the inhabitants which are not always of the same type. In Figure 207 we can clearly see that some communities are satisfied with the traditional type of hustreets and husquares with the same heights of buildings, while other communities prefer the notion of one or more symbolic towers as we see in a big square building near the center and a bigger one at the northern side.

In this unit we can see a large Industrarea (southern coast) which, because of its dimensions, its rocky soil and the fact that it serves more needs by sea with special boats entering directly into factories and not disturbing any other area, is not underground as were the ones we saw in the polis (Chapter 11) and in the central parts of the metropolis (Chapter 12). This area is properly isolated from the Anthropareas by a green Naturarea.

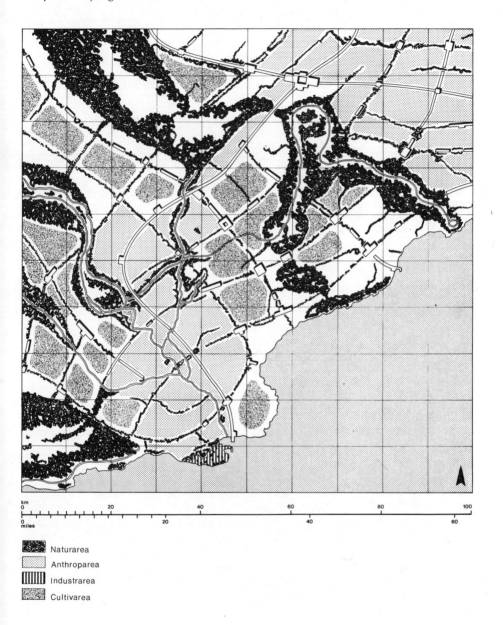

km
0   20   40   60   80   100
0   20   40   60
miles

Naturarea

Anthroparea

Industrarea

Cultivarea

207. the larger metropolis

The same area of the metropolis is also seen as a system of Networks where certain parts and characteristics appear which do not exist in the smaller areas. In such a complete metropolis, the Networks of higher class connect it not only with the megalopolis (ekistic units 11 and 12 as we saw it in Figure 191) but also with the whole eperopolis where it belongs (ekistic units 13 and 14).

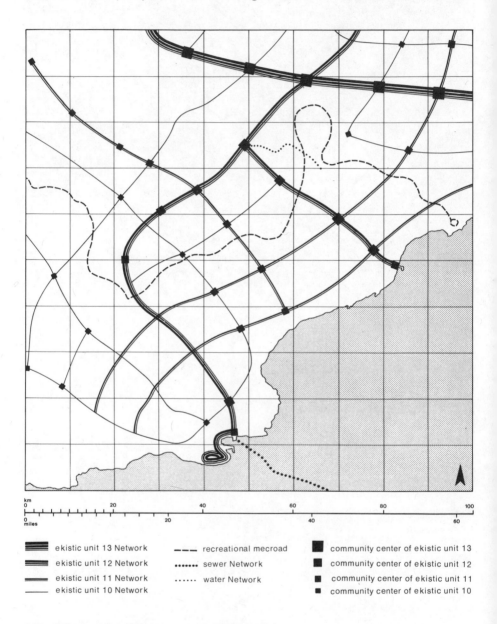

≡≡≡ ekistic unit 13 Network	――― recreational mecroad	■ community center of ekistic unit 13
≡≡≡ ekistic unit 12 Network	•••••• sewer Network	■ community center of ekistic unit 12
══ ekistic unit 11 Network	•••••• water Network	■ community center of ekistic unit 11
── ekistic unit 10 Network		■ community center of ekistic unit 10

208.   the metropolis as a system of Networks

The general system of Networks can be better understood by comparing Figure 207 with Figure 208. The hierarchical structure, which in the previous scale covered corridors from ekistic unit 9 to ekistic unit 12, now covers from ekistic unit 10 to ekistic unit 13. Second, the systems are not only land systems, but have become LANWATER (LAND-WATER) systems, as the corridors class 12 terminate in sea ports for direct transmission from auto-cars into auto-boats and from auto-containers into corresponding types of boats. In the same way the corridor class 12 serves the Industarea existing on the southern coast, by turning below it to serve a great number of industrial plants.

On the other hand we see the very important LANWAIR knot serving all three types of transportation that is land, water and air[53]. These will be the great knots of the future, serving all human needs in the best possible way.

Two types of mecstreets appear here, both of which are on the surface and are not deepways. The first one is purely commercial and is meant to help people who are searching for contacts with major commercial installations inside service corridors which sell large quantities or large size products (refrigerators, auto-cars, etc.) so that they can visit many of them by auto-mobile and not on foot. This happens in the corridor class 12 where the big deepways run, but it happens above them. This street cannot be seen from the air (Fig. 207), because it is covered in order to allow the visitor to move in an open auto-mobile and see all around, as this is really a big exhibition. Thus, it is called an exhibition mecstreet versus the normal hustreets (see Chapters 10 and 11). When we drive on it, it looks like an elongated pyramid so that everyone in an auto-mobile can look at the surfaces of the exhibition building (Fig. 209).

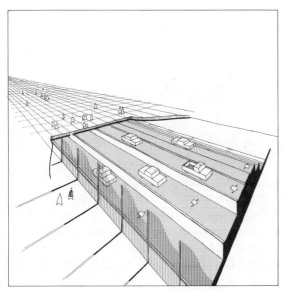

209. the exhibition mecstreet

The second type of surface mecstreet or mecroad, which appears here for the first time since it did not exist in lower scales, is the recreational mecroad which allows people to visit Nature and enjoy it on a larger scale than only by walking. It can be seen in Figure 207 and Figure 208 as a special line which gives the opportunity to explore along the river in the West, along the green corridor in the middle and up to the eastern hills until it reaches the coast, as well as in the southwest. This mecroad serves all those who cannot walk over large distances (babies, the disabled, old, tired, etc.) to be in contact with Nature and learn about and enjoy it. Speeds up to 50 km (30 mi.) are allowed on it and only special motors which cannot attain a higher speed are permitted to use it. This mecroad can be seen in Figure 210.

210.   the recreational mecroad

Also in this scale we can see the structure of utility corridors which coincide with all the mecstreets and never with the huroads or the recreational mecroads. They are all underground in the same tunnels so that they can be visited through the mecstreets. The cases where they go beyond them are only for connections with sources of water, energy etc., which also take place in deep underground corridors, as we see in Figure 188 where water comes down from the eastern hills and some of the rainwater goes deep into the sea in order not to pollute the coast with surface waste, as the other part is recycled.

13. Megalopolis

Ekistic Population Scale	Name of unit	Population range	Ekistic units covering this chapter	Kinetic field	Com. class	Ekistic unit
1	Furniture			a		1
2	Room			b		2
5	House	3 - 15		c		3
40	Housegroup	15 - 100		d	I	4
250	Small Neighborhood	100 - 750		e	II	5
1,500	Neighborhood	750 - 5,000		f	III	6
10,000	Small Polis	5,000 - 30,000		g	IV	7
75,000	Polis	30,000 -200,000		A	V	8
500,000	Small Metropolis	200,000 - 1.5 M		B	VI	9
4 M	Metropolis	1.5 M- 10 M		C	VII	10
25 M	Small Megalopolis	10 M- 75 M	▒▒▒▒	D	VIII	11
150 M	Megalopolis	75 M- 500 M	▒▒▒▒	E	IX	12
1,000 M	Small Eperopolis	500 M- 3,000 M		F	X	13
7,500 M	Eperopolis	3,000 M- 20,000 M		G	XI	14
50,000 M	Ecumenopolis	20,000 M and more		H	XII	15

The present situation

There are now already many small megalopolises (ekistic unit 11) and megalopolises (ekistic unit 12) which are human settlements connecting, absorbing and
influencing many metropolises, polises, etc. into one broader system which began
to take shape after 1940. An analysis of megalopolises, especially of the larger
ones, is given in *Ecumenopolis: the Inevitable City of the Future*[54] and thus I
will only describe them here in terms of their connections with the other human
settlements. They now contain from 5 to 75 million inhabitants and in the classification of ekistic units they will reach up to 500 million. They cover areas which
can be seen in frames of a few hundred kilometers to 1,000 kilometers. People
have already begun to commute daily even within areas of about 200 by 200 km
and reach up to a radius of 60 km[55] and thus the metropolises which are sometimes
not located at large distances from each other begin to be interconnected into
broader systems.

There are certainly people who pretend that the megalopolises can be avoided, but they have no idea of the first two principles of human settlements (see Chapter 1). There are others who support the idea that megalopolis also means huge buildings rising up to 500 stories and containing 50,000 persons each, but they have no idea what Anthropos is and what he needs. The only reasonable policy to slow down the very quick formation of megalopolises (which is taking place at very high speed because of an unprepared mankind) is regional decentralization and the development of rural areas. These are reasonable actions as long as it is recognized that we cannot and should not reverse natural trends, and that we should study the realistic and inevitable trends and make them more useful for Anthropos.

Some countries have begun to understand these needs. Even in some high-income countries such as the U.S.A. there have lately been movements for "a sound balance between rural and urban America. The Congress considers this balance so essential to the peace, prosperity, and welfare of all our citizens that the highest priority must be given to the revitalization and development of rural areas"[56].

The conclusion is that megalopolis is inevitable and that some few people are beginning to understand it, starting with Jean Gottmann in 1961[57] and some others who are beginning to plan for it as in the case of the Great Lakes Megalopolis which we are studying[58]. We are beginning to open our eyes, but no action has yet been taken. This is where we stand.

The megalopolis of the future

As even the present-day megalopolises[59] have only begun to take shape, the real megalopolises belong to the future. Thus, unlike in the previous chapters (6-12), where we studied the future and how we could move to it, step by step and with different changes of existing human settlements, in the present case we really see only the process leading towards megalopolises, the steps and the changes that have to take place for their ultimate formation. The larger the ekistic unit we speak of, the more general our presentation will be because we can now design in detail (and do) a house and a polis of the future, but an entopian approach for the future megalopolis requires a very general concept and a specific application in very concrete cases.

Here I will briefly present the theoretical concept as a continuation of the theoretical structure we followed from room to metropolis, and then turn to specific cases. These will be shown in three scales as was done for the metropolis, that is at 200, 500 and 1,000 km.

The first image we get is Figure 211, where we see the last metropolis (Fig. 207) in the lower right-hand corner. As happened in that case, where we saw for the first time all four types of areas, we now see these areas even more extended and in a better balance, as there are more Naturareas in this larger scale. It is quite clear that in the megalopolis scale, there is no longer any human scale, as even our eyes do not keep us in contact with what happens over such distances. In terms of Shells, we can see the major service corridors which incorporate almost all types of buildings as we have seen before.

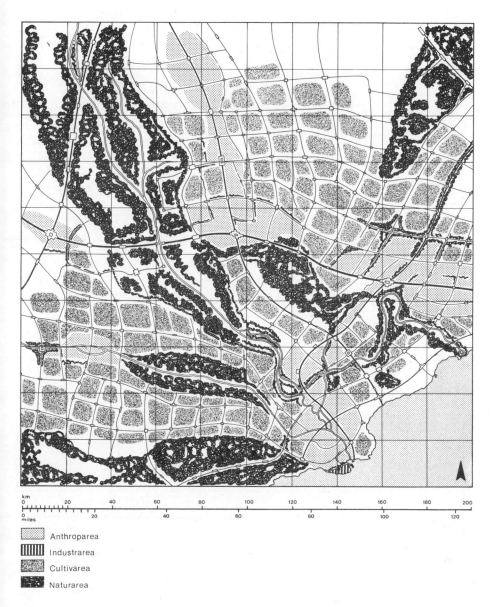

km
0   20   40   60   80   100   120   140   160   180   200

0   20   40   60   80   100   120
miles

Anthroparea

Industrarea

Cultivarea

Naturarea

211. the megalopolis of the future

At this scale we can study a very specific case which has been studied for its future evolution. It is the Urban Detroit Area[60] (Fig. 212) which we have already discussed earlier in this book.

This plan demonstrates how in reality there can be complete harmony between all four types of areas, even within an urban system that suffers so much today from great mistakes due to the industrial explosion.

Nature

human energy

212. the Urban Detroit Area, U.S.A.

In a larger area (Fig. 213), the megalopolis appears in an even better harmony and balance of the four areas because all four of them, the Anthropareas, the Cultivareas, the Naturareas and the Industrareas have their normal locations without problems arising between them.

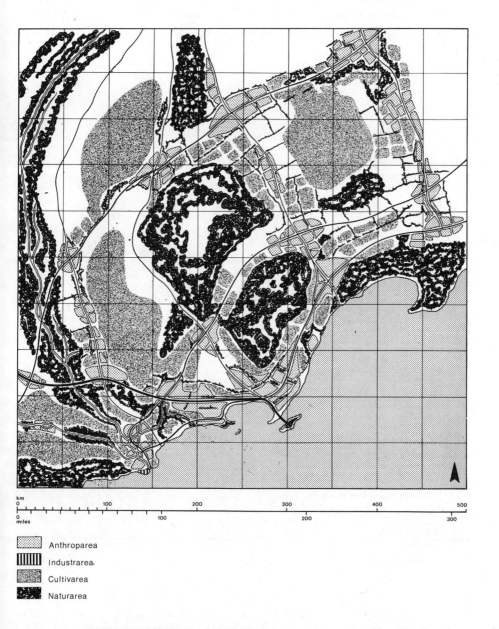

▨	Anthroparea
⦀	Industrarea.
▨	Cultivarea
▨	Naturarea

213. the larger megalopolis of the future

We can see how megalopolis is already developing at this scale in the following five cases: two from the U.S.A., two from Europe and one from Asia. There are many more[61] but I insist on presenting only the ones I have personally visited and studied, as I am certain about them. The first one we see here is representative of a megalopolis that is not yet suspected as such, but will turn into a strong one along the Caspian coast of Iran (Fig. 214) and the second one is a megalopolis that is beginning to be conceived as such along the southern coast of France[62] (Fig. 215).

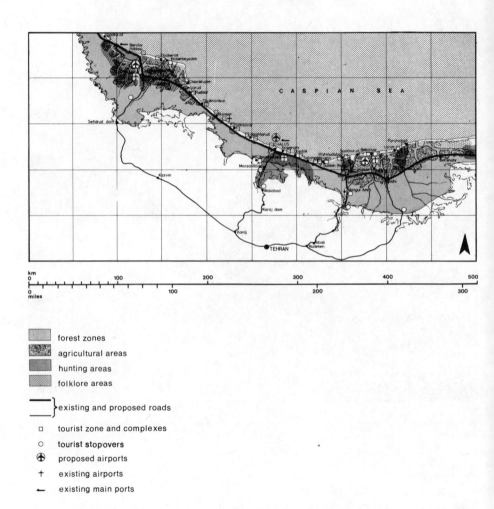

forest zones

agricultural areas

hunting areas

folklore areas

existing and proposed roads

□   tourist zone and complexes

○   tourist stopovers

⊕   proposed airports

+   existing airports

—   existing main ports

214.   Caspian Sea Coast, Iran: proposed land use for the year 2000

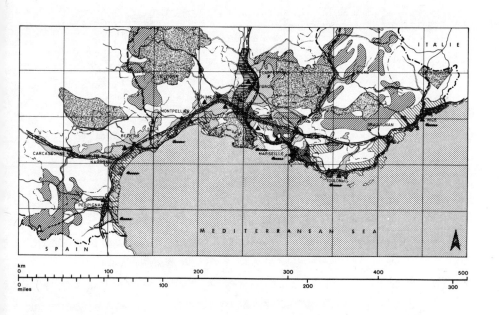

km
0   100   200   300   400   500

0   100   200   300
miles

▨ urban centers
░ agricultural areas
▨ national and regional parks
▤ industrial poles
▨ tourism and summer resorts
▨ tourism
── air train
--- principal road Network
▲ airports
⬎ ports

215.   Mediterranean France: prospective development for the year 2000

Next to the French megalopolis is the Catalonian one (Fig. 216) which in the future will be united with the French one, but at present is only beginning to be so. It has already though been conceived as a unified system between the three provinces of Barcelona, Gerona and Lerida[63].

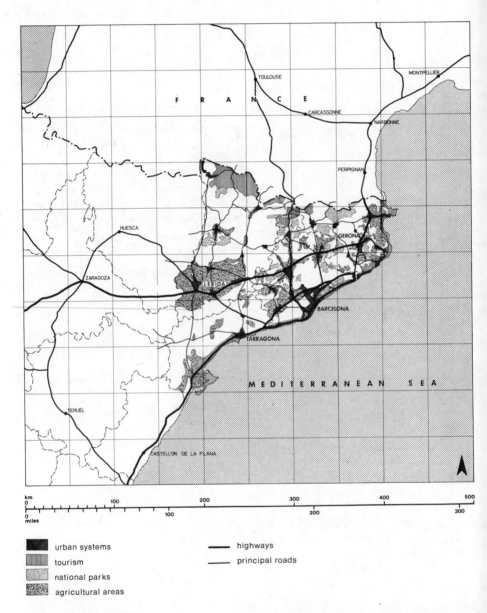

urban systems

tourism

national parks

agricultural areas

highways

principal roads

216. Barcelona, Gerona and Lerida Provinces, Spain: proposed development for the year 2010

One of the several American megalopolises is taking shape around Cleveland, and covers the whole of Northern Ohio and connects with Pennsylvania in the East and Michigan in the West. It is called the Northern Ohio Urban System (NOUS) and has already connected several metropolises and polises together and is preparing its future development (Fig. 217).

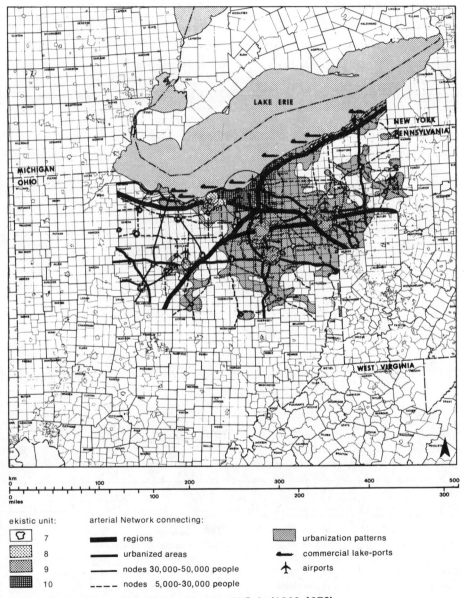

ekistic unit: arterial Network connecting:

7	▬▬ regions	▨	urbanization patterns
8	▬▬ urbanized areas	⬳	commercial lake-ports
9	▬▬ nodes 30,000-50,000 people	✈	airports
10	▬ ▬ nodes 5,000-30,000 people		

217. the Northern Ohio Urban System, U.S.A. (1960-1970)

The Urban Detroit Area which we have seen at the smaller scale (Fig. 212), is now shown at the larger one (Fig. 218) as planned for the year 2100 in an entopian way. This will save the city of Detroit from disaster by developing a twin center to its North and helping developments in certain directions to satisfy all future needs, to save Nature and to achieve the best marriage between the city that is the exploding Anthroparea, and the Naturareas.

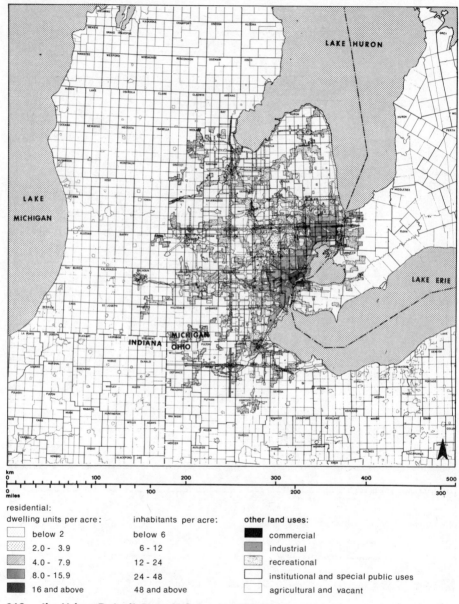

residential:

dwelling units per acre:	inhabitants per acre:	other land uses:
below 2	below 6	commercial
2.0 - 3.9	6 - 12	industrial
4.0 - 7.9	12 - 24	recreational
8.0 - 15.9	24 - 48	institutional and special public uses
16 and above	48 and above	agricultural and vacant

218. the Urban Detroit Area, U.S.A.: master plan

219.   Britain from 435 kilometers (270 mi.) up

The study of these megalopolises can now be greatly facilitated by the proper use of photographs taken from a great height such as the one of Britain (Fig. 219) taken by the Skylab space station from 435 km (270 mi.) which demonstrates the Wash (small indentation on coast at center right); the Thames Estuary (far right of picture); the Isle of Wight (light diamond shape off south coast at right); Portland Bill (small peninsula in center of south coast); Lyme Bay (large half-moon shape on south coast); the Bristol Channel (large waterway at left of land-mass); the

North Sea is at the top, stretching away to the land-mass of Europe, which is under a cloud. At bottom right is the English Channel, at left, the start of the Atlantic[64].

Such a photograph helps in two ways, first by convincing Anthropos that such a size of space is also a unit; in the same way as the farmer was convinced about his village when he saw it from a hill, and second by giving a very good image of many parts which are already interconnected into a system.

The largest scale of megalopolis can be seen in Figure 220 which incorporates all previous units (Chapters 6-12) and the smaller sizes of megalopolises (Figs. 211 and 213) in the lower left-hand corner. By moving to such a large scale that covers countries, such as the whole of France, we see all types of areas with the Naturareas controlling the situation, the Cultivareas following and the Anthropareas and Industrareas covering a smaller and smaller area. For Industrareas, especially, we now see some completely isolated places which are not inhabited but can be reached in a few minutes from the Anthropareas where their personnel lives.

What is now clear is that this future megalopolis depends on topography and related factors (Nature), on organized or disorganized growth (Society) and on the systems of Networks which can destroy or save Anthropos and Nature, and the whole system of life. The organization includes at this scale the problem of national security and the Networks include the full LANWAIR[65] system first seen in Chapter 12 which now also runs on the surface to help people visit Nature for training and entertainment. It is at this scale that adolescents try to conquer Nature and satisfy many of their great needs[66].

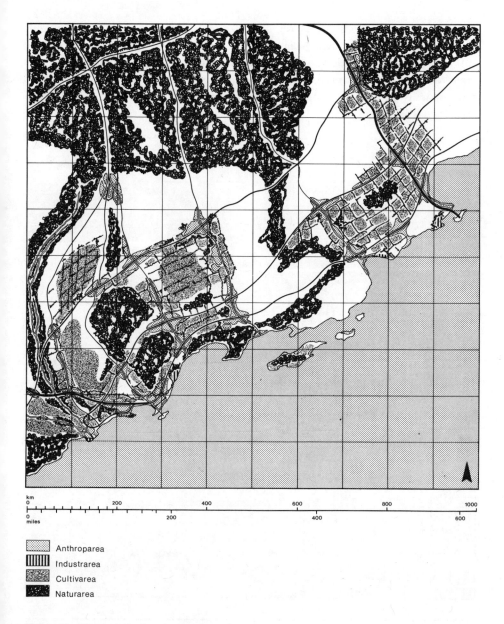

km
0   200   400   600   800   1000

0
miles   200   400   600

- Anthroparea
- Industrarea
- Cultivarea
- Naturarea

220.   the largest scale of megalopolis

In practice we may see two very different megalopolises at this scale of 1,000 km. One is in Greece (Fig. 221).* Even in small countries like Greece, which in classical times had many hundreds of city-states, we witness the formation of the present-day Greek megalopolis which unites the classical capital of Athens with the Byzantine one of Salonica (Thessaloniki) and with many others such as the ancient

213

Greek, Roman and modern Corinth, etc. into one system containing nine million people today — a system which cannot reasonably surpass twenty million.

It is Nature that prevails here, first because of the seas and then because of the great mountains (Naturareas) and the few but highly productive Cultivareas. The Anthropareas are concentrated mostly along the coasts for many reasons already explained (Chapters 3, 4 or 5).

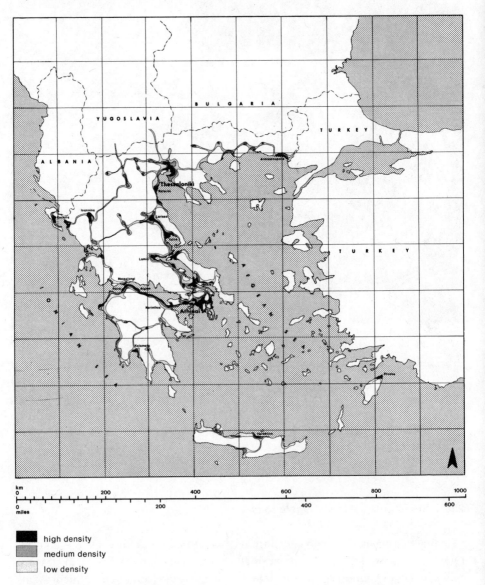

high density
medium density
low density

221. the Greek megalopolis

A completely different case is the Great Lakes Megalopolis which is now under study, as already mentioned[67], and which is beginning to become apparent when we see how Chicago, Illinois has been already connected with Milwaukee, Wisconsin, and Indianapolis, Indiana (West and South of Lake Michigan); how Detroit is connected with Windsor, Ontario and Toledo, Ohio, and how Toronto, Ontario is connected with Buffalo, New York, etc. (Fig. 222).

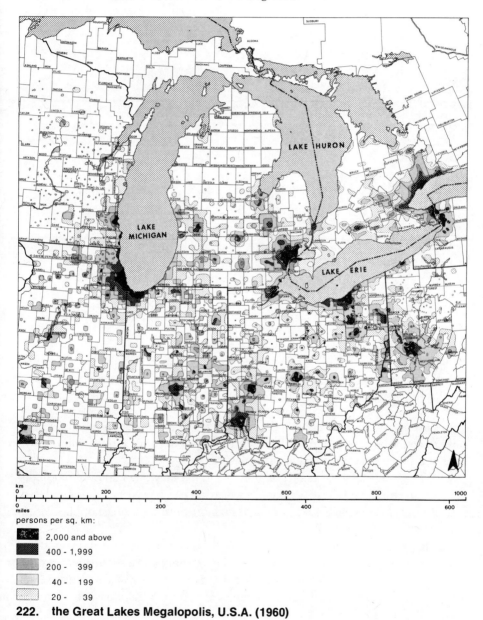

persons per sq. km:

- 2,000 and above
- 400 - 1,999
- 200 - 399
- 40 - 199
- 20 - 39

222. the Great Lakes Megalopolis, U.S.A. (1960)

In dealing with the different types of human settlements so far we have been able to see their future and final structure. In dealing with the megalopolis we cannot achieve the same thing for two reasons:

1. No specific study has been completed and the only one I know about under way is the Great Lakes Megalopolis which needs a few years to be completed.
2. The most prevailing force in the formation of a large megalopolis is geographic and topographic formation.

For these reasons and because all present-day megalopolises are really dyna-megalopolises, we can only conceive a final megalopolis as a static one in a completely indicative way and this is the meaning of Figure 223 which gives an indication of how a static megalopolis like the Great Lakes Megalopolis may probably look.

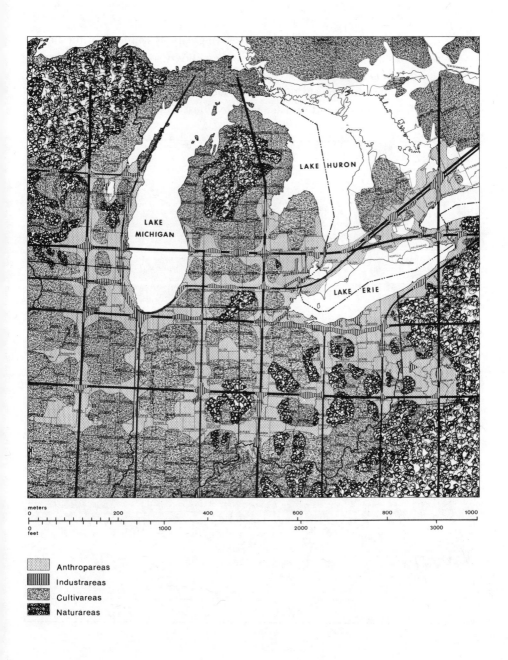

meters
0   200   400   600   800   1000

0   1000   2000   3000
feet

Anthropareas
Industrareas
Cultivareas
Naturareas

223.   the Great Lakes Megalopolis, U.S.A.

We do not yet know how the Great Lakes Megalopolis will look in the future as the study has not been completed, but we see here two extreme cases proving how we can proceed to the research for the entopian megalopolis. The first extreme case is to let the present trends continue forever (Fig. 224), and this alternative will lead to chaos and disaster for all values. This is definitely a feasible

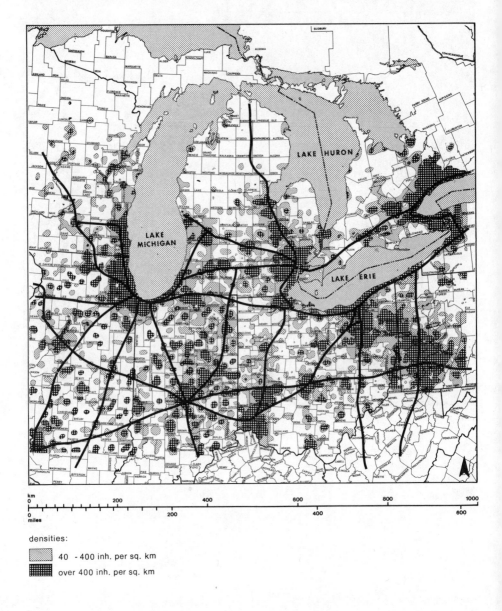

densities:

40 - 400 inh. per sq. km

over 400 inh. per sq. km

224. **continuation of present trends in the Great Lakes area**

and undesirable alternative. Another extreme case is to impose on the whole area a geometric network (Fig. 225) and let things happen along it. This is unrealistic in several ways and in other ways an undesirable alternative. The entopian megalopolis is a different alternative and will appear and be presented after the completion of our study.

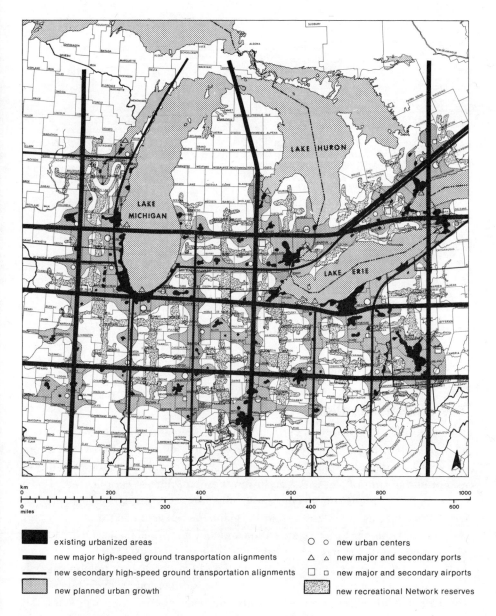

km					
0	200	400	600	800	1000

0	200	400	600
miles			

■ existing urbanized areas

▬ new major high-speed ground transportation alignments

— new secondary high-speed ground transportation alignments

▨ new planned urban growth

○ ○ new urban centers

△ △ new major and secondary ports

□ □ new major and secondary airports

▨ new recreational Network reserves

225. imposition of a geometric Network on the Great Lakes area

14. Eperopolis

Ekistic Population Scale	Name of unit	Population range	Ekistic units covering this chapter	Kinetic field	Com. class	Ekistic unit
1	Furniture			a		1
2	Room			b		2
5	House	3 - 15		c		3
40	Housegroup	15 - 100		d	I	4
250	Small Neighborhood	100 - 750		e	II	5
1,500	Neighborhood	750 - 5,000		f	III	6
10,000	Small Polis	5,000 - 30,000		g	IV	7
75,000	Polis	30,000 -200,000		A	V	8
500,000	Small Metropolis	200,000 - 1.5 M		B	VI	9
4 M	Metropolis	1.5 M- 10 M		C	VII	10
25 M	Small Megalopolis	10 M- 75 M		D	VIII	11
150 M	Megalopolis	75 M- 500 M		E	IX	12
1,000 M	Small Eperopolis	500 M- 3,000 M	░░░	F	X	13
7,500 M	Eperopolis	3,000 M- 20,000 M	░░░	G	XI	14
50,000 M	Ecumenopolis	20,000 M and more		H	XII	15

The present situation

The eperopolis (ekistic units 13 and 14) contains several megalopolises, metropolises and minor human settlements and covers a large part or the whole of any one of the continents (*eperos* in Greek). Today the eperopolis does not yet exist except in the form of Networks, and even these are not yet coordinated. This is because, first, there is still no concept for the LANWAIR system (see Chapter 12) which I first proposed for Europe[68] in 1973, and has not yet been studied. Second, no continent belongs to any single nation and thus no overall plan even for a single element of a continent has been made on a continental basis.

The eperopolises are five, if we stick to the old notion that our globe has only five continents; but if we think of a better spatial subdivision for our globe we can consider that there are seven continents and each one of them will some day have its own name:

Africa	—	Africapolis
North America	—	North Americapolis
South America	—	South Americapolis
East Asia	—	East Asiapolis
West Asia	—	West Asiapolis
Europe	—	Europolis
Oceania	—	Oceanopolis

The smaller eperopolises (ekistic unit 13) covering parts of one or two continents can also have their names, at least as long as our globe is divided by nations, races, etc. Thus we can have a Chinapolis, Indiapolis, Russopolis, Arabopolis, etc. In a similar way we can speak of Hellenopolis (the Greek city), or Zambiapolis, to serve the total national concept of a city as in ancient days when the word polis was first used to mean both the city-state and its capital.

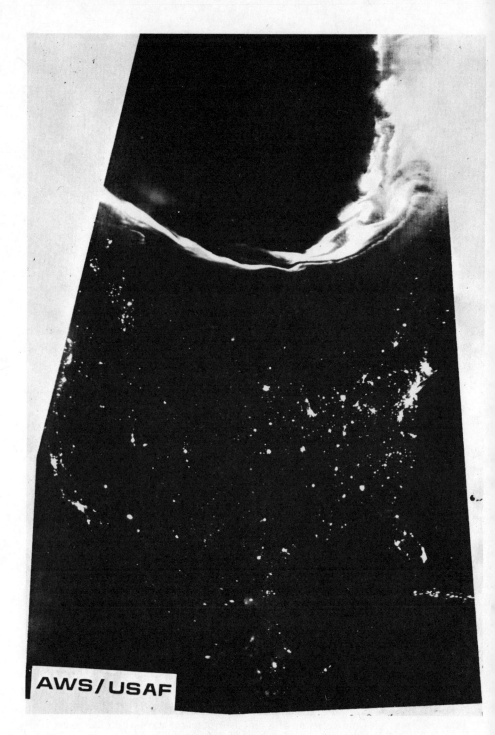

226. photograph of the U.S.A. taken by satellite

The eperopolises do not yet exist, but if we look at the U.S.A. from space at night (Fig. 226) we can see how the eperopolis is beginning to appear along the eastern and western coast. In the same way we can see the appearance of the Europolis in its northwest corner where southeast England connects with the northwest continent and will be even more connected now that the Channel tunnel connecting France with England has been decided but postponed.

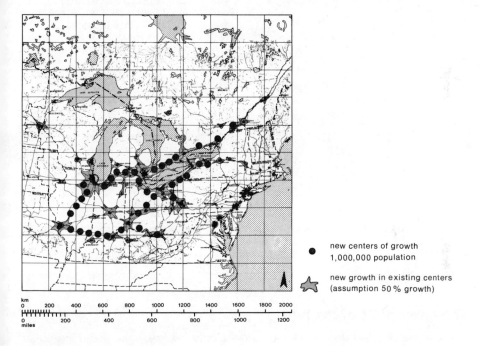

● new centers of growth
1,000,000 population

✩ new growth in existing centers
(assumption 50 % growth)

227. nucleus of an eperopolis, Northeastern U.S.A. and Canada

There are some studies which are now beginning to cover larger scales than the megalopolises, giving an image of the upcoming nuclei of eperopolises. The first is the northeastern U.S.A. and Canadian one (Fig. 227), where we can see how an eperopolis will be formed if every megalopolis (the northeastern one, the Great Lakes Megalopolis and southern unnamed one) allows the organized growth of their metropolises, but without any overall concept of eperopolis. The second case is the Rio de la Plata basin in South America which covers large parts of five countries (Argentina, Paraguay, Uruguay, Bolivia, Brazil) and is beginning to be conceived by the Inter-American Development Bank[69] as one water system (Fig. 228).

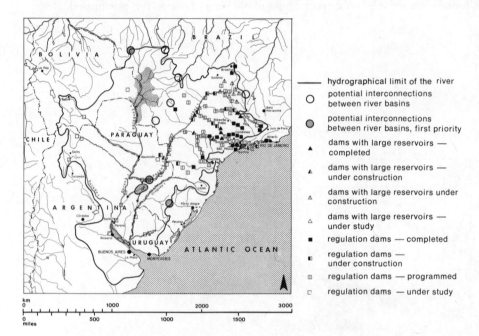

	hydrographical limit of the river
◯	potential interconnections between river basins
◍	potential interconnections between river basins, first priority
▲	dams with large reservoirs — completed
◬	dams with large reservoirs — under construction
△	dams with large reservoirs under construction
△	dams with large reservoirs — under study
■	regulation dams — completed
◧	regulation dams — under construction
⊞	regulation dams — programmed
▭	regulation dams — under study

228. **nucleus of an eperopolis, Rio de la Plata, South America: major hydraulic projects**

The eperopolis of the future

The real eperopolises do not yet exist and the only thing that has been done so far are the studies carried out by the Athens Center of Ekistics and its collaborators to analyze their most probable location. This has happened during the process of studying habitability (Fig. 229), proving where the city can naturally go, and has been presented in *Ecumenopolis: the Inevitable City of the Future*, both for eperopolises and Ecumenopolis[70]. Gradually we will have measures preventing the eperopolis from invading the areas that have to be saved because we need them for cultivation, for ecological or cultural reasons[71] (Fig. 230). The final location in an entopian world will be the eperopolis shaped according to what is possible (Fig. 229) and what is desirable (Fig. 230). The result can be seen in Figure 231.

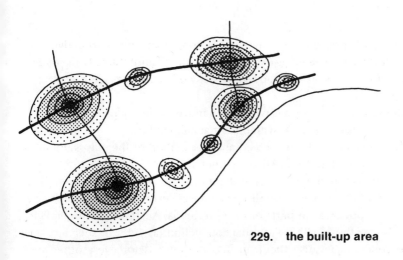

229. the built-up area

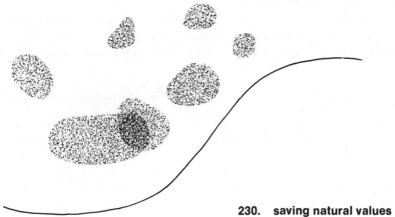

230. saving natural values

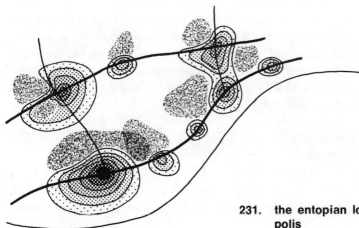

**231. the entopian location of epero-
polis**

When speaking of eperopolis we have to remember that it will start as dynaeperopolis and will remain dynamic for several generations until it finally becomes a static and final eperopolis, as will happen to many of its parts, as we have seen in previous chapters.

To reach the entopian eperopolis we have to move by the following steps:
1. Immediate analysis of the areas with potential habitability.
2. Examination of values to be preserved and declaration of them as Naturareas.
3. Proper evaluation of 1 and 2 and their synthesis.
4. Proper structure within the synthesis of all three in the broad sense of LANWAIR.

Such an effort must be made for all eperopolises, even for those which have not yet begun to appear, as in parts of Brazil, Canada, Australia, Rio de la Plata, Africa, etc., even for those with no internal connections as yet. For such areas we need a fresh concept, because they can become models for every other area. Geography decides; the past plays a small role, we can have an ideal marriage of city and wildlife and also an ideal organization.

In the same way that Chang'an or Peking were much better cities than imperial Rome, as they were conceived as a whole, the eperopolises in the non-connected parts can become a model for the others — if conceived in the proper way.

Since we cannot yet present the eperopolises in those parts of our globe which do not yet have any metropolises, we will study the Europolis (Fig. 232), which is beginning to take shape especially along the coastal areas and rivers, such as the Rhine, by the natural and definitely unplanned expansion of its metropolises. It is clear that geography and economic growth have taken all decisions (subconsciously for Anthropos) which lead to such a formation. The final formation will depend on decisions to be taken on:
1. How to respect and protect Nature.
2. How to organize growth.
3. How to organize Networks.
4. How to organize social contacts.
5. How to help Anthropos to conquer Nature by entering it, not with machines, but as a natural animal, in order to learn about Nature and its laws by respecting it.

226

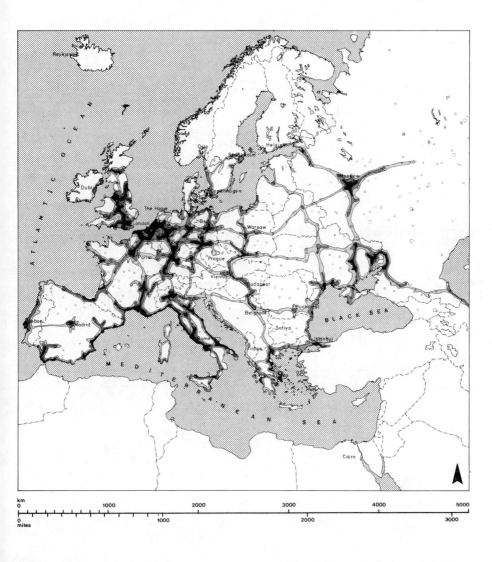

■ high density
▓ medium density
░ low density

232. Europolis

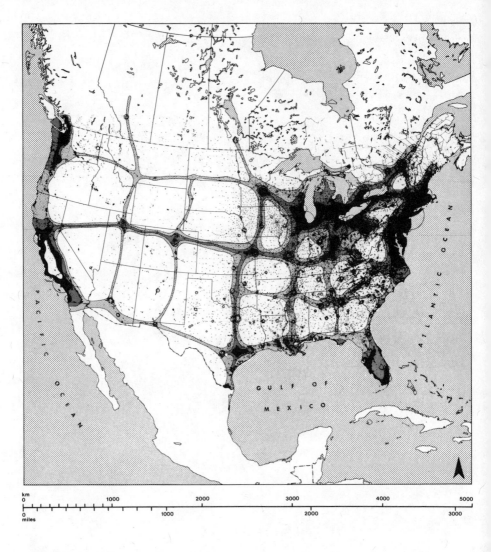

high density
middle density
low density

the Eastern Megalopolis and especially the Great Lakes Megalopolis have been studied in some detail; the other areas can only be roughly estimated because they have not been studied in detail.

233. North Americapolis

A similar case is the North Americapolis (Fig. 233) which we see here in the form that will certainly occur along the coastal areas and the Great Lakes. This is indicative only for all other parts, because no proper study has been made. There is as yet no possibility of forming any final opinion about the major corridors to be created by the movement Networks, nor about very special centers corresponding to all future needs from isolation and recreation, to science and industry.

After having studied the parts of two eperopolises at the 5,000 km scale (Figs. 232, 233), we can now look at a whole continent at the scale of 10,000 km. Our example is Africapolis (Fig. 234), for which the only study we have made is a first concept of its future LANWAIR system[72] which will immensely influence its future. Having been exploited for centuries by colonizing forces, Africa has almost all its major centers located along the coastal areas; although it needs, as do all other continents (for example also South Americapolis) a better development of its inner part.

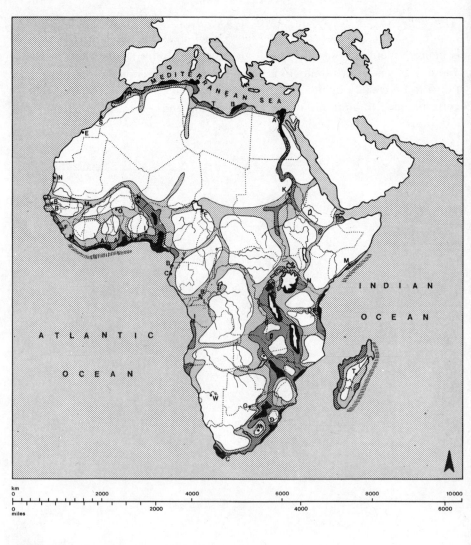

high density
medium density
low density

234. Africapolis

15. Ecumenopolis

Ekistic Population Scale	Name of unit	Population range	Ekistic units covering this chapter	Kinetic field	Com. class	Ekistic unit
1	Furniture			a		1
2	Room			b		2
5	House	3 - 15		c		3
40	Housegroup	15 - 100		d	I	4
250	Small Neighborhood	100 - 750		e	II	5
1,500	Neighborhood	750 - 5,000		f	III	6
10,000	Small Polis	5,000 - 30,000		g	IV	7
75,000	Polis	30,000 -200,000		A	V	8
500,000	Small Metropolis	200,000 - 1.5 M		B	VI	9
4 M	Metropolis	1.5 M- 10 M		C	VII	10
25 M	Small Megalopolis	10 M- 75 M		D	VIII	11
150 M	Megalopolis	75 M- 500 M		E	IX	12
1,000 M	Small Eperopolis	500 M- 3,000 M		F	X	13
7,500 M	Eperopolis	3,000 M- 20,000 M		G	XI	14
50,000 M	Ecumenopolis	20,000 M and more	▨▨▨	H	XII	15

The present situation

Ecumenopolis does not yet exist today, but it is certainly already under formation if we consider the space capsules which pass over it in about an hour. This is as long as it took the farmer to reach his fields and form a village. Although we have been speaking about it for fifteen years, and have presented many documents about it[73] I doubt if it is yet properly understood, because many people believe it is a utopia, and almost all are afraid of it.

One of the reasons for the misunderstanding about the real and entopian Ecumenopolis is that many people speak about a shrinking world, and this creates great confusion. It is true that the air trips over the Atlantic have shrunk from 17.5 hours in 1947 to 6.5 hours in 1973, that the trade between free-world nations has changed from $56 billion in 1950 to $371 billion in 1972, that the travelers across the oceans have increased over 1000% from 1950 to 1972 and that the overseas telephone calls have increased from 900,000 in 1950 to 35,000,000 in 1972[74] but the world is not shrinking. What is true is that Anthropos is expanding and turning his globe into Ecumenopolis.

This change has already begun in many ways and in a few generations it will be completed, because we are in the middle of the explosion that has created all our problems and has already lasted 150 years. We need an equal time to overcome all our problems, as I explained in Chapters 1-5 and in *Ecumenopolis: the Inevitable City of the Future.* A fever that develops from a virus over one week may well need another week or a longer period for therapy.

Ecumenopolis is under way, but we lack the overall concept and the courage to guide Ecumenopolis rather than just letting it happen by chance and necessity.

Ecumenization

The road to Ecumenopolis leads from civilization to ecumenization and this has to be properly understood because it is the greatest change since civilizations were born. This change is much greater than the one which led to civilization and I present here three out of the many reasons explaining this statement.

First: because Anthropos is expanding in terms of spatial relationships, as I have already explained in so many cases, and this has not happened with civilization but only through better organization without any technological change.

Second: because in civilization most of the enemies leading to wars were outside the walls or outside national or imperial boundaries; that is outside the organizational units of Anthropos. Now with new technology the enemy, even if it is another nation, is inside Ecumenopolis.

Third: the jump from hunters' clans and villages to polis was much smaller than from polis to Ecumenopolis. With an average clan containing 70 people and villages of a few hundreds of inhabitants we jumped to the polis of a few thousands or tens of thousands. This was a jump up to a hundred times higher population over thousands of years. When we remember though that ecumenization started in 1825 (see Chapter 1) and that with very few exceptions the city was at the level of tens of thousands, and that by 2125 we will be more than ten billion, we see that the jump is of the order of one million. For civilization we jumped one hundred times and for ecumenization one million times; that is ten thousand times more. Moreover, the first jump lasted thousands of years while the present one has lasted only 300 years (1825-2125). The difference in the magnitude of the explosion is so big that we can understand the great confusion we are in. Nothing similar has ever happened before, and as it now happens at a time when human minds are much more trained, it is time to understand that there is no need for any pessimism and we can face the future with reasonable optimism.

The inevitable and frightening Ecumenopolis

Once we are led towards ecumenization, the question may arise whether the Ecumenopolis will not be a huge round city somewhere in Africa (the more central continent), with the whole global population within it. This is not possible because the forces which have gradually shaped our city since the machine was developed are of three kinds, those of attraction by urban systems, of lines of transportation and of esthetic forces[75] (Fig. 235). In this way Ecumenopolis will spread all over the globe as we saw in Chapter 1 by night (Fig. 1) and now we see in daytime (Fig. 236).

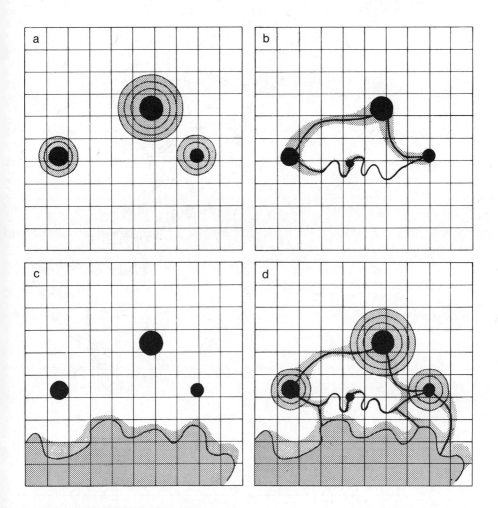

a. the attraction of existing systems
b. the attraction of existing lines of transportation
c. the attraction of esthetic forces
d. the total system of attractions

235. the three forces conditioning the shape of urban systems

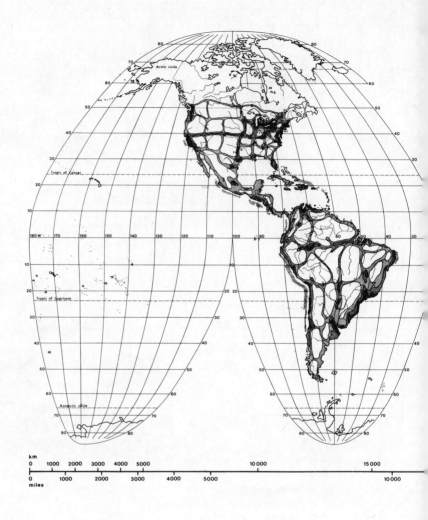

km
0   1000 2000 3000 4000 5000   10 000   15 000
0   1000 2000 3000 4000 5000
miles

236.   Ecumenopolis

234

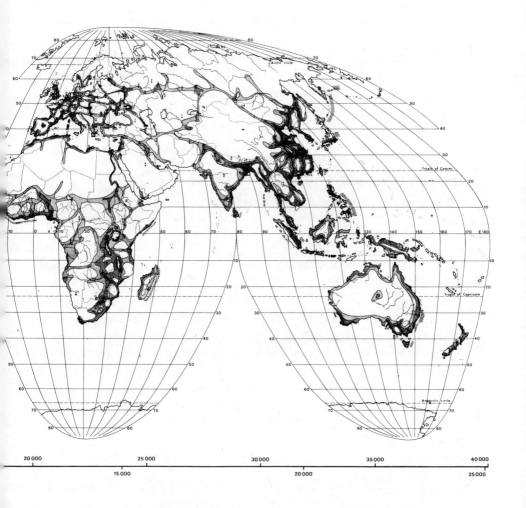

relative degree of elaboration by region (highest = 1)

1. Europe
2. North America
3. Australia, Japan, Egypt
4. Africa south of $0°$, S.E. Asia
5. other

 high density

medium density

low density

deep ocean waters (practically no continental shelves)

deep ocean waters (greater depths)

Such a map frightens those people who see the probable distribution of the global population in terms of densities and do not understand such statements as Arnold Toynbee's, "the most obvious problem menacing the world today is Ecumenopolis — that is, the coming world-city in which one day all present cities will merge"[76]. But on the one hand the map also presents very low densities and on the other hand they have not understood that Toynbee makes such a statement in order to help us to open our eyes and change the fate of Ecumenopolis and of Anthropos.

The desirable and entopian Ecumenopolis

If, instead of being frightened and starting screaming, we start action for an entopian Ecumenopolis, as we call its entopian parts (Chapters 6-14), then we will have the ideal Ecumenopolis of a quality much higher than any city of the past. To achieve this we must remember all five principles guiding human settlements (see Chapters 1, 2) and instead of letting only the first two principles guide us, as happens today, we must satisfy all of them in the same way.

In this way we can realize that we can reach an ideal not by limiting ourselves to a solution which will be under the control of one set of forces, but to a solution which will not be under the control of any single set of forces. The entopian solution can only be found when we reach a balance between all forces which influence the life of settlements. We can head towards it only if we reach a balance between the forces conditioning the present and the forces that will condition the settlements of the future. By thinking in these terms we are gradually heading towards the formation of an ideal entopian city, the city which will achieve a balance between Anthropareas and Naturareas. The balance will be such as to allow for the maximum number of people to live on this earth under the best possible conditions.

This ideal entopian city will be a static one as it will have reached the point of complete balance between its own forces and the forces of Nature. To reach this static phase Ecumenopolis will pass through many phases of dynamic development, that is as dynapolis or more accurately as dynaecumenopolis in many of its parts. We should never forget that when we speak of a woman or a man they may look static, but they have passed through many very dynamic phases and that even in an apparently static phase they are always changing for better or worse. Within Ecumenopolis the Anthropareas will cover the unproductive areas of our globe. The best parts of the plains, the best parts of valleys and hills, will remain completely free for cultivation, which will take place in a very rational, very organized way. The best types of landscapes, the best types of forests, the most beautiful river and lake shores, the tops of the mountains and other areas which are not good for cultivation or residence, will remain free as Naturareas of different categories.

In such a way Ecumenopolis will be married to the global garden or Ecumeno-kepos[77] and those frightened by a plan like Figure 236 will understand that most of the areas of Ecumenopolis (over 94.10% of the earth will be wildlife and cultivation) will be controlled by Nature as we can see in most of the plans of Chapters 6-14.

Inside Ecumenopolis, Anthropos will have the great advantage (for the first time in his history) of living only in the human scale, and at the same time when he needs to be further out of his own area he can use the machines to jump into another human scale area. In this way the globe will turn into a human globe, giving Anthropos a maximum of choices which he never had before or when he did, only inside very small areas corresponding to his daily kinetic fields (a few square kilometers). In this way Anthropos will be of higher quality and will have much greater happiness, having the choice as an Ecumenanthropos to select the best quality for his life.

Inside Ecumenopolis, Society will operate in an ideal entopian way because Anthropos will organize it much better than in his small polis, for two reasons. By reopening his eyes he will re-establish all natural human contacts in the best possible way which have been lost in our era since 1825. Also, the new technology will help the organization of the huge scales created today, which presently lead to confusion (Figs. 16-21). Thus Anthropos will have the whole range of natural contacts from the human scale ones to the Ecumenocontacts.

In the same way, through completely understanding human needs and the real new possibilities, Ecumenopolis will have the best Anthropareas with completed systems of Shells and Networks serving all human needs, from material ones to such high-level ones as the symbols of ecumenization.

How the difficult task of the full conception of entopian Ecumenopolis, with all its elements and parts in balance, can be carried out, depends on our ability to look at Ecumenopolis as a system which will become our goal and this is presented in the next part (Chapters 16-22).

Part Three

The system of Entopia

16. The need for a system

In closing the description of all basic units of Entopia, I stated that we will see them merged into a system. This system will be very complex, but unless we conceive it as a whole and build it as such, we will not attain the Anthropopolis we need, but instead chaos. If we assume that somewhere there exist architecturally perfect buildings by different architects from different cultures, we have a ridiculous situation. If we have the most perfect neighborhoods without proper connections between them we do not have a city, but nomadic life in a jungle.

We have seen the units and parts of the system at all levels, but now we have to see how they are interconnected. To achieve this we have to see their connections by elements. In the Anthropocosmos model (see Chapter 4, Fig. 56) we have seen the vertical parts, that is the ekistic units, and we now have to see the five basic horizontal ones (Nature, Anthropos, Society, Shells, Networks) and then their interconnection into a total system. This is done in the following chapters.

I will begin by presenting the basic need for organized systems, because otherwise we are led to chaos.

After clarifying the concept of Entopia: i.e. what is inevitable and what is desirable, and after defining some basic solutions for all units and parts of Entopia, we can take one more step to discover how to move from several concepts and units and parts to the whole. We have already seen the ten units of our city, from furniture to Ecumenopolis, and in describing them we have seen their five elements, from Nature to Networks. We know that we must bring all five elements into harmony at all levels, because if this harmony exists only in our home, or only in our small city, we will not achieve anything. The reason is that, all over the globe we depend on one another. It is not possible for a city to survive if the water all around it is polluted, or for any country to survive if the global atmosphere becomes poisonous. We all depend more and more on each other inside our biosphere, or the world of living things, which constantly changes.

These statements bring to mind the problem of independence which was the ideal in many cultures, and expressed by many philosophers such as the half mythical Chinese sage, Lao-Tzu (6th century B.C.), Plato who supported the really isolated city-state (4th century B.C.) and Aristotle who supported only a few connections with other city-states (4th century B.C.), and Thomas More who described his isolated *Utopia*, up to our days and the concepts of Skinner's *Walden Two* and Huxley's *Island*.

In the past "independence", at least from other people, was much more possible than today. People lived in isolation as hunters, farmers, citizens and sometimes even as nations, as was the case for China and Japan for centuries on the basis of their policies. Today this is no longer possible at any scale because with every day that passes we all depend more and more on each other's actions, as we have seen in the patterns of people moving far out (Chapter 2) and as is clear when we think of global energy resources or military weapons. There is no longer any independence and the harmony we are seeking depends on the proper degree of dependence. The ancient Chinese symbols of yin and yang bring us closer to the notion of a balance through continuous dependence with changing degrees at different times (Fig. 237). But this is a very simple symbolic presentation of our present situation which is so complex in every respect, from spatial dimensions to numbers of interacting and changing elements, that it leads to chaos.

237. ancient Chinese symbols of yin and yang

There is only one way to avoid this chaos and this is to organize a system of life, as we have learned from physics, biology, anthropology and our present-day life. There is some confusion about the term "organization" and such terms as "control", "information", "coordination", "regulation", etc., as we learn from biology[1]. I will use the term "organization" here not in its limited and usually static literary sense but to represent the "over-all pattern and behavior"[2] or structure and function of human settlements. It is well known that "The fundamental problem in development is the capacity of the living system to organize the material available to it"[3]. It is true that in biology experts speak of "that mysterious principle known as 'organization'"[4] but it is also clear that all expressions of life from molecules and multicellular organisms are hierarchically organized systems and operate hierarchically[5]. Anthropos represents the highest form of organization[6] and his social evolution depends on his organizing ability. This creates many problems as to how organization can best be achieved without limiting the individual's freedom. It is quite clear, however, that successful social organization always increases human freedom[7]. The broad types of organization, as we learn from biology, tend to persist indefinitely[8]. The conclusion from biological and social experience is clear: to avoid chaos we must organize our system of life, here represented by human settlements.

Because there are many doubts today, held especially by some artists, whether organization, or in morphological terms synthesis, requires a certain order or can be completely disorderly, I use the example of spiders' webs created normally (Fig. 238), or after receiving dextroamphetamine (Fig. 239). For those who do not have the experience of creating a structure or building a city may thus wonder why I insist on building orderly hierarchical systems my statement is clear: there is no other way to get out of the chaos that we create today except by building orderly organized systems of life. They may look stiff and geometric in some of their aspects, but as a whole they are as non-geometric as a human body is, and only thus can they give Anthropos maximum flexibility and freedom. Only such systems can give us the maximum of choices (first principle, p. 6); that is, the greatest possible freedom in the most economic way in terms of time, energy, money, etc. (second principle, p. 6), satisfy our need for proper space, (third principle, p. 24), give us a real synthesis of all five elements, (fourth principle, p. 24) and a balance between all four principles, (fifth principle, pp. 24-26).

 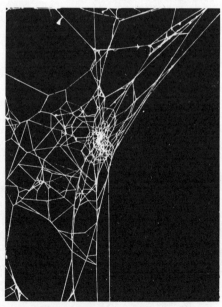

238. a normal spider's web

239. the web spun after the spider had received a dose of dex-troamphetamine

17. The system of Nature

The general concept

The first and prevailing element of human settlements is Nature, and although Anthropos does not create it he is obliged to see it as an organized system. The reasons are many and well-known by now, although they have been forgotten or were seen in a very narrow and limited way since the beginning of our explosion in 1825. They range from biological reasons for the survival of the whole biosphere, to human needs for recreation. We cannot allow any kind of plants or animals to disappear, nor can we allow the pollution of any part of Nature that cannot be cleaned in time by a normal process. We cannot allow any method of spoiling Nature, even when we pretend that it serves social or national goals as many countries do by writing for example their slogans in huge letters and symbols on the hill-sides. Such actions mean, among other things, that we have not yet understood what Nature is or its relation to Anthropos.

We are now beginning to be aware of the truths about Nature, and many scientific efforts are being made which have never been made before. Scientists begin to observe and study carefully all sorts of phenomena of flora and fauna. Animals become agents of such research, as when penguins with radio backpacks provide information on such phenomena as blood flow and pressure under varying conditions. Climate also is not only being studied but occasionally changed, and many people emphasize the need for looking at Nature as the area of adventure, especially for young people or as a well studied area for rest and recreation as Innokenti P. Gerasimov proposed in A Soviet Plan for Nature[9].

The great change that has lately been achieved, which facilitates far better understanding and action, is due to the overall image of the situation that we are able to get from photographs and films taken from space because they demonstrate very clearly the existing situation and its changes. This was reported lately by the Skylab-3 astronauts to Congress, who presented "a view of an earth scarred by the activities of man, an assault on the environment that they said future missions might help control"[10].

The organized system of Nature is extremely complex, but we can study here its basic relationship to the City of Anthropos. To achieve this we must first look at its parts: land, water, air, climate, flora and fauna; second, at their dimensions and characteristics and third, at their marriage with the city and the formation of a total natural system.

In general (as already stated in Chapter 4) we should divide our environment into four types of areas affecting all parts of Nature and their relationship to Anthropos. These are:

1. The natural areas or *Naturareas* where Nature prevails with its main characteristics.
2. The cultivated areas or *Cultivareas* where Anthropos uses Nature in his own way.
3. The so-called built-up areas where Anthropos prevails with his action, and as they are of many types and also exist on water we call them *Anthropareas*, where Anthropos is very active.
4. The heavy industry and waste areas or *Industrareas* where Anthropos has to build problem-creating factories or to pile waste material until it can be used again by recycling.

1	2	3	4	5	6	7	8	9	10
type of area	zones	% of Nature and Wildlife in each zone	Anthropos's intervention	% of cultivation by Anthropos	the role of the machine	Shells (buildings)	Networks	% of global land	% of global land
Naturareas	One	100	only scientists for research	—	—	—	—	40	67
	Two	100	crossing by foot or boat	—	—	—	—	17	
	Three	95	crossing, staying temporarily	3	—	tents	—	10	
	Four	95	crossing, staying temporarily	4	—	camps	—	8	15
	Five	90	crossing, staying temporarily	5	motorcars	hotels, houses	roads	7	
Cultivareas	Six	20	staying permanently	70	motorcars, tractors, light industry	houses, buildings of many kinds	roads	5.5	10.5
	Seven	20	staying permanently	60	motorcars, tractors, light industry	houses, buildings of many kinds; covered cultivation areas	roads, railroads	5	
Anthropareas	Eight	20	staying permanently	40	for entertainment	hotels, sports-buildings	roads, railroads, airplanes	5	5
	Nine	10	staying permanently	30	motorcars	homes, second-homes, buildings	roads, railroads, airplanes	1.3	2.5
	Ten	10	staying permanently	20	motorcars	homes, buildings	roads, railroads, airplanes	0.7	
	Eleven	—	staying permanently	10	motorcars	homes, buildings	roads, railroads, airplanes	0.3	
Industrareas	Twelve	—	for work only	10	every possible role	industrial waste disposal	roads railroads, airplanes	0.2	

240.   the twelve global land zones

246

The twelve land zones

Land is the most important part of Nature affecting the City of Anthropos, but we don't use it properly, although Anthropos achieved a proper use in the past and this is why he survived. Even a permanently surviving village had decided that its land consisted of three zones, the built-up one, the farms and the forests for hunting and supply of timber and wild flora and fauna. In our case, and in the new dimensions of the City of Anthropos, we have to move from three to twelve zones with their own characteristics and define their dimensions. My first attempt leads to the following proposal about the characteristics and dimensions of the twelve land zones on a global scale[11] (Figs. 240, 241).

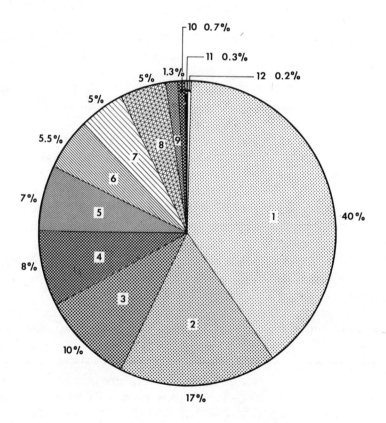

241.   the twelve global land zones (percent of area occupied by each zone)

Zone One: Real Wildlife (40%): Anthropos is not allowed to enter here with the exception of authorized scientists for research purposes. For many reasons (such as biological) we need the preservation of this zone in its virgin state.

Zone Two: Wildlife Visited (17%): Anthropos enters this zone, but without machines, without matches and lighters, and does not stay in it.

Zone Three: Wildlife Embraced (10%): Anthropos enters this zone without machines, matches and lighters, and stays in temporary camps without mechanical installations.

Zone Four: Wildlife Invaded (8%): Anthropos enters this zone without machines, matches and lighters and lives in permanent well-built camps with mechanical installations restricted to the camps.

Zone Five: Wildlife Conquered (7%): Anthropos gets control of it so as to protect it and enjoy it with all his facilities and conveniences.

Zone Six: Natural Cultivation (5.5%): Anthropos cultivates in the open air and enjoys the landscape.

Zone Seven: Industrial Cultivation (5%): Anthropos cultivates and has the right to cover the cultivated area, to control climate and production.

Zone Eight: Physical Human Life (5%): In free land, Anthropos lives as close as possible to Nature and has "sexual" relations with it, from swimming, to becoming a nudist and athlete or a golf player.

Zone Nine: Low Density City (1.3%): In this zone are included those areas which we sometimes call suburbs or small towns, with proper gardens.

Zone Ten: Middle Density City (0.7%): Those regions which can be called "normal human built-up areas".

Zone Eleven: High Density City (0.3%): Settlement approximately like the old traditional city which we now admire, or like the contemporary central business district.

Zone Twelve: Heavy Industry and Waste Zone (0.2%): These are the regions which ought to be separated from Anthropos's everyday life because they disturb him in every way.

In this way we give 66.8% or about two-thirds of the land total of Ecumenopolis solely to continuous wildlife, a large part of which in any case cannot be visited by Anthropos. These are the first three zones.

An even larger percentage, 81.37% of the total, is given to different types of Nature, including isolated special regions, as well as Naturareas between built-up settlements. These are the first five zones that make up the total of Naturareas.

The total percentage of Nature comes to 94.10% if we add the regions cultivated by Anthropos, no matter where they are in all twelve zones (Fig. 242, column 7). Anthropos keeps control of 33% (Zones Four to Twelve) of the surface of the earth but builds cities only on 2.5% (Zones Nine to Twelve). This is not phantasy! It is based on calculations and pragmatic estimates of future needs on the basis of existing data and calculations made for Entopia[12].

1	2		3	4	5	6	7
type of area	zones	% of Nature and Wildlife in each zone	% of global land area by zone	% of Wildlife on global basis	% of cultivation by Anthropos in each zone	% of cultivation on global basis	% of global Wildlife and cultivation
Naturareas	One	100	40	40	—	—	40.00
	Two	100	17	17	—	—	17.00
	Three	95	10	9.5	3	0.30	9.80
	Four	95	8	7.6	4	0.32	7.92
	Five	90	7	6.3	5	0.35	6.65
Cultivareas	Six	20	5.5	1.1	70	3.85	4.95
	Seven	20	5	1.0	60	3.00	4.00
Anthropareas	Eight	20	5	1.0	40	2.00	3.00
	Nine	10	1.3	0.13	30	0.39	0.52
	Ten	10	0.7	0.07	20	0.14	0.21
	Eleven	—	0.3	—	10	0.03	0.03
Industrareas	Twelve	—	0.2	—	10	0.02	0.02
	Total	—	100 %	83.70	—	10.40	94.10

242. the role of Nature (Wildlife) and total Nature (Wildlife and Cultivation)

The first five of these zones are Naturareas, the sixth and seventh are Cultivareas, the eighth, ninth, tenth and eleventh are Anthropareas and the twelfth comprises the Industrareas.

These twelve zones form a system which starts with the home gardens (Figs. 85, 107) continues into the housegroup (Fig. 119) and gradually forms Networks beginning with green corridors and parks (Figs. 153, 168b) which can be seen as complete systems in the metropolis (Fig. 188) and in different forms in the megalopolis

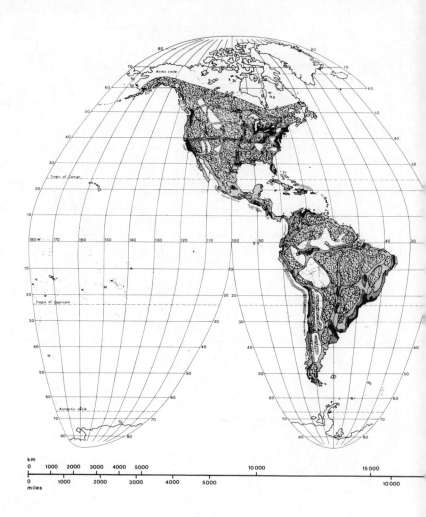

243. Ecumenopolis and Ecumenokepos

(Figs. 211, 213) and the eperopolis (Fig. 231) and end up in a global scale where we can speak of the great global garden or Ecumenokepos (Fig. 243). This total system consists of forest empires and desert or glacial empires some of which reach into the city, like the forest empires, whilst others are kept out of it.

The conclusion of this proposal is very clear — there is no problem about the availability of land in general; the difficulty is in how we use it and how it is connected with the City of Anthropos. The only answer is the formation of a system like the one proposed in all scales from the global one to the single house.

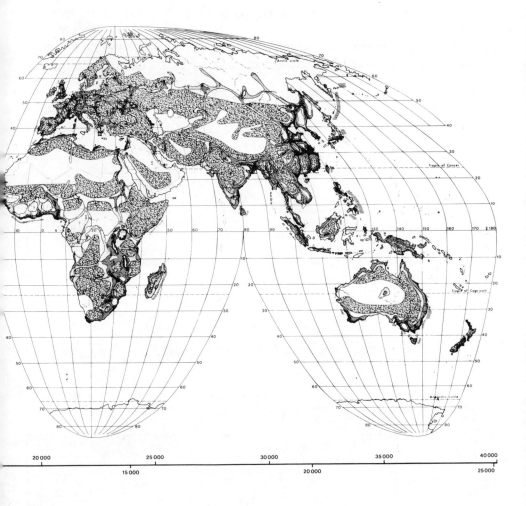

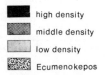 high density

middle density

low density

Ecumenokepos

251

The twelve water zones

There are similar proposals for twelve water zones. We have to follow the same policies for all our water resources. Let us not forget that 71% of the entire surface of the earth is covered by water, and that our own bodies are made up of 65-70% water. We need lakes and rivers and parts of the ocean which should be kept virgin, as well as other similar parts which will support invasion. We ought to form twelve water zones.

In this effort we ought to bear in mind that the water zones are three-dimensional, and recognize the difference between surface and deep water uses. I am not yet able to suggest percentages for each zone, as I have done for the terrestrial zones. For this reason I suggest that the most urgent necessity is the preliminary indicative definition of the dimensions of each zone (Fig. 244)[13].

1	2	3	4
type of area	zones	characteristics	Anthropos's intervention
Naturareas	One	real virginity	only scientists for research
	Two	natural crossing	only with his body
	Three	crossing, staying temporarily	without machines
	Four	crossing in groups	with machines under control
	Five	crossing in groups	creation of ports
Cultivareas	Six	fishing, food production	creation of installations but no pollution
	Seven	food production	very special installations
Anthropareas	Eight	entertainment	special installations
	Nine	commerce and transportation	traditional small ports
	Ten	commerce and transportation	large ports
	Eleven	commerce and transportation	very large ports
Industrareas	Twelve	waste disposal zone	installations for recycling

244. the twelve global water zones

Zone One: the most difficult to be created in the oceans: Only scientists are permitted to enter this zone, and only for research purposes. This can be obtained for lakes, rivers, and as far as possible for some natural sea harbors which may be isolated from pollution coming either from the land or from the sea. There is no reason preventing countries like Canada from declaring it illegal to approach certain lakes by any method, including swimming. This is more difficult for countries like Greece, but not impossible. There is no reason why each country cannot achieve this, at least for the upper parts of its rivers.

Zone Two: Wildlife Visited: Here Anthropos enters as a primitive animal, he can swim, float in wooden vessels, but cannot bring food with him or any object produced mechanically or industrially.

Zone Three: Wildlife Embraced: The limitations of Zone Two still apply here with the added point that Anthropos can live here in traditional types of ships, can fish using traditional methods, but without using chemical products or machines.

Zone Four: Wildlife Invaded: Here apply all the same limitations as in Zone Three. In addition, only certain types of ships with few or many passengers are allowed to cross this zone, with low and controlled speeds. Neither the ships nor the visitors have the right to throw any kind of material in this zone. All their wastes must be carried outside the zone, to special regions of the land, or to Zone Twelve.

Zone Five: Wildlife Conquered: Similar conditions apply as with Zone Four; however, permission can be given for the creation of harbors for ships of Zone Four type and in combination with terrestrial Zone Five.

Zone Six: Natural Fishing: This is the zone of cultivation of fish and other living sea organisms. Every action of Anthropos is permitted as long as vessels and methods eliminate every possibility of pollution of the flora and fauna.

Zone Seven: Industrial Mariculture: This is a revolutionary type of zone. Special lakes and rivers and natural or constructed harbors will be dedicated to the production of flora and fauna for the benefit of Anthropos. Conditions in general can also be changed as in land Zone Seven so as to change the old idea of fish-collecting into producing food and other materials for Anthropos.

Zone Eight: Physical Human Life: In this zone, action of Anthropos is allowed for every purpose related to his organized recreation. That is all types of small and large-scale installations for Anthropos's performance on all types of athletic training instruments.

Zone Nine: Low Density Water Zone: Here are small harbors for every type of boat which allow Anthropos to live near them and to enjoy them. In some ways Zone Nine resembles Zone Eight, but here commerce and transport are added to recreation.

Zone Ten: Middle Density Water Zone: This is one step up from Zone Nine; larger harbors and larger ships are permitted up to 30,000 tons. The land around is more connected with exchange, commerce and trade.

Zone Eleven: High Density Water Zone: Very large harbors for every type of ship, including new types, and special installations for containers so as to permit full interconnection with the commercial city and with every type of industry.

Zone Twelve: Waste Disposal Zone: This is a new type of zone that we must establish for the future in general or at least for a few generations. This is the waste disposal zone. Here will be gathered the wastes today thrown into the oceans; and some day, through chemical processes, the polluted water and the waste will be converted into materials useful to Nature, and certainly progressively useful to Anthropos, for their correct recirculation. This zone will be completely isolated from any other water zone until the moment comes when recycling will allow the clean water to run out of it into the land or water zones it is meant for.

All twelve zones form the global system of water or Ecumenohydor. The way in which it is married to land has been decided by Nature; but it can be reshaped by Anthropos as was already started thousands of years ago[14] and is continued today, but not in the proper scale. The City of Anthropos can be much better if it is married to water, such as in cases like Venice and Amsterdam down to simple canals for recreation, and from big dams and revolutionary irrigation systems as in China[15] down to specific ones.

Again we can locate the first five zones as Naturareas, the next two as Cultivareas, followed by the four which are Anthropareas and the twelfth one which is the Industrarea (Fig. 244).

The twelve coastal zones

Apart from the land and water zones there is an imperative need for the definition of the twelve coastal zones, as coastal areas are those which attract the greatest part of the global population (Fig. 236) and may be the first to be spoiled. These zones are:

Zone One: Truly Natural Shore: Of course, this will be limited in extent in relation to the corresponding land zone, because one can never prevent a ship from approaching the shore in a time of storm and danger. This zone applies to coastlines which correspond to land and water Zones One and covers a percentage of these coasts.

Zone Two: Visited Natural Coast: Accessible only in the ways allowed for land and water Zones Two.

Zone Three: Natural Wild Coast for Habitation: Corresponding to land and water Zones Three, only more extended as far as possible.

Zone Four: Protected Coast with Permanent Establishments: This zone is controlled by the hotels (which are supported by the state and usually destroy the natural environment, as happened in many traditional human settlements in the Mediterranean where hotels were allowed to be built as skyscrapers which destroyed the total environment).

Zone Five: Protected Coast With Full Development: Comparable to Zone Four, but with denser settlement, as when it occurs near cities, etc.

Zone Six: Natural, Productive Developed Coast: The coasts which created the fishing villages. They should be supported in every way so as to preserve their character and protect them from the imposition of touristic constructions.

Zone Seven: Coast suitable for up-to-date fishing methods and their establishments, corresponding to water Zone Seven.

Zone Eight: Zone of natural life, corresponding to land Zone Eight.

Zone Nine: Urban development coast with low density.

Zone Ten: Urban development consisting of first or second homes.

Zone Eleven: Full urban development.

Zone Twelve: Coast for industrial and other bothersome development based on movement of goods, pollutants, etc.

Again the first five zones are the Naturareas, the next two the Cultivareas, the other four Anthropareas and the twelfth is an Industrarea.

Air and climate

Out of all the elements of Nature, these are the most difficult ones for Anthropos to regulate for many obvious reasons. It is true that Anthropos is now polluting air as never before, but this is a purely technological phenomenon which can and will be solved. Anthropos is also exercising an influence on climate in his cities, positive in winter when he raises the temperature slightly and negative in summer. But this is now happening in a coincidental way.

In the future it can be planned and arranged so that we will have many places protected from winds, from house courtyards to big private and public squares (Figs. 111, 165), warm and dry streets in winter and cool ones in summer. This will happen in market streets and more generally in service corridors and office and administrative centers, where the quality of the air and climate can definitely be regulated by the existence of auto-roofs, which will be closed when needed to allow warm or cool air to enter and to prevent rain and snow. We should not forget that centuries ago people created the big bazaars in the Middle East, not with mechanical air-conditioning but with roofs covering the commercial streets and structures allowing for much greater protection from the climate and a better climate inside them. If Anthropos managed to find solutions at incomes of $100 per capita, it is ridiculous to believe that much better solutions are not realistic.

The bazaars of the future, as well as many other Shells, will provide Anthropos with much better conditions in terms of air and climate, and these will form a system as in Figure 187, showing the human scale where such intervention is needed.

Flora and fauna

The twelve land, water and coastal zones give the answer to how we will handle flora and fauna. This solution creates the opportunity to save the species of flora and fauna that must be saved in the proper scale, as well as the opportunity for Anthropos to exploit them for his own benefit by developing, cultivating and using the species that he needs for many purposes related to his survival and development.

The total system

After seeing the different parts of Nature and the partial systems they form, we can see the total system of Nature as it appears on the surface of our globe at least with land, water, flora and fauna. Air and climate require a more elaborate presentation which is not within the scope of this study.

We can see this total system and how it changes by following Nature's surface appearance in spatial units from 50 m to 40,000,000 m (Fig. 245a-g) where we see that the synthesis exists in very different forms. It starts in a completely free and natural way as in small scales, it turns into very geometric forms as in Figure 245b, c and again it turns into natural forms from Figure 245d on. It ends up with the very natural form that geography imposes on the whole globe. We should never see Nature as spots of green, no matter what their scale (pots with flowers or big parks in a city), but only as a continuous system consisting of all sorts of parts in all scales.

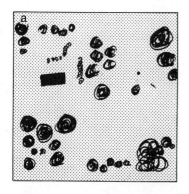

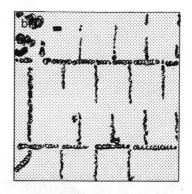

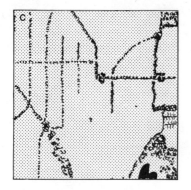

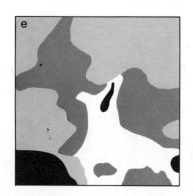

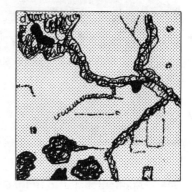

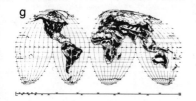

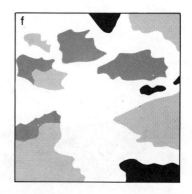

245. Nature's surface appearance
in spatial units from 50 m to
40,000,000 m

257

If any doubt remains about the possibility of an Ecumenokepos we can study the change brought about by the Apollonion, already presented in previous chapters, within a two-year period where a very rocky coast and hillside (Fig. 246) turned into a natural garden with a residential neighborhood married to it (Fig. 247).

246. Apollonion, Porto Rafti, Greece (1972)

247. Apollonion, Porto Rafti, Greece (1975)

18. The system of Anthropos

The body of Anthropos

In the same way in which the first element, Nature, is one of the systems of the city, Anthropos is also a system even if we do not understand it and make all our great mistakes. In the same way as we did for Nature, we must look first at the different parts of Anthropos, like body, senses, mind and psyche, second at their dimensions and characteristics and third at their marriage with the city and the formation of the total human system.

The parts of Anthropos are such that their dimensions and characteristics differ enormously. Where his body is no more than a bubble of up to 2 m (6 ft 7 in.) diameter and his touch does not go beyond, his ears can receive messages from many kilometers distance, his eyes can see up to the stars and galaxies and his mind goes beyond. The system of Anthropos is therefore very different depending on which part of him we look at. To study the whole requires a much longer effort; but to illustrate it in relation to the city, I will present here some indications about its parts and one specific case of them as a system.

The easiest part of Anthropos to be conceived as a system is his body and most of the buildings and building codes take care of his body's dimensions and safety, although this is completely overlooked in the streets. The answer to this last remark has been given in Chapter 5, page 66 where I proposed the separation of hustreets and mecstreets. The hustreets complete the system of Anthropos inside the city which starts with furniture and room. It is only with the husystem that we can overcome the great problem already created by elimination of muscular effort as we have forgotten the reality brought back by Alexis Carrel's statement that "By doing away with muscular effort in daily life, we have suppressed, without being aware of it, the ceaseless exercise required of our organic systems in order that the constancy of the inner medium be maintained"[16].

Other parts of the systems of Anthropos depend on his senses, like touch, which is connected with the system of hustreets as it matters what walls we touch and how or what we walk on with bare feet or shoes. The system based on taste is naturally very important, but limited only inside the mouth. The systems of smell and hearing need very special protective measures to save Anthropos from all sorts of smells and noises which torment him today.

The systems of mind and psyche are very complex and relate to the whole system of life that we build, as I present it in this study, because both depend on the total of messages, both positive and negative, that Anthropos receives from his city.

To illustrate some aspects of all these systems and their parts, I will deal next with Anthropos's system of sight in general. It is only one example of the total system of Anthropos on our globe, because every single action of ours is a part of the system of Anthropos even if expressed in machines. Thus we make a basic distinction between the terms Anthropocosmos and Anthroposystem which cover the total space inhabited by Anthropos and the humane cosmos or system (husystem) which is the expression of the total in terms of quality. A plant is a part of the Anthroposystem but it does not belong to the husystem.

Anthropos looking at his city

As Anthropos does not live in the jungle he needs to feel open space, an open world for him to look far out, and to think and imagine a wide world. At the same time though, he needs to enclose himself inside his own shell and to feel as isolated as possible. The present-day city does not give us the first possibility as we can never see far out. Even one of the largest city parks, the Central Park of New York, gives you the feeling of enclosure. You cannot see far out of it as it is surrounded by skyscrapers. In our city you cannot even see far up either during the day because of air pollution or at night also because of the lights. There is no longer a moon or stars in our sky.

The solution is, apart from cleaning the air which is well known (I speak of this in the latter part of this chapter), to create a system of spaces giving Anthropos all the opportunities to be and feel in different types of space from the smallest possible unit (third principle) to the largest possible one (first principle). This has already been formulated in Chapters 6-15 describing the city and explained in the units of room (Chapter 7, pp. 86-95) and housegroup (Chapter 9, pp. 116-125) and can be followed throughout the corresponding sketches and plans. Especially in Chapter 11, pp. 154-157 we can find several types of huspaces which help us to understand the notion of a system.

The system of Anthropos's sight starts with the completely enclosed space on all six sides (Fig. 248), continues with its gradual opening by auto-walls and auto-roofs and is followed by the open courtyard (five sides in Fig. 249), the open garden looking into the hustreet (five sides in Fig. 250), the hustreet itself (four sides in

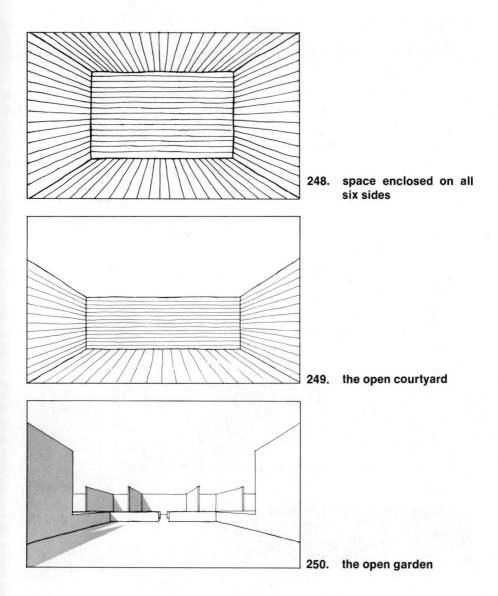

248. **space enclosed on all six sides**

249. **the open courtyard**

250. **the open garden**

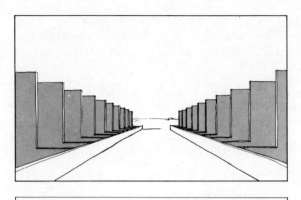

251. the hustreet

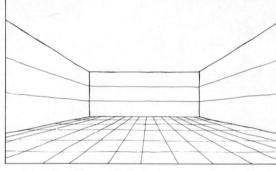

252. the public square

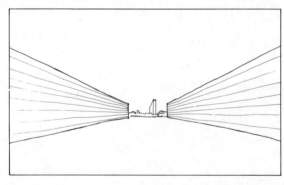

253. the hu-avenue

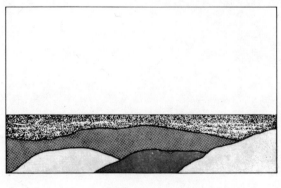

254. the hill

Fig. 251), the public squares (five sides but the three or four are low ones, in Fig. 252), the hu-avenue (three sides in Fig. 253) until it reaches the hill from which only one side is enclosed, that is the soil (Fig. 254). This has always existed in the past on the hills of the small town or the Acropolis. Even when there were no such opportunities to climb up, as in big plains like in Mesopotamia, Anthropos created the ziggurats, or in Peking where the altar of the Temple of Heaven was created with a completely open view all around.

This is the one aspect of the system of Anthropos inside the city that we have to build and has been a basic rule for the Entopia I propose in this study.

In designing it we must take into consideration that "None of us can take in at the same time everything that is striking our eyes and our ears. There seems to be a kind of filter inside the head which protects the central systems against being overloaded."[17] This is true, but when our eyes, ears and other senses are struck by too many things over too long a time, the filters may get tired and this is why we are not protected as much as we need, we are overloaded, turn nervous, etc. This is why we really need a well-conceived human system.

19. The system of Society

How to look at Society

I begin with the clarification that I consider Society as a total system of relationships between people which are either visible or invisible and which form networks. On this I do not agree with the idea of Society as consisting only of people,
because if we take all the people of London into a desert they no longer form a
Society and they are in a chaotic situation; the particles are there, but no longer
Society. On this point I think that Society can be considered as the "total network
of relations between human beings" as Toynbee stated so well in his *Study of
History*[18] and I follow him when he quotes F.A. Hayek stating that "individuals are
merely the foci in the network of relationships"[19].

In this way Society can be seen as a total system consisting of many parts, as also
happens with Nature and Anthropos, parts which are completely interrelated and

can be subdivided further and further. Thus we are again dealing with one element of human settlements which is a subsystem of the total, consisting of many sub-sub-systems of a lower and lower order. Following the method used for Nature and Anthropos, we must first look at the different parts of Society, such as social contacts, aggression, safety and security, organization, administration and leadership, etc.; second, at their dimensions and characteristics; and third, at their inter-marriage with the city and the formation of a whole social system.

We now live in the middle of a complete confusion about the whole system of Society and the city. If the experts know the answers to our many questions they have not yet transmitted them to the many members of our Society who are in the middle of a confusion. On this occasion I refer to the problem of "blue" people that is now so confusing and to the misunderstanding of a case like the Woodstock movement

If we assume that one out of 500 persons of this earth is "different" from the others, let us say a blue person, this means that in the era of villages with green people there would be one blue person per village who was sometimes called "crazy" by the others, even if he was the genius of the era, was isolated and more often than not declined. In the big city of red people the same blue people are many, they can unite and express a certain new movement which for the majority can be good or bad, right or wrong. In the same way we can understand that an urban system of ten million people has 20,000 blue people who can create many groups of new movements and that a country with 200 million can easily assemble 400,000 for any movement, be it blue, or red or yellow. The Woodstock pheno-menon is therefore a very normal movement and there will be many such ex-pressions from liberation movements to political parties like the "dwarfs" of Holland, some of which will have greater influence than others. If we remember that we do not have only blue people but also orange and violet and many other colors we will better understand the formations that come into life in an urban era.[20]

My conclusion as a non-expert on Society is that we are badly in need of a clearer view of the complex system of Society and the city we live in. Out of this very complex system and its many sub-systems or parts I select three for their presenta-tion in relation to the city. I have already dealt indirectly with several in dealing with the units of the city as in Chapter 11, where I describe the polis of the future as achieving the best possible system for all central functions, including democracy (which is really created by the human contacts).

The three parts I will deal with here are only sub-systems, but they are very im-portant ones and have today been completely overlooked. They are the sub-systems of person-to-person natural contacts, of safety from other individuals and of hierarchical organization. I selected them as very important and characteristic ones because the natural contacts define the stimulation that an individual needs in order to develop his identity and creativity; safety is imperative for survival and without organization there is no hope for any system.

Natural contacts between people

Today we are confused when talking about contacts between people because we say that they have been increased in the new huge cities and because we always think of telecommunications. We forget two things. First, that we may see millions of people in a central city, but this does not mean that we have real contacts with them — we are simply exposed to them and we may suffer from them. Second, contacts by telecommunications are very useful but not complete; by telephoning my wife or children I do not satisfy four of my senses and thus neither body, mind or psyche are completely satisfied. If we consider Anthropos as a system of four equal parts (body, senses, mind and psyche), the telephone satisfies 25% of Anthropos's senses but also a part of the anxiety of mind and psyche — but never more than a certain percentage. It is a simplified presentation of a complex phenomenon but it transmits the meaning of the truth about it.

It is a fact that very soon we will communicate by telephone that will also serve our eyes, that is a total of two fifths of our senses and gradually even more.

The conclusion is clear and thus we can see that we now have decreased natural contacts; but in the future we can re-establish them in a very natural way in the system of hustreets up to the size of polis (Chapter 11) because we will not normally walk beyond it. On the other hand, developing technology will increase our additional contacts and instead of creating problems it will, however, solve many for contacts over larger distances — either because the transportation systems will take us very quickly and easily to our people or because we will be able to hear and see them (perhaps someday to smell them) by developing telecommunications.

We thus have to understand the system of natural human contacts and how it works. At this point it is useful to remember the old Confucian concept of jên or "human heartedness" related to Anthropos's dealings with others which was a combination of the symbols of "man" and "two" indicating its connection with human interaction[21]. Thus we have to understand how this natural interaction works. We see it here in three cases, in a home-street of a housegroup (Fig. 255) in a hustreet of a neighborhood (Fig. 256) and in a hustreet of a big service corridor (Fig. 257). What we see in all these figures is the line connecting each person with another in terms of quality, that is of degree of interaction which is strong in the first case (friendship or even the opposite), weaker in the second case and chaotic in the third. Such an illustration helps us to understand how natural contacts can be meaningful in a small unit and simply confusing in a very big one and explains what we now miss by elimination of the small units of natural contacts.

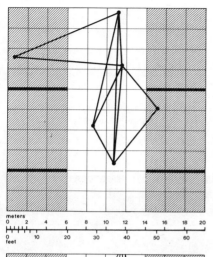

255. degree of interaction between people: a housegroup homestreet

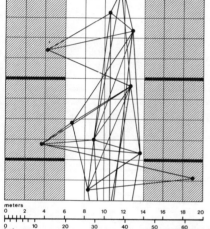

256. degree of interaction between people: a neighborhood hustreet

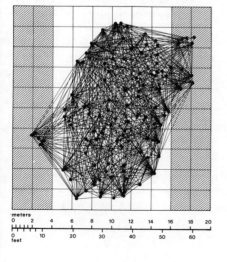

257. degree of interaction between people: a big service corridor hustreet

A similar case can be understood by the interaction which exists between people at the same level, where the connection is complete (Fig. 258), at different levels but in small distances on narrow streets (Fig. 259) and at different levels and huge avenues (Fig. 260) where there is no hope of natural contacts. It is now clear that people living in towers are really enclosed in fortresses.

258. interaction between people at the same level

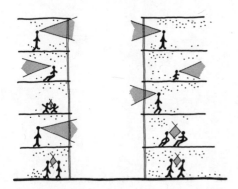

259. interaction between people at different levels in small distances

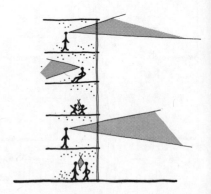

260. interaction between people at different levels in great distances

Following such an analysis we understand how the ancient systems of natural daily contacts at home, in the street, in the public square (agora), etc. (Fig. 261) have now been replaced by a system creating gaps and problems (Fig. 262), and how the whole system can again be very natural and extended (Fig. 263). In this way the city helps people to see as many people as is natural in their own or other areas and gives them the chance to meet the whole of mankind *if* and *as* they want. Having left the traditional system, we now live in no system, but we can have an excellent one.

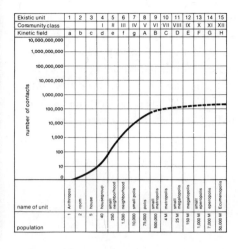

natural contacts

261. daily contacts in the past (before 1825)

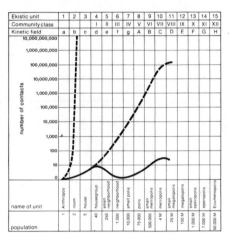

natural contacts

- - - contacts by using transportation means

- - - contacts by using telecommunications

262. daily contacts at present

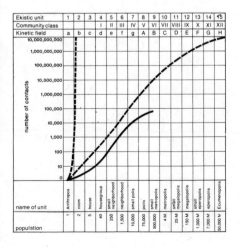

natural contacts

- - - contacts by using transportation means

- - - contacts by using telecommunications

263. daily contacts in the future

Such an analysis of the social system helps us to understand the problem of densities which depend on several factors, the most important of which are physiological and social. These densities can be better understood if rather than saying so many people per hectare (acre), we study the distance between people in space and see what is a usual case today (Fig. 264), and what are the probabilities for the future (Fig. 265). What has to be decided in Entopia is the optimum average at each ekistic unit and in each case for building up the proper social system.

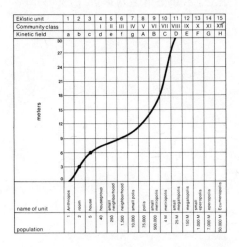

264.   distances between people today

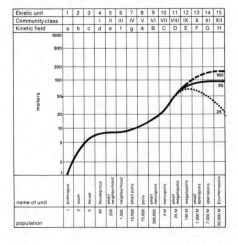

265.   distances between people in the future

Safety from Anthropos

One of the greatest social problems for Anthropos is his safety from other men. It is clearly expressed by the third principle of protective space (page 24) and has always been faced in many ways ranging from walls, doors and keys for the house to city walls or the Great Wall of China. In addition to this, Anthropos has organized his police forces and armies, but here we deal only with the physical aspects which have to create a protective system from human aggression by individuals or groups, as the mass aggression of nation against nation is a different matter. Today we don't have a real system of safety that is expressed in relation to the human settlements. We can get a simple image of the social protective system of safety when looking at the single individual's room (Fig. 266) where he is 100% safe (white), at his house where he may even feel a bit unsafe from his relatives, e.g. when speaking over the telephone about his secrets (light gray), the courtyard, garden, home-street, etc. where the degree of safety decreases. The image we have made demonstrates how we hope to feel safe some day, that is 100% in our room and necessarily less and less in larger units. The ideal is to decrease the danger to zero everywhere, but the realistic goal is to decrease it as much as possible in the larger units where humans are necessarily exposed to more and more dangers.

We know very little today about crime and the city[22] and it is doubtful if the official statistics can be used in the proper way as they differ greatly from country to country and even city to city, as we have not agreed on what the real city is. From a recent World Health Organization survey[23] we learn that Venezuela and the U.S.A. have the top homicide rates and that in Communist Hungary violent

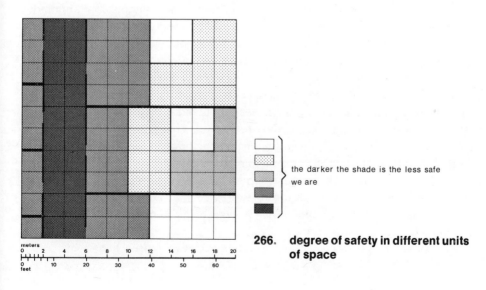

the darker the shade is the less safe we are

266. degree of safety in different units of space

crime is more frequent than in any other West European country. It is quite clear that we cannot connect crime only with incomes or political systems. On the other hand there are theories that the larger the city the higher the rate of crimes, but there is also the view that Tokyo, one of the five largest cities of our globe, is the safest city[24].

There are many recent studies connecting crime with incomes, races, social problems, sex, drugs etc. but we cannot draw any conclusions from them. The ones which are more important from our point of view are those connecting crime with physical structures like Oscar Newman's *Defensible Space*[25]. From such studies we learn that no matter what the other factors are, if we live in towers we are less safe than if we live in row houses. From such experiences we can learn enough to build the proper safety system inside our city.

The system begins with the house which ought to open as much as possible to the outside world but must also become a fortress which will be 100% safe and this can be achieved if the auto-walls are created with such materials that nobody can break or cut through from outside. In the courtyard Anthropos can be made safe by a proper structure of the dividing walls so that nobody can cut through them (this is why they have to be prefabricated from very special reinforced concrete) or jump over them. This can be achieved both by making the tops of the walls sharp and by electronic devices which will call for help if any one passes over them.

This is not enough, though, as Anthropos is also in danger in the street and square. The answer to this is the organization of larger spatial units in a safe way. This can be done in the housegroup by making the gate to the outside world completely safe or even guarded by special people living next to it. Walls and their electronic systems can guarantee full security.

In the past, the first great cities planned by Anthropos introduced a system of division into districts with their own walls and protected gates like in Chang'an, the first big capital of China[26], and later in Peking where people could not move from one district to another at night. This makes it clear that crime in the big city is dangerous because in our proximity to other people we are exposed to more criminals, as we can see by comparing 10 million people living in a city like New York and in a big region (Fig. 267). It is clear that we have to take more measures than in the countryside where the danger — let us assume — is the same in terms of percentages of criminals, but our chances of meeting them are much less. How far these measures have to reach, whether we should have protective walls in every size of ekistic unit (one for the house, one for the housegroup, one for the neighborhood, one for the city, etc.) is something that I can support theoretically at such an early stage. It will take us quite some time to understand what each one of these walls means and how it is ideally expressed. For a house, it certainly has to be a structural wall, but for polis a wall may mean an automatic electronic warning or recording system. The fact is that we have to conceive and develop the proper system of protective "walls". What is certain is that we must start as soon as possible with at least a double protective system at the level of the house and at one higher level protecting Anthropos in the hustreet. The future of the mecstreets does not create any danger from aggression as all the auto-mobiles will run in corridors where no one can pass, or stop or attack the other.

The conclusion is clear: we need a social protective system, at least in the smaller ekistic units, to save Anthropos, living and moving in huspace.

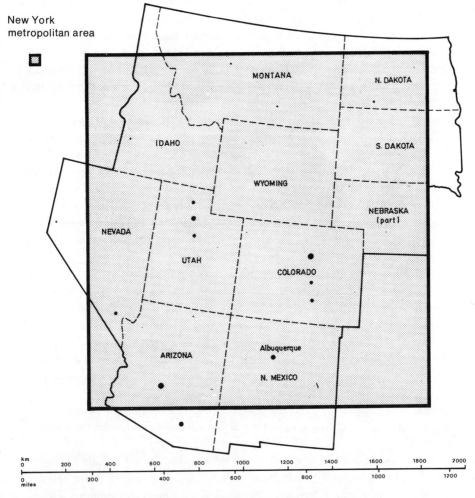

New York
metropolitan area

in metropolitan New York ten million people live in an area of 3,127 sq. km or 1,208 sq. mi.

in the north of the U.S.A. we have to cover almost eleven states in an area of 2,371,000 sq. km or 1,055,000 sq. mi. to find ten million people

this is the reason we hear so much about crime in the one area and not in the other

267. comparison of two areas of ten million people shown on the same scale

Hierarchical organization

The hierarchical organization is imperative for all sorts of social functions, for the very simple reason that the more the people the higher is the type of function they need and can support. If 5,000 or 50,000 people can support a first-aid station, hundreds of thousands are necessary to support a complete hospital and millions are necessary to support difficult research in specialized centers. This does not mean that people cannot enter immediately a high-order research center, but it does mean that it is a center of much higher order than a first-aid station and small clinic. This is valid for all social needs and stresses the need for a proper hierarchical organization of all functions. If we do not achieve it as the basic structure of the social system, there will be no hope for the solution of any of the other social problems, like those of contacts and safety as already mentioned. There is an imperative need for social organization from the housegroup to Ecumenopolis.

Theoretically this means that we need a twelve-level hierarchical social system since we have twelve levels of communities[27] but it does not mean that all functions start from the lowest level or end up at the highest. We cannot support a clinic at the level of a housegroup and the lowest medical unit may start at a large neighborhood (ekistic unit 6) or town or polis (ekistic unit 7 or 8). We may also not need one very central hospital at the level of Ecumenopolis (ekistic unit 15), although some day we may be able to support a huge research center on very difficult questions at such a level only.

Such a hierarchical system is valid for all functions taken together, but this again does not mean that every social function will exist at every level. We may need schools at level 4,5 or 6, such as a kindergarten, but we may also be able to have a lower degree at level 4 where the local mothers will be in charge one day each for the three-year-olds and then at level six for all children of four and five years. The elementary school can then exist at level seven, the high-school at level eight, but the college at level ten. Depending on numbers, incomes, systems and cultures every social function will find its proper level, but all of them taken together form a completely hierarchical system. After all, though we may not need a school at level nine, this does not mean that we don't need a clinic or club at that level.

As one example of how the different ekistic units are interrelated in terms of size and hierarchy, we have seen a first sketch showing how an urbanized part of a continent that is an eperopolis (ekistic unit 14) like North America (Fig. 61) is divided into small eperopolises (ekistic unit 13) and these into megalopolises (ekistic unit 12), small megalopolises (ekistic unit 11) and metropolises (ekistic unit 10) and how these metropolises (Fig. 62) are divided into small metropolises (ekistic unit 9), polises or towns (ekistic unit 8) and smaller polises (ekistic unit 7) and smaller communities, that is larger or smaller neighborhoods (ekistic units 6 and 5). This presentation is indicative only of the system that we are lacking, because the real situation is a very confusing one. This can be seen in several cases, as in Fridley, Minnesota, where there are eleven levels from the city to the U.S.A. (Fig. 268) instead of a maximum of seven that could serve it in an ideal way[28].

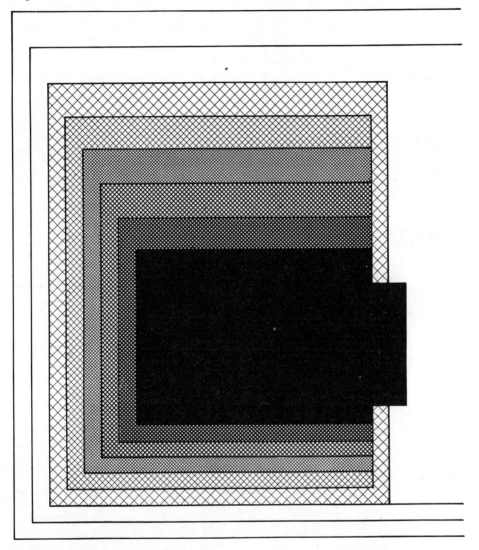

1. City of Fridley — population 15. 173
2. Independent School Districts
3. North Suburban Sanitary Sewer District
4. Minneapolis - St. Paul Sanitary District
5. North Suburban Hospital District
6. Soil Conservation District
7. Anoka County
8. Minneapolis - St. Paul Metropolitan Airports Commission
9. Metropolitan Mosquito Control District
10. State of Minnesota
11. United States of America

268. layers of government in Fridley, Minnesota, U.S.A.

In recapitulation we can see that while the system of Society in terms of contacts looks like Figure 262, in terms of safety like Figure 266 and every other aspect looks different, we can conceive its total system in many ways with superimposed systems. We cannot standardize and unify all relationships and every individual may belong to one family (Fig. 269) love a person more in another and feel a member of political, religious and other groups lying far out.

When we superimpose all systems of Society we see that many of them cannot be expressed in the city and only basic ones, like contacts and safety, can lead to the practical system that we need.

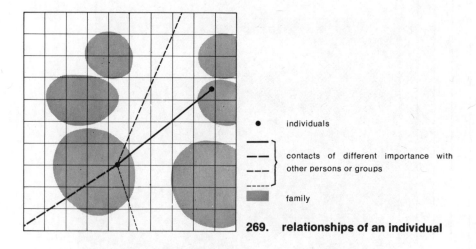

- • individuals

- contacts of different importance with other persons or groups

- family

269. relationships of an individual

20. The system of Shells

The continuous Shells

The proper system of Shells can be better understood than the system of Society in Chapters 6-15 because Shells can be seen, and those who know about them do not need any further explanation. But as this book is not addressed only to real builders (called architects, engineers, planners, etc.), I present two basic notions about the system of Shells within Entopia.

The first notion is that the city always means a continuous system of Shells. We know that Anthropos started in several ways ranging from very separated Shells, as in many Paleolithic (more than ten thousand years ago)[29] settlements, to very compact ones as in Catal Hüyük where people did not even have streets and had to jump into their houses from the roofs. The fact is that all the civilizations ended up with continuous built-up systems no matter how they started. We also have to remember that all the cities and villages humans admire today consist of continuous systems of Shells forming streets and squares as well as inner courtyards.

There are many reasons which can be understood by the second principle (saving energy) and the fourth and fifth ones (see Chapter 2). There is no question that in Entopia we will return to the system of continuous Shells, as we can see in a housegroup in a hustreet (Fig. 119), or in the special neighborhoods (Fig. 148) or in a metropolis (Fig. 182) where we see the new notion of service corridors of all sorts which save human and industrial energy to the maximum possible degree.

The heights of Shells

Today we are in a chaotic situation in terms of the heights of Shells as we allow feudal towers to be mixed with normal houses and lower buildings. It is gradually being understood how many crimes these towers represent, both against their inhabitants (they are inhuman, they waste energy, etc.) and against the city as a whole.

In Entopia it will be clearly understood that we no longer live in a feudal era and three-dimensional space will belong to the city as a whole[30] and thus only buildings serving the communities of various sizes will rise above the common buildings. Of course central areas, special buildings like hotels, offices, etc., will rise above the two or three-story normal houses for the same reasons for which the *attic*, which is a two-story building, was created by the "great" classical city of Athens in Attica[31]. But their height will not be expressed in towers but in continuous systems of four, five, six and more stories depending on the class of the service center and corridor. Any building rising above them will have a symbolic character as a tower, as was the case in many past civilizations.

In this way the entopian city, in terms of heights, will have a system of Shells with three concepts.

    a. the normal hu-areas up to three stories as continuous Shells;
    b. the service centers and corridors with more stories as continuous Shells;
    c. the symbolic buildings rising above a. and b. as isolated towers.

The three-dimensional concept

On the basis of the concepts of Shells as continuous systems and of their height, or third dimension, we now conceive the total system of Shells as a three-dimensional one. It will be an evolution of what has been created in famous villages or cities of the past. The houses are its cells and all other buildings form special parts such as corridors or centers.

In this way we start with lower, continuous systems with lower densities in terms of humans, social contacts and Shells (Fig. 270), and gradually form service corridors (Fig. 271) reaching higher up in all three ways (human, social, Shells systems) and end up with much higher centers again in terms of all three: human densities, social interaction and physical heights (Fig. 272).

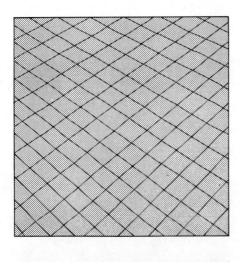

270. the three-dimensional system of Shells: lower continuous systems

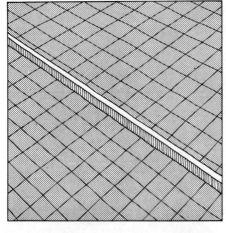

271. the three-dimensional system of Shells: service corridors

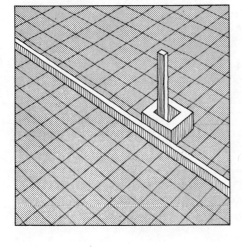

272. the three-dimensional system of Shells: the symbolic higher centers

21. The system of Networks

The proper concept

What has not yet been understood will be very clear in Entopia, that is the proper concept of an ecumenic system or ecumenosystem of Networks including all types of Networks from hustreets to transport, energy, etc., etc. This system will not be a new invention, as we must remember that in ancient days they managed to coordinate all Networks (hustreets, water pipes, sewers) on the same corridors. The change will be a change in scale. What Anthropos achieved in the past inside the city walls must be achieved in Entopia in an ecumenic scale, as his city will be Ecumenopolis. This will require some basic changes.

The *first* basic change will be that people will no longer make the mistakes of the present in speaking of transportation, assigning the tasks to transportation experts only and thus forgetting that Anthropos does not live by transportation, but by movement, since he walks in order to do the most important things in his life such as to develop his muscular system, to walk inside his home, to his bed, to his fellow human, even to his motorcar. Transportation is only a part of Anthropos's movement and we overlook this truth to the benefit of machines causing him many losses. Anthropos's mobility has increased through modern transportation networks, but in general, have lowered the quality of the city and destroyed the equality between its inhabitants. In small settlements all people can interact in space in similar terms (Fig. 273). In settlements larger than a certain size, some people are free to make the contacts they choose, and some are not (Fig. 274).

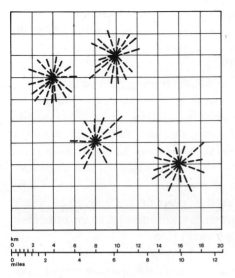

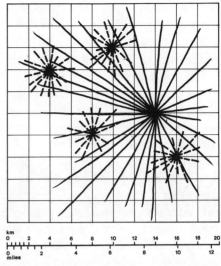

273. in the past every human had the same opportunities in his small world

274. now some people using means of transportation have the choice of all contacts, while others have very limited ones

In Entopia the change will be that all Networks will be called Movement Networks (see Chapter 10), including human movement or transportation as well as the movement and transportation of all goods, energy and messages.

The *second* basic change will be the complete separation of natural human movement from every type of human transportation through the creation of the husystems and mecsystems, as has already been explained in previous chapters, by eliminating even the words street, square, etc. and replacing them with hustreet and husquare as well as with mecstreet and mecsquare, the first ones meaning human and the second mechanical. We cannot survive as humans unless we separate the huspace from the mecspace.

The transportation Networks

The transportation Networks will be organized in a hierarchical way beginning with the movement of one or a few persons in a real auto-mobile (as we have seen in Chapter 9 for small scales) and ending with a total ecumenosystem. The hierarchical organization will not exist only in Society (Chapter 19) and Shells (Chapter 20), but very clearly also in Networks as they must serve all human needs and this can be done only in a hierarchical way.

The *third* basic change in Entopia will be that the present-day conflict between personal and mass transportation will cease to exist because both will be co-ordinated into one system. People today need mass transportation when they do not have the economic power or time to own a private motorcar. On the other hand, they all dream of a private car as under normal conditions it serves them much more by giving them the freedom to select the best type of connection from point to point, from door to door instead of from station to station. The solution will be that the auto-mobiles (owned or used by every person through automatic payments or being charged) will move in the same corridors together with public transportation and thus the system will be both private and public with the advantages of both and no disadvantage at all. This will mean a very well organized system, as we have seen in Chapters 10 to 15, and a huge number of real auto-mobiles.

The *fourth* basic change relates to the larger scales where there is now no co-ordination at all between all types of transportation systems. They are not conceived as integrated systems, as they should be. Highways and ferryboats are not coordinated. There is no country nor any example where the transportation network has been conceived, realized and operated as an overall system in the most economic way in terms of time, energy and cost for the benefit of the country as well as of the individuals.

If any one doubts this statement, I will ask where we can find a bus service which issues tickets for the boats of the harbor it takes the people to, or where an airport exists enabling people to descend from the airplane and get straight into the motorcar and then to the boat. Our Networks are not unified. They are simply connected by auxiliary lines (Fig. 275).

In Entopia there will exist the new concept of LANWAIR (Land-Water-Air) systems[32]. The meaning of this is that we must realize that in the future there will be a growing need for a much closer coordination between all Networks moving people and goods, which should be conceived as unified systems. An example is the unification of ports, airports, etc. They should be brought together as LANWAIR knots (Fig. 276). Such a proposal has been submitted to the Greek Government and is now under examination. It consists of the creation of the new airport of Athens on an island near Sounion connected with Attica by a 2.5 km dam which will create the two new ports of Greece and will save Athens and Piraeus from many problems (Fig. 277).

In this way people will fly from any place into the LANWAIR knot and will simply walk to a boat for an island or cruise, or will walk to a car or train with their baggage following them automatically. It will be a big change.

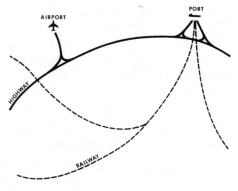

275. the present uncoordinated system

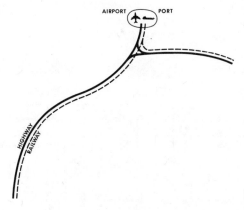

276. the LANWAIR system

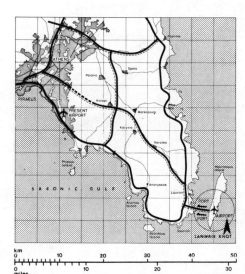

277. the new LANWAIR proposal for
the Athens area, Greece

283

The *fifth* change will be the gradual creation of new types of direct connections between land areas over the water like the bridge connecting Europe and Asia in Constantinople which already operates, or below the water like the Channel to connect England with France, originally planned to operate in 1980 and which has been postponed. In this way the LANWAIR systems will have many more connections by the same vehicle, without the need for flying, which will remain the service for long distances.

The *sixth* basic change will be the transfer from the completely uncoordinated air connections (Fig. 278) to coordinated systems (Fig. 279) which are presented here in a schematic way only because no such study has been carried out in detail.

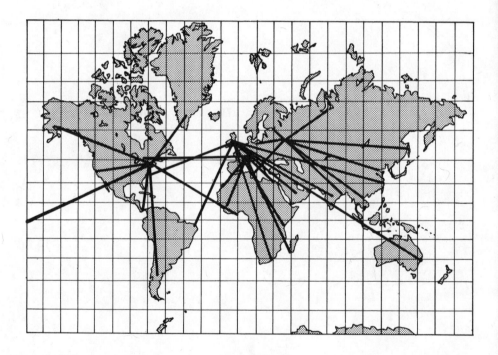

278.   uncoordinated air connections

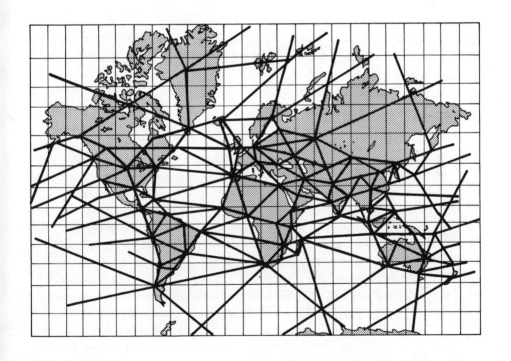

279. **coordinated systems**

The utility Networks

The *seventh* change will be the creation of coordinated hierarchical utility Networks. The big mistake most commonly made today is that when we speak of transportation we think only of persons and goods. We forget the existence of water, clean or otherwise, moving in pipes, of gas, oil, electricity, messages, the telephones, etc. The result is that we waste a lot of space and Networks. We have proved this in many studies for many cases, especially in Europe and the U.S.A. Here I present the examples of the Urban Detroit Area and of Athens, Greece where one can see the chaotic situation created by uncoordinated Networks of all sorts (Figs. 280, 281). The cause of this and other problems already explained is that before the last war there were few dense Networks beyond major cities. After the last war, however, everything expanded very quickly beyond cities; and everywhere each agency or company studied its own network in the best possible way for its own purposes and immediate needs without due consideration for other Networks.

The solution in Entopia will be the full coordination of all utility systems within the same corridors, as several studies began to present in the 1970s[33].

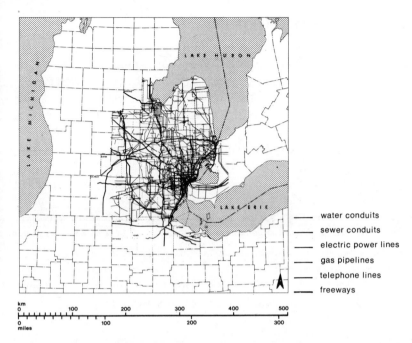

———	water conduits
———	sewer conduits
———	electric power lines
———	gas pipelines
———	telephone lines
———	freeways

280.   uncoordinated Networks of all sorts in the Urban Detroit Area, U.S.A.

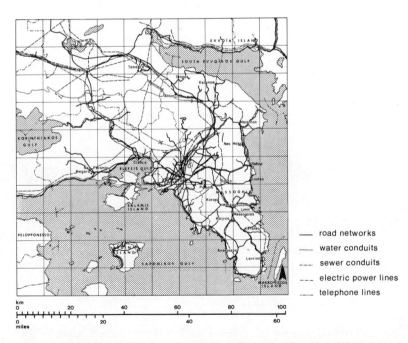

———	road networks
....	water conduits
– – –	sewer conduits
– – –	electric power lines
....	telephone lines

281.   uncoordinated Networks of all sorts in the Greater Athens Area, Greece

287

The complete system of Networks

The *eighth* and most important change will be the complete coordination of transportation and utility corridors. We call them transutilidors. When this is done the savings in land will be higher than 80% of the total area occupied today, as we can see from the Urban Detroit Area study which was carried out in detail and with the full coordination of all agencies and companies concerned on the U.S.A. and the Canadian side (Figs. 282, 283) and also from the Athens, Greece study (Fig. 284). The savings in environment and quality of life in the countryside will be even greater.

This change will lead to the need of placing all Networks underground and cover them. This is not an invention — it is what has always happened. Dead human bodies were first left inside the caves, then they were buried. Water was left running on the surface of the streets, then it was sent underground in pipes. Sewers were originally on the surface and then were placed underground. Electricity and telephones were in the air (see Chapter 5, Fig. 68) and now they are underground. In the same way we will travel in underground tunnels in bubbles at very high speeds and in an automatic way go anywhere we want.

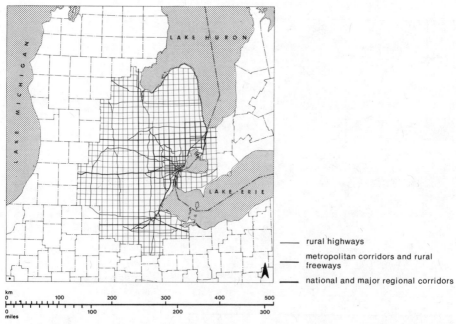

rural highways

metropolitan corridors and rural freeways

national and major regional corridors

282. possible system of coordinated Networks in the Urban Detroit Area, U.S.A.

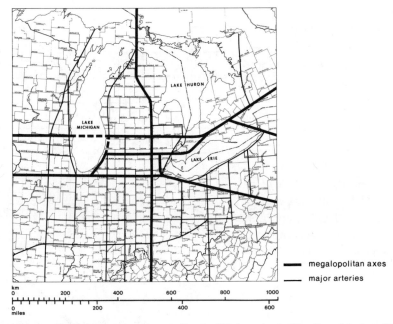

megalopolitan axes
major arteries

```
km
0        200       400       600       800       1000
0              200            400             600
miles
```

283. possible system of coordinated Networks in the Great Lakes Megalopolis, U.S.A. and Canada

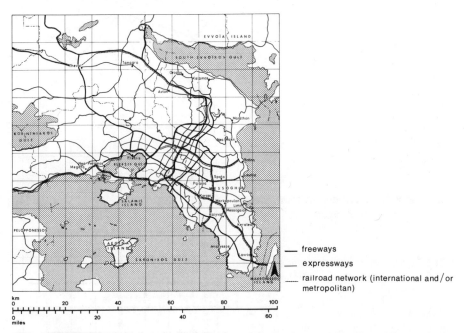

freeways
expressways
railroad network (international and/or metropolitan)

```
km
0        20        40        60        80        100
0              20             40              60
miles
```

284. possible system of coordinated Networks in the Greater Athens Area, Greece

We can see in the following figures
how this complete system which starts
with hustreets and ends with electronic
safety systems guaranteeing Anthropos
and Shells from house to city (depending up to what class of unit we want)
is conceived. In the first one (Fig. 285a)
we see the comparison from the point
to point gradual extension to the orderly organization of the whole area.
In the second one (Fig. 285b) we see
how instead of the conflicting systems
of transportation and utility corridors
we have to move towards a completely
coordinated system (Fig. 285c).

a

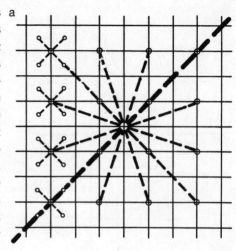

b

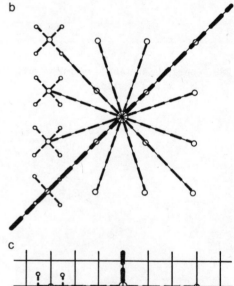

c

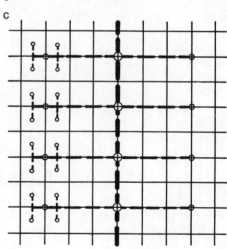

**285. how the complete system of Net-
works is conceived**

a. transportation Network follows a grid
pattern while utility Networks follow a different pattern

b. transportation and utility Networks follow the same pattern but not the grid

c. transportation and utility Networks follow the same grid pattern

22. The total system

From the parts to the whole

We have already seen Entopia in all its parts from furniture to Ecumenopolis (Chapters 6-15) and we have seen the systems created by its five elements (Chapters 17-21) and why we need a total system of organization (Chapter 16). We now have to understand how all parts and elements form a total system.

I will use two examples. The first one demonstrates the difference between the scales and the synthesis inside them. A modern new capital like Islamabad consists of a system of polises forming a metropolis. Each sector or polis incorporates one of the famous cities of the past (Fig. 286), such as classical Athens (upper part), Renaissance Florence (right part), Paris within its walls (lower part) and ancient London (left part) and this is only a small part of the present-day metropolis (Fig. 196). The scale and the synthesis of the city changes continuously, but it can be very successful if we understand what the change in scale means.

The second example demonstrates how the five elements are connected into a system. We have already seen this in previous chapters, but I will use here the case of three types of areas which can marry together in one very successful synthesis, as in Figure 287 where we have set a goal as in Chapter 10, for the Naturareas to penetrate into Anthropareas which are organized in communities (size of polis) some of which spread out and marry with Cultivareas.

In this way we understand how the synthesis can be guided by such desires as easy access to Nature, variety and diversity and how it can lead to unifying systems as we discussed in the symposion on a City for Human Development[34] and to systems for hospitality and travel[35].

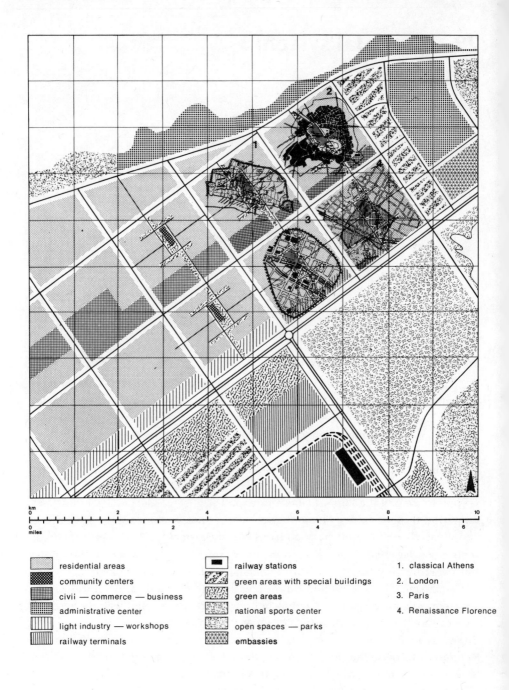

km
0   2   4   6   8   10

0   2   4   6
miles

residential areas	railway stations	1. classical Athens
community centers	green areas with special buildings	2. London
civii — commerce — business	green areas	3. Paris
administrative center	national sports center	4. Renaissance Florence
light industry — workshops	open spaces — parks	
railway terminals	embassies	

286.   first sectors of Islamabad, Pakistan, planned in 1960

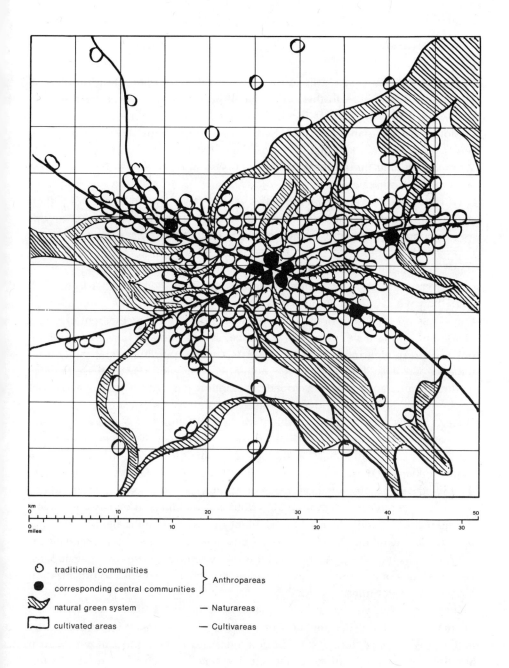

km
0   10   20   30   40   50
0   10   20   30
miles

◖	traditional communities	⎫ Anthropareas
●	corresponding central communities	⎭
🖎	natural green system	— Naturareas
▭	cultivated areas	— Cultivareas

287.   synthesis of Anthropareas, Naturareas and Cultivareas

The synthesis

Having stated that a synthesis must be achieved in all scales and between all elements, we now turn to the most difficult part, or how this can be achieved. I have been working on this for 40 years and have already presented my conclusions in practice and several of them appear in this book. Here I will explain how it evolved. In 1963, that is 11 years ago, I started the effort to present the system explaining the synthesis of the total system of all forces shaping human settlements at all scales.

I first studied several hundred cities, and I have gradually increased their number to about one thousand. I did not make my first announcement on this assumption until 1968, after it had been repeatedly checked[36]. I have continued improving my experience and ideas and in 1969 I presented the fourth assumption[37]. Continuing my work, I presented the fifth one in 1972[38].

I have recounted the evolution of these assumptions here in order to demonstrate how we can improve our knowledge by continuously testing our assumptions, because the future of our cities depends not on the development of "great ideas" but on the development of a science, and in this way I have reached the point of presenting my sixth assumption[39]. It does not differ significantly from the previous ones, but it is definitely better. I can now present all these findings in the seventh and more developed assumption (Fig. 288) where we see the eleven forces in the five groups of the five basic elements (Nature, Anthropos, Society, Shells and Networks) which we can call the $N.A.S.SH.NE.$ System.

What is the value of studying the elements in order to arrive at ekistic synthesis for each scale of settlement? In the case of a small town or polis the forces of Nature are very important (land, water, air, climate). Other factors also play roles: the biological and physiological needs of Anthropos and his social organization; the need of proper form (appropriate layouts for building); the forces of growth (economic, etc.); the systems of movement of people (kinetic fields, etc.); and organization (whether there is a large city hall, cathedral, or a regional administrative center, etc.). As the small town grows into a metropolis, megalopolis, etc. the values of the forces change: Nature, growth, movement and organization play much greater roles.

Humans in the past had in many places developed the ability for a synthesis in small units. I will just mention one case out of the many I admired in my lifetime. When we enter the small port of the island of Ios in the southern Aegean Sea there is, on our right hand, the small, isolated church of St. Irene. Its unknown builder has managed to transmit a message of isolation and beauty, a message that prepares you to talk to yourself and, if you can, to God. Sitting on the wall of the small courtyard, unaware of the hails from the departing sailboat, I found myself envying this unknown builder, who, in managing to build this church, perhaps fulfilled a lifetime's dream. He did not have a tenth of the infor-

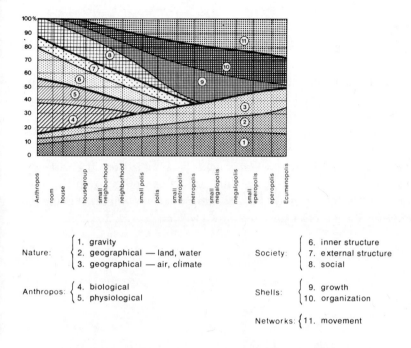

Nature:	1. gravity 2. geographical — land, water 3. geographical — air, climate	
Anthropos:	4. biological 5. physiological	

Society:	6. inner structure 7. external structure 8. social
Shells:	9. growth 10. organization
Networks:	11. movement

288. probable validity of the forces of ekistic synthesis (assumption seven)

mation possessed by any architectural student today, nor did he have any of the techniques that today's builders possess, but he had the ability to transmit the right message in the right way because his ideas, his processing, and his transmitting were in balance. What he did have was the ability to make a synthesis between the rough and rocky landscape, the knowledge of the needs of the human body and even more of the senses, mind and soul. Who has these abilities today when we deal with the large scale human settlements as we are obliged to do?

The conclusions are clear: human settlements are higher order complex organisms which, as growing ekistic systems, develop a different relationship with Nature because their dimensions change, and they depend to an even greater extent on certain types of human action, such as Networks and organization. As a result, the overall synthesis of the system changes and so does its structure, and finally a different form is produced. This form may become confused unless we analyze its evolution in a systematic way and understand the total system and its principles and laws[40].

The foundations

Before closing this chapter I want to state very strongly that what I present is a real Entopia and not only a theory because together with my associates in Doxiadis Associates and the Athens Center of Ekistics, we have worked with reality in 40 countries, and we have studied human settlements in more than one hundred. I may be wrong in some conclusions or parts of some conclusions as some theoreticians may say, but the fact is that what I say is based not on theories and "intellectualism" but on hard work applied to over 1,000 cases in the big hospital that we see here (Fig. 289) where patients have come from long distances and doctors (including a few surgeons) dedicated themselves to ameliorating human settlements. What I present is a real Entopia, and we will see it in the following chapters in illustrations explaining how it will look.

289. the Doxiadis Organization building in Athens, Greece

Part Four

The real Entopia

23. The great dystopia of 1984

We will never understand all the characteristics of Entopia 2121 A.D., which we will see in the next chapter, if we do not compare it with the present-day dystopias we live in. I will start in the proper historical order, that is with the present-day dystopia and move next to the Entopia that will replace it. Out of the many dystopias which exist today, I have selected the one built exactly where the Entopia will appear; and in order to avoid any confusion about the notion of today, I select the year 1984. The reason is that we have been more prepared to accept the year 1984 as the symbol of the worst that can happen ever since George Orwell opened our eyes to it. In this dystopia (Fig. 290), we can clearly see a whole metropolis. If there is any question why I call a small group of buildings a metropolis, my answer is that this is how it looks because the air pollution covers the main part of it. So let us be realistic and see and understand the character and quality of our dystopian metropolis.

To the right I see the forces which lead to dystopia. It is the big corporation which built the tower on top of the small hill which tells me: "Fly ABC fortresses!" Airplanes have to be built like fortresses to avoid skyjacking attacks by passengers.

The corporation continues with its messages: "Eat only ABC food" and ends up with "Sleep only with ABC women". On the other sides of the tower it has many more messages to impose on the city as its symbols.

290.   dystopia 1984 covered with pollution

Below the tower I see the hotel *Belle Vue,* which when built had a beautiful view which has now been replaced by the multi-story garage and the many signs which are very interesting and prove the chaos we live in. The great competitor insists on flying only XYZ. Down below I can see the night club called *Oh! Oh!* to tell us how beautiful life is; we then have in Greek the message: "Buy Greek!" and next to it the Japanese and Italian messages. With all these languages it is very clear how harmonious the environment is now.

Finally I see the motorcar reaching the other machines to the left. It is owned by its driver and has the sign, "long live my machine". I cannot see beyond this level. Pollution takes care of the task of hiding the dystopian city. In this respect pollution can be called useful as it hides the ugliness, but we also have to breathe it and we do not know how long we will live in such an atmosphere. Then the wind blows and in a few moments we feel that it is clean and we start breathing vigorously. When I open my eyes I see a large part of the city, as the pollution has been blown away (Fig. 291). I see now the second hill where the effort has been made for a harmonious synthesis; but, as I learned later, a lot of money was lost as the market relied on the towers. I then notice the factories invading the beautiful plain from the right where the big harbor lies beyond what we see. Behind them I do not understand what happens or why. There is a great mixture of old beautiful fields, factories, towers, small buildings. I do not really understand what the "city" means here.

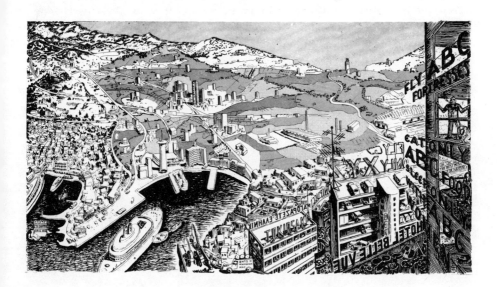

291.   dystopia 1984

When I turn to the middle and see the highways and the towers around them I begin to understand. The old story that this area will be saved because of its cultural tradition is over. Some "able" businessmen managed to get permission to build their towers. For the sake of the area, the regulations changed and the metropolis which was supposed to be stopped to the right is now spreading everywhere, into all types of areas. I now see where the new explosion or, as some people call it, the freedom for creation is leading. The ability for synthesis which I see in the buildings of this harbor in the middle is unique. Even the Paleolithic humans did not make such mistakes. They tried all possible sorts of buildings, but only one type in every human settlement. The units were not ideal but the total made sense because of its unity. Now everyone pretends to build the "best building", but the total is chaotic. Any ability for synthesis has been lost.

In the harbor we see the big boat entering, and I witness how we have forgotten the meaning of scale. What is now left of the view from the hotel which advertised, "Come to see the beautiful sea in front of you"? To the left of this big boat we see the formerly beautiful beach which existed outside the traditional harbor. Even this harbor has been invaded by new types of boats and has lost its scale. This is not happening only in the sea. I see the big hotel which destroyed all traditional values of the age-old small traditional town. And this is not the only change. I can see many frightening ones.

I am frightened and I turn to the very small island which I always remember as having the most beautiful beach and I am even more frightened by the change. It is now simply the basis for the big sign "Come to our beautiful village". Tourism, I see, means signs and advertisements and no more values. This is the great dystopia 1984. Do not try to see it before or after 1984. It is so dynamic that it changes from day to day.

24. The real Entopia 2121 A.D.

Although I have already described in detail the real Entopia of the future and explained how we will lay the foundations in order to build it for our future, although I have already given an analysis of many of its parts and systems, I have now reached the point of speaking about how it will look. I do this for two reasons:

1. Because we usually speak about the cities we visit in terms of how they look.
2. Because the non-experts who read this book may feel unable to understand some of the partial drawings and how they connect into a complete system.

In order to achieve this goal I visited several cities in the year 2121 A.D., and as I cannot present all of them I will here describe my experiences in the Mediterranean region. I name the region which has inspired this drawing of mine (Fig. 292) because, although all cities of 2121 A.D. have the same basic characteristics, as the 1984 dystopias also tend to do, they certainly look different in small scales and details. I had to select a specific region and I chose the Mediterranean megalopolis because many of its parts, like southern France, Italy and Greece are quite well known internationally and thus the Entopia will be better understood.

What we see is one metropolitan area out of the many which form the megalopolis. In order to understand it properly and to connect it with what already has been presented I follow the process introduced in Part Three (Chapters 16-22); that is, I analyze a total system of human settlements consisting of five subsystems and many more sub-subsystems.

I start with Nature. We can see large areas of it such as hills and mountains in the background, and many parts such as the hill to the left or the parks and the river to the right. In front of us we can see another expression of the sea kingdom of water. We see two harbors and when we observe them carefully we will notice that they are very different. The one to the left is the traditional

292.   **Entopia 2121 A.D.**

harbor built before machines were invented and is only suitable for sailing boats. This is how it is used now, no big boat or even small motor-powered one is allowed to enter it. The other harbor to the right is meant for any kind of modern boat, provided it is quite small and does not disturb the scale. The harbor of the metropolis for big boats and large-scale movements is to the right, and we cannot see it. Each harbor belongs to a different type of water zone (see Chapter 17).

These major parts of the land and water kingdoms are interconnected into a continuous system by smaller areas of land and water. We see small parks, including cemeteries, big areas covered by grass, to the right, and many corridors covered with trees as well as major and minor rivers of which we see the major one to the right. In such a way we see the whole system of Nature (we do not see the air, because it is not polluted), as a really continuous and meaningful system starting with the mountains and the sea on a metropolitan scale (ekistic unit 10) and going down to corridors of small polis, like the ones running parallel in the area around the square with the tower, to the left of the river and park (ekistic unit 7). We can follow the system into smaller units by seeing the planted roads inside the community to the right of the hill on the left (ekistic unit 5), and even into smaller ones in hustreets on the hill to the right, and houses and courtyards (ekistic unit 3). In such a way we can conceive the total system of Nature from the oceans, and the Ecumenokepos which we do not see, down to the metropolis which we start to see and down to the smallest units of houses and their rooms containing Nature inside their courtyards (as we can see them in the right hand lower part) in the form of small plants. Thus Nature controls the largest part of Ecumenopolis, starting with Naturareas and going down to small units even as small potted plants inside rooms. It starts with ekistic unit 15 and goes down to ekistic unit 2.

After Nature, we move to the subsystem of Anthropos. Unlike Nature, where we started with the big units and went down to the smallest ones in order to understand how the Naturareas infiltrated the city, we now move from the smallest unit of one human gradually to reach the largest ones.

Mother and child stand on their veranda, lower right, nude, as they enjoy the climate better and they are allowed by law to go nude without creating any problems for anyone. The reason that they are allowed to do so is that they live in a community (ekistic unit 5) where everyone is nudist at home (which is different from the nudist community where everyone is allowed to be nude also in their own streets and squares).

Below the mother and child (ekistic unit 2) we see people walking in the hustreet (ekistic unit 5) of their neighborhood and to their square where they meet in the coffeeshop to contact each other after buying in the small local shops. In between them we see the small hustreet (ekistic unit 4) entering into the lower housegroup.

303

We can see the same hustreets on the next hill which is covered by a small neighborhood (ekistic unit 5).

When we move to the harbors we see the larger hustreets all around them, which are class 8 as they surround the small polises behind them. In both cases we see husquares at one point of the hustreets, which are the connections of the outside world with the inner community, that is the polis. It is here that the maximum traditional number of human contacts takes place. Thus we understand the huge system that starts with the isolated person inside her room or courtyard, where if she wants she cannot see or be seen by others. Using the proper auto-walls or auto-roofs she continues with her family or home contacts of a few people, walks on the hustreet with contacts with a few tens of people, until she reaches the larger hustreets and squares where she can contact a few thousands, especially on occasions like festivities, political gatherings, demonstrations, etc. We start with ekistic unit 1 and end up with ekistic unit 7 or 8 as in the bigger square built on a human scale which can serve up to tens of thousands of people, that is the ekistic unit 8 or polis.

We can see the polis behind the second hill on the right, with its big central square and tower for the 80,000 people who live between the sea, the river and the big corridor we see behind the pyramid, running as a horizontal line through the whole picture.

When we move to larger units for hundreds of thousands or millions we no longer have the physical system of a husquare, because it does not really have a meaning. It has become so big that there is no reason for humans to gather. They may be able to hear a political leader, but beyond the tens of thousands they cannot see him. From here on, that is from the small metropolis on (ekistic unit 9), we do not have natural contacts between people and the husystem relies on machines, either for meetings with more people by proper movement to many gatherings, or on telecommunications like television for one-way contacts and transmission of messages to the many.

Now we move to the third subsystem, that of Society. From the description of the two previous subsystems and from the overall picture, we begin to understand that what characterizes it is the hierarchical organization. In front of us to the right we see the housegroups (ekistic unit 4) forming small neighborhoods (ekistic unit 5) each on its own hill. The front one is for nudists at home and the next one for a very puritan group which is praying at this moment, and thus we do not see anyone in the street. Together with other small neighborhoods behind them they form the complete neighborhood (ekistic unit 6).

Then we see several polises (ekistic unit 7) on the left. The oldest one runs from hill to harbor, and the younger and commercial one is in the youngest harbor. And then we can see the one with the big central square for all sorts of gatherings, from political to cultural ones, with the big tower.

They are all parts of the polis (ekistic unit 8) and they are separated from each other by green corridors, seven of which we can see forming the polis. They are the one to the lower right with which we started the description, the other three, traditional, younger commercial and youngest with the big center and the three behind them. We do not see the eighth one, which is to the right.

Then we see other polises, one behind and one more behind it until we reach the hills, and several to the right. All those to the left of the river and parks form a small metropolis (ekistic unit 9), while to the right of it we have another small metropolis. They are together with some others which we do not see to the right and the left parts of the metropolis (ekistic unit 10) of which we see the center symbolized by the pyramid of the people, upper right.

Thus we have seen the whole system of social organization also expressed physically, from the lowest ekistic units up to the metropolis (ekistic unit 10) and this continues up to Ecumenopolis with natural areas playing greater and greater roles as dividing lines. This is the hierarchical organization that guarantees the greatest freedom to the people; by far greater freedom than the chaotic system which exists today. Only such an organization allows every individual to select his own ekistic unit where the local laws and regulations allow him to live as he pleases: as a nudist or well dressed, with traditional families or in communes, with several sexes (e.g. homosexuals) expressing themselves freely in front of others or not, with religious rules imposed on streets and squares or not, etc. etc. Only an ideal organization can give to every human the maximum of choices. The best system gives the greatest freedom, and not the lack of it as some theoreticians of cities pretend.

The organization of Anthropos and Society which we have seen help us to understand the next subsystem, that of Shells. In every very small community or ekistic unit, we see that all buildings are equal, in terms of heights, regulations, etc. When we move to the larger units we begin to see some buildings emerging above the others and the larger the unit the more they emerge. On the second hill to the right we see the small church becoming the highest symbol of the puritans. In the oldest community of all, the one to the left, we see the old monastery and church at the top forever the symbols of a broader culture.

Looking at the whole settlement we can recognize the hierarchy of all buildings and understand that the most important buildings are the symbols of the communities or ekistic units they belong to. Thus there are traditional churches, which are symbols of ekistic unit 5 (to the right) or even ekistic unit 7 (to the left), and many other churches, temples, mosques, etc. or commercial, administrative, cultural centers which are symbols of increasingly larger ekistic units, until we reach the great pyramid of the people which is the symbol of the center of the whole metropolis (ekistic unit 10). On the saddle of the heights to the right, from where the full panorama of the metropolis can be enjoyed, the pyramid of the people is the center and symbol of the whole city, as every community has its own center and symbol, religious, cultural, social or political.

Looking at the whole city we can see that its Shells belong to many eras from many centuries. On the left we can see the traditional polis which was saved and restored after what happened in dystopia 1984 (see Chapter 23, Fig. 290). There are also very recent Shells such as several of the great symbolic buildings and the modern housing schemes to the lower right and the polis around the administrative square and tower behind the second hill.

These are the types of houses, housegroups and neighborhoods we have seen in Chapters 8, 9, 10, Figures 109, 119, 148. They represent the best effort to save space, which we badly need, and energy which was always badly needed even if we have forgotten it now (second principle), while at the same time giving their inhabitants the best quality that can be given within the city.

But where are the industrial plants? The probable answer, that our picture does not include the Industrarea, that is, Zone 12 (see Chapter 17) is not completely correct. The reason is that a substantial part of industries is located here, but is below the buildings (Chapter 10, Fig. 158) and a larger part is below the park to the right. It is the automated industry which has been built underground and is guided by the personnel working in the straight line of buildings which we see inside the park. Because of the underground buildings the park does not have trees where the roofs exist underground and thus there is enough isolation from heat and cold and saving of energy. The factory costs more to build underground, but its operation does not disturb the city at all. The surface is saved for the city to breathe and the people to enjoy it and all the liquids and air that have to come out are guided by underground Networks for recycling, and other uses. Technology and a better understanding of the total system and how it can become economic lead to the proper solution for industry within the city.

The fifth subsystem is that of Networks. By carefully following the description of the previous four subsystems we can easily understand it, because although it is mostly underground it can be clearly seen on the surface.

We can see the high-speed lines (darker shade) and some very few lines of the lower speed branches serving special buildings, homes, etc. If we place them all, we will be unable to see and understand anything. Think how we illustrate our cardiovascular system in order to understand it. It starts in the smallest units, as happened in our history, and reaches up to Ecumenopolis in ekistic unit 15 and even goes beyond to ekistic unit 16 with the spaceships that connect us with the cosmos, even in a very limited way.

By looking at the infiltration of Naturareas inside the Anthropareas we can understand where the major transportation and utilities corridors are, like those of class 12, which run below the hills from the left to the great people's building to the right, connecting the present metropolis with the other parts of the megalopolis of which it is a part. In the same way, by following all natural corridors, we come down to Networks class 8 surrounding the polises. In this way if at

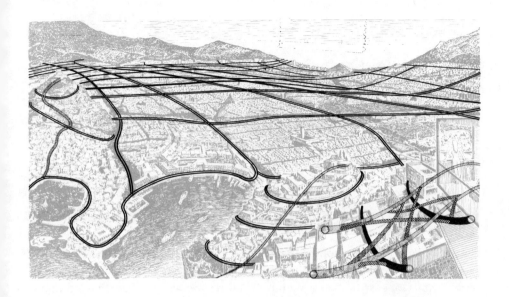

293. underground Networks in Entopia

any time there is a need for a major change of the underground channels, there is no need to destroy any buildings. What happens is that by special equipment the trees and plants are lifted to one side, an opening of the underground corridor takes place and the changes are made without disturbing anyone and without stopping any function because the corridors operate all around in many directions. A simple sketch (it is early for details) (Fig. 293) demonstrates the type of underground network that serves the movement of people and some bulky goods. This also explains how the system is built below the hustreets after leaving the natural corridors which reach down to ekistic unit 8. Thus by understanding how the movement of people takes place on the surface, how Nature infiltrates the Anthropareas and how Society and Shells are organized, we can see the whole subsystem of Networks.

This last example of how one subsystem can be understood by the others demonstrates the existence of the total system of human settlements as one unified system with a real synthesis of all parts for the sake of all humans in the broadest sense, not only for a short period but forever. This means that for the sake of humans a true balance has been achieved with Nature which is as rich as possible for the sake of the broadest human interests. This is the city that makes people happy and safe and helps them to develop more and more.

Epilogue

If in building Entopia we follow the guidelines of the present book, we will lead humans back to the harmony they badly need. This harmony will fulfill many more human needs than at any time in the past when people achieved many very harmonious human settlements, from camps to villages and cities, but without serving all their needs such as social equality, scientific and technological services, the best health conditions, the greatest possible mobility on our earth. Harmony was there and this is why we now admire so many human settlements of the past, but we should not forget that we admire only what we see, that is the harmony between Nature and Shells and Networks as well as the human scale. What we miss seeing and what we forget is that this harmony made people safe in terms of their relationship to Nature and gave them a human scale to live in, but not necessarily freedom and services for many of their needs such as education. The fact that this was achieved to a certain degree in classical Athens does not mean that it lasted forever or that we should forget the feudalism, the kingdoms, the dictatorships, political, religious, etc. that deprived the humans of many of their other natural desires. Humans became aware of all these needs and began trying to serve them with the scientific revolution and the technology which followed. It brought in so many new forces that the great explosion took place; and we are in the middle of it. One of the results of this explosion was the lack of balance between so many old and new elements and the complete loss of harmony, and our confusion on so many things expressed in human settlements. We now open our eyes, we see the explosion, we understand the confusion and its causes, we have an exact diagnosis of our disease and we can begin the therapy, not by nervous and uncoordinated magical solutions, but by properly conceiving and trying to build the Entopia we badly need. The process has begun. Someday it will be completely understood and then we will see that building Entopia is our great task and we will carry it out. There is no reason for any pessimism when humanity learns the truth. We are on the proper road for the best harmony that humanity has ever achieved.

Glossary

Anthroparea: Term coined by C.A. Doxiadis from the words *Anthropos* (human being) and *area*, meaning the so-called built-up area or area mostly used by Anthropos in his daily life.

Anthropocosmos: Term coined by C.A. Doxiadis from the Greek words *anthropos* and *cosmos*, (human being and world), meaning World of Anthropos as distinguished from the great world or cosmos beyond Anthropos's reach.

Anthropos: One of the five ekistic elements, it is the Greek word for human being, used instead of the English word, "Man", since it has no connotation distinguishing sex or age, but means men and women equally belonging to all age-groups. See note 31, Part One for further clarification.

Community class: Based on a systematic classification of human communities expressed in the ekistic logarithmic scale (els), starting from class I, which corresponds to housegroup, and ending up with class XII, corresponding to Ecumenopolis.

Cultivarea: Term coined by C.A. Doxiadis, meaning the cultivated areas.

Dynapolis: Term coined by C.A. Doxiadis and used since the early fifties in his teaching and writing; meaning dynamic city or dynamic "polis". The ideal dynapolis is the city with a parabolic uni-directional growth which can expand in space and time.

Dystopia: From the Greek words *dys* and *topos. Dys* signifies difficulty or evil. It is the opposite of *eu* — good. In this combination and context, *dystopia* is another and much more precise word for what anti-utopia was supposed to mean.

Ecumenopolis: Term coined by C.A. Doxiadis from the Greek words *ecumene,* that is, the total inhabited area of the world, and *polis,* or city, in the broadest sense of the word. It means the coming city that will, together with the corresponding open land which is indispensable for Anthropos, cover the entire earth as a continuous system forming a universal settlement.

Ekistic elements: The five elements which compose human settlements: Nature, Anthropos, Society, Shells and Networks.

Ekistic logarithmic scale (els): A classification of settlements according to their size, presented on the basis of a logarithmic scale, running from Anthropos (ekistic unit 1), as the smallest unit of measurement, to the whole earth (ekistic unit 15). The ekistic logarithmic scale can be presented graphically, showing area or number of people corresponding to each unit, etc., so that it can be used as a basis for the measurement and classification of many dimensions in human settlements.

Ekistics: Term coined by C.A. Doxiadis from the Greek words *oikos,* and *oikō,* "settling down", to mean the science of human settlements. It conceives the human settlement as a living organism having its own laws and, through the study of the evolution of human settlements from their most primitive phase to megalopolis and Ecumenopolis, develops the interdisciplinary approach necessary to its problems.

Entopia: Term coined by C.A. Doxiadis from the Greek words *en* and *topos,* "in" and "place", to mean place that is practicable — that can exist.

Eperopolis: Derived from the Greek words *eperos,* "continent" and polis, "city", it replaces the old term "urbanized continent", which corresponded to ekistic unit 14 and community class XI, with a population of 5,000 million.

House and housegroup: These terms replace "dwelling" and "dwelling group", which corresponded to ekistic units 3 and 4, with a population of four and 40 people respectively. Housegroup corresponds to community class I.

Hustreet (husquare, hu-avenue, etc.): Term coined by C.A. Doxiadis to signify the division of the human from the mechanical. A hustreet is a street reserved for human beings only, and prohibited to machines.

Industrarea: Term coined by C.A. Doxiadis meaning the industrial areas.

LANWAIR: Land, Water, Air. Term coined by C.A. Doxiadis to mean the transportation Network conceived as a unified system, in which ports, airports, etc. are brought together as LANWAIR knots, enabling people (and goods) to move from airplanes to boats, cars, and trains without any extra formalities or difficulties. See also note 32, Part Three.

Mecstreet (mecsystem, mecarea, etc.): Term coined by C.A. Doxiadis to denote the mechanical from the human. A mecstreet is a street reserved for machines only.

Megalopolis: Term used since ancient Greek times when the small city of Mega-lopolis was created in Arcadia. Jean Gottmann gave a special meaning to this ancient term in 1961 in his book, *Megalopolis: the Urbanized Northeastern Seaboard of the United States.* A megalopolis is a greater urbanized area re-sulting from the merging of metropolises and cities into one urban system. Its population is calculated in tens of millions. It corresponds to ekistic unit 12 and community class IX.

Nature: One of the five ekistic elements corresponding to the natural environ-ment of Anthropos as it exists before he starts remodelling it by cultivation and construction. It provides the foundation upon which the settlement is created and the frame within which it can function.

Networks: One of the five ekistic elements corresponding to the Anthropos-made systems which facilitate the functioning of settlements, such as roads, water supply, electricity.

Polis: Corresponding to ekistic unit 8 and community class V, it has a population of 50,000 and replaces the term "city".

Shells: One of the five ekistic elements corresponding to all types of structures within which Anthropos lives and carries out his various functions.

Society: One of the five ekistic elements corresponding to human society with all its characteristics, needs and problems, where each individual is examined only as one of its units.

Bibliography

Carrel, A., *Man the Unknown*, Hamish Hamilton, London, 1961.

Clarke, G. and Piggott, S., *Prehistoric Societies*, Hutchinson, London, 1965.

Eiseley, L., *The Immense Journey*, Vintage Books, New York, 1957.

Fitzgerald, C.P. and the HORIZON MAGAZINE eds., *The Horizon History of China*, American Heritage Publishing Co., Inc., New York, 1969.

Gardner, J.W., *Self-Renewal: the Individual and the Innovative Society*, Harper & Row, New York, 1964.

Giedion, S., *Architecture, You and Me*, Harvard University Press, Cambridge, Mass., 1958.

Gottmann, J., *Megalopolis: the Urbanized Northeastern Seaboard of the United States*, MIT Press, Cambridge, Mass., 1961.

Hayek, F.A., *The Counter-Revolution of Science*, Allen & Unwin, London, 1952.

Huxley, A., *Island*, Chatto & Windus, London, 1959.

Newman, O., *Defensible Space*, Collier and Macmillan, New York, 1972.

Simpson, G.G., *The Meaning of Evolution*, Yale University Press, New Haven, Conn., 1967.

Sinnott, E.W., *The Problem of Organic Form*, Yale University Press, New Haven, Conn., 1963.

Skinner, B.F., *Walden Two*, Macmillan, New York, 1963.

Toffler, A., *Future Shock*, Random House, New York, 1970.

Toynbee, A., *A Study of History*, one-volume edition, Oxford University Press in association with Thames & Hudson, London, 1972.

Weiss, P., *Dynamics of Development: Experiments and Inferences*, Academic Press, New York, 1968.

Wilde, O., *The Soul of Man under Socialism*, Crescendo, Boston, Mass., 1969.

Wright, A.F., "Changan", *Cities of Destiny*, edited by Arnold Toynbee, Thames & Hudson, London, 1967.

Books and publications by the author

Between Dystopia and Utopia, Trinity College Press, Hartford, Conn., 1966; Faber & Faber, London, 1968; Athens Publishing Center, Athens, 1974.

Urban Renewal and the Future of the American City, Public Administration Service, Chicago, Illinois, 1966.

"Water and Human Environment", *Water for Peace*, U.S. Government Printing Office, Washington D.C., 1967.

Emergence and Growth of an Urban Region: the Developing Urban Detroit Area, The Detroit Edison Company, Detroit, Michigan; Vol. I, 1966; Vol. II, 1967; Vol. III, 1970.

Ekistics: an Introduction to the Science of Human Settlements, Oxford University Press, New York, 1968.

"The Future of Human Settlements", *The Place of Value in a World of Facts*, edited by Arne Tiselius and Sam Nilsson, Wiley Interscience Division, John Wiley & Sons, Inc., New York, 1970.

"Ekistics: the Science of Human Settlements", SCIENCE, Vol. 170, October 23, 1970.

"Ecumenopolis: the Inevitable City", "Isopolis: the Desirable, Humane City", "Entopia or the City We Can Build", The Whidden Lectures, McMaster University, February 17, 18, 22, 1971.

"Order In Our Thinking: the Need for a Total Approach to the Anthropocosmos", EKISTICS, Vol. 34, No. 220, July 1972.

The Two-Headed Eagle: From the Past to the Future of Human Settlements, Lycabettus Press, Athens, 1972.

"The Formation of a Human Room", EKISTICS, Vol. 33, No. 196, March 1972.

313

"Human Settlements in Space and Time", *Nature in the Round*, edited by Nigel Calder, Weidenfeld & Nicolson, London, 1973.

The Great Urban Crimes We Permit by Law, Lycabettus Press, Athens, 1973.

"The Structure of Cities", EKISTICS, Vol. 36, No. 215, October 1973.

Anthropopolis: City for Human Development, Athens Publishing Center, Athens, 1974 and W.W. Norton, New York, 1975.

"The Four Explosions of Our Cities", EKISTICS, Vol. 38, No. 228, October 1974.

"Movement and City", EKISTICS, Vol. 37, No. 223, June 1974.

"The Ecological Types of Space That We Need", ENVIRONMENTAL CONSERVATION, Vol. 2, No. 1, Spring 1975.

"Human Settlements and Crimes", EKISTICS, Vol. 39, No. 231, February 1975.

"The Great Danger", EKISTICS, Vol. 39, No. 230, January 1975.

(with J.G. Papaioannou), *Ecumenopolis: the Inevitable City of the Future*, Athens Publishing Center, Athens, 1974 and W.W. Norton, New York (in press).

Notes and References

No. Page

Part One

1   2   C.A. Doxiadis, "The Great Danger", EKISTICS, Vol. 39, No. 230, January 1975, Fig. 1.

2   2   We began with the term *settlement* in order to remain open-minded. Then we found that this settlement was to be an urban system, and in keeping with the ancient tradition which created the term *polis* and formed *metro-polis* and *megalo-polis*, we decided to use *polis* as the suffix of our new term since it would be universally understood. We examined several alternatives, such as *geo-polis* — which had to be excluded because the new city will cover the whole earth — or *cosmo-polis* — which had to be excluded because we do not at present foresee going into space beyond the moon, and if we do, then *cosmo-polis* will be needed for a much larger unit than this present one. We ended with the term *Ecumeno-polis*, since it serves our realistic goals best. (See also Glossary).

3   3   Aristotle, *Politics*, I.i, 8-9, trans. by H. Rackham, The Loeb Classical Library, William Heinemann Publishers, London, 1944, pp. 8-9.

4   6   C.A. Doxiadis and J.G. Papaioannou, *Ecumenopolis: the Inevitable City of the Future*, Athens Publishing Center, Athens, 1974 and W.W. Norton, New York (in press).

5   6   C.A. Doxiadis, "The Future of Human Settlements", *The Place of Value in a World of Facts*, edited by Arne Tiselius and Sam Nilsson, Wiley Interscience Division, John Wiley & Sons, Inc., New York, 1970, pp. 307-338.

6   8   A series of three lectures entitled Whidden Lectures delivered at McMaster University, February 17, 18 and 22, 1971, under the following titles: "Ecumenopolis: the Inevitable City", "Isopolis: the Desirable, Humane City", "Entopia or the City We Can Build".

7   12   C.A. Doxiadis, *Ekistics: an Introduction to the Science of Human Settlements*, Oxford University Press, New York, 1968, pp. 208-215.

315

No.	Page	
8	16	J. Gottmann, *Megalopolis: the Urbanized Northeastern Seaboard of the United States*, MIT Press, Cambridge, Mass., 1961.
9	16	The Great Lakes Megalopolis research project started in 1965, and was initiated within the framework of the Developing Urban Detroit Area research project when it was felt necessary to undertake a series of studies of the broader regions encompassing the Urban Detroit Area to place it in its proper setting and perspective. During the early stages of this work, a zone of more or less intense urban-type phenomena running from Illinois to Pennsylvania could be clearly distinguished from its surrounding area. It was then suggested that this Great Lakes zone might constitute an emerging megalopolis analogous to the Eastern Megalopolis, the urbanized northeastern corridor studied by J. Gottmann. This view was soon confirmed by further findings and the study of this megalopolitan zone, due to its relevance to the Urban Detroit Area, became an important constituent element of the Urban Detroit Area research project.
10	21	See note 5, p. 312.
11	21	FINANCIAL POST (Canada), May 15, 1974.
12	22	Alvin Toffler, *Future Shock*, Random House, New York, 1970.
13	26	Aristotle, *The Nicomachean Ethics*, VIII.i, 6, trans. by H. Rackham, The Loeb Classical Library, William Heinemann Ltd., London, 1968, Vol. XIX, p. 453.
14	26	INTERNATIONAL HERALD TRIBUNE, December 1-2, 1973.
15	28	There are now several like *The Quality of Life Concept: a Potential New Tool for Decision-Makers* by The Environmental Protection Agency, Office of Research and Monitoring, Environmental Studies Division, 1973, which presents many views.
16	28	C.A. Doxiadis, "Order in our Thinking: the Need for a Total Approach to the Anthropocosmos", EKISTICS, Vol. 34, No. 200, July 1972, pp. 43-46. C.A. Doxiadis, "Human Settlements in Space and Time", *Nature in the Round*, edited by Nigel Calder, Weidenfeld & Nicolson, London, 1973, pp. 90-100.
17	28	C.A. Doxiadis, *Ekistics: an Introduction to the Science of Human Settlements*, pp. 27-31. C.A. Doxiadis, *Anthropopolis: City for Human Development*, Athens Publishing Center, Athens, 1974 and W.W. Norton, New York, 1975. See also p. 45 of this book.
18	29	C.A. Doxiadis, *The Two-Headed Eagle: from the Past to the Future of Human Settlements*, Lycabettus Press, Athens, 1972, pp. 46-48, 50-53.
19	29	C.A. Doxiadis, *Between Dystopia and Utopia*, Trinity College Press,

No. Page

Hartford, Conn., 1966; Faber & Faber, London, 1968; Athens Publishing Center, Athens, 1974.

20   30   Paul Vieille, "Les Enfants et l'An 2000", REVUE 2000, No. 11, December 1968, drawing appearing on p. 33. Reproduced by permission of REVUE 2000, Paris, France.

21   30   "Scientists discuss biology's new threats to mankind", THE TIMES (London), September 20, 1974.

22   32   B.F. Skinner, *Walden Two*, Macmillan, New York, 1963.
Aldous Huxley, *Island*, Chatto & Windus, London, 1959.

23   32   Oscar Wilde, *The Soul of Man under Socialism*, Crescendo, Boston, Mass., 1969. Reprinted by permission of Crescendo Publishing Co., Boston, U.S.A. 02116.

24   32   C.A. Doxiadis, *The Great Urban Crimes We Permit by Law*, Lycabettus Press, Athens, 1973, pp. 12-17.

25   34   George Gaylord Simpson, *The Meaning of Evolution*, Yale University Press, New Haven, 1967 (rev. edition), p. 143.

26   34   Alexis Carrel, *Man the Unknown*, Hamish Hamilton, London, 1961, p. 184.

27   34   C.A. Doxiadis, *Anthropopolis: City for Human Development*.

28   34   See note 6.

29   35   René Dubos, "Humanizing the Earth", SCIENCE, Vol. 179, February 23, 1973, p. 770. Copyright 1973 by the American Association for the Advancement of Science, Washington D.C., U.S.A.

30   35   The Editors of FORTUNE, *The Mighty Force of Research*, McGraw-Hill, New York, 1956, p. 3.

31   38   For years I thought that "Anthropos" (the ancient Greek word for human) would be better than the English word "Man" to describe human beings or mankind, because the word "Man" is also confused with the masculine gender. Now the American Anthropological Association has passed a resolution (November 1973) and has taken the following decision: "In view of the fact that the founders of the discipline of anthropology were men socialized in a male-dominated society which systematically excluded women from the professions and thereby prevented their participation in the formation of our discipline, including its terminology; and being trained as anthropologists to understand that language reinforces and-perpetuates the prevailing values and socio-economic patterns that contribute to the oppression of women; we move that the American Anthropological Association:

a.   urge anthropologists to become aware in their writing and teaching that their wide use of the term "man" as generic for the species is conceptually confusing (since "man" is also the term for the male) and that it be replaced by more comprehensive terms such as "people" and "human being" which include both sexes;

b. further urge that members of the Association select textbooks that have eliminated this form of sexism which has become increasingly offensive to more and more women both within and outside the disciplines.

I agree with this basic goal and throughout this book have used the word *Anthropos* (and where necessary the Greek plural *Anthropoi*) as meaning human of both sexes. Unfortunately, however, because of the grammatical structure of the English language, in several instances it has been impossible to avoid the use of masculine pronouns when referring to *Anthropos*.

32 38 Gay Gaer Luce, *Body Time: Physiological Rhythms and Social Stress*, Random House, Pantheon Books, New York, 1971.

33 38 See "Prehistory" in *Encyclopedia of World Art*, McGraw-Hill, New York, Vol. XI, 1966, p. 614.

34 38 Edward T. Hall, *The Silent Language*, Doubleday, New York, 1959.
Edward T. Hall, *The Hidden Dimension*, Doubleday, New York, 1966.

35 41 C.A. Doxiadis, *Anthropopolis: City for Human Development*, pp. 101-190.

36 43 C.A. Doxiadis, *Ekistics: an Introduction to the Science of Human Settlements*, pp. 212-213, 364-371, 467-479.

37 45 C.A. Doxiadis, *Ekistics: an Introduction to the Science of Human Settlements*, pp. 27-31.

38 45 C.A. Doxiadis, *Anthropopolis: City for Human Development*, Fig. 134, p. 193.

39 46 C.A. Doxiadis, *Ekistics: an Introduction to the Science of Human Settlements*, pp. 27-28.

40 49 C.A. Doxiadis, *Anthropopolis: City for Human Development*, pp. 103-106.

41 50 C.A. Doxiadis, "The Structure of Cities", EKISTICS, Vol. 36, No. 215, October 1973, pp. 277-281.

42 54 See note 5, pp. 334-335.

43 55 There is a more complete form of the Anthropocosmos model which was published in EKISTICS, Vol. 38, No. 229, December 1974, pp. 405-412, but I limit myself here to this one because we can see the total model in one page whereas the complete one needs four pages for its simplest presentation.

44 57 Paul Weiss, *Dynamics of Development: Experiments and Inferences*, Academic Press, New York, 1968, p. 18.

No. Page

15   115   See note 5.

16   115   C.A. Doxiadis, "Ekistics, the Science of Human Settlements", SCIENCE, Vol. 170, October 23, 1970, Fig. 13.

17   115   C.A.Doxiadis, *Anthropopolis: City for Human Development*, Fig. 64.

18   115   C.A. Doxiadis, *Anthropopolis: City for Human Development*, Fig. 98.

19   115   Janet Bloom, "Changing Walls", FORUM, Vol. 138, No. 4, May 1973, pp. 20-27.

20   115   Daniel Cappon, "Mental Health in the Hi-rise", EKISTICS, Vol. 33, No. 196, March 1972, pp. 192-195.

21   115   Eric Kroll, "Folk Art in the Barrios", NATURAL HISTORY, May 1973, pp. 56-65.
"Art City", THE GUARDIAN, May 28, 1973.
Judy Hillman, "Designed for Living — In a Motorway Wall", THE GUARDIAN, May 29, 1973.

22   116   Jonathan Steele, "A Better Life in Siberia", THE GUARDIAN, September 20, 1974.

23   117   "Pulling up Young Roots", *Story of Life*, The Marshall Cavendish Encyclopedia of the Human Mind and Body, London, 1969 and 1970, p. 2616.

24   117   Albert Eide Parr, "To Make the City a Child's Milieu", THE NEW YORK TIMES, July 4, 1971.

25   119   "One in 10 London Boys Found to Enjoy Acts of Violence", INTERNATIONAL HERALD TRIBUNE, August 24, 1973.

26   119   S. Giedion, *Architecture, You and Me*, Harvard University Press, Cambridge, Mass., 1958, pp. 123 ff.

27   119   Plato, *The Republic*, 8, XIV, trans. by H. Rackham, The Loeb Classical Library, William Heinemann Ltd., London, Vol. II, 1963, pp. 309-310.

28   120   E.E. David, Jr. (Bell Telephone Laboratories, Murray Hill, New Jersey), presentation for "The Future Technology of Communication and Communication Centers", Wayne State Centennial, Wayne State University, May 8, 1968.

29   131   C.A. Doxiadis, *Anthropopolis: City for Human Development*, pp. 163-169, Fig. 40.

30   134   Aristotle, *Politics*, II.iv, 13-v.1, trans. by H. Rackham, The Loeb Classical Library, William Heinemann Ltd., London, 1959, p. 121.

31   134   C.A. Doxiadis, *Ekistics: an Introduction to the Science of Human Settlements*, pp. 348-349.

32   134   Arthur F. Wright, "Changan", *Cities of Destiny*, edited by Arnold Toynbee, Thames & Hudson, London, 1967, pp. 138-149.

33   134   "The Human Community", EKISTICS, Vol. 20, No. 117, August 1965, pp. 83-112.

No.   Page

34   135   Judy Hillman, "Pupils taut", THE GUARDIAN, May 31, 1974.
35   151   C.A. Doxiadis, *Urban Renewal and the Future of the American City*, Public Administration Service, Chicago, Illinois, 1966.
C.A. Doxiadis, *Ekistics: an Introduction to the Science of Human Settlements*, pp. 403-413.
36   152   C.A. Doxiadis, *Emergence and Growth of an Urban Region: the Developing Urban Detroit Area*, The Detroit Edison Company, Detroit, Michigan, Vol. 3, 1970, pp. 330-334.
37   152   Edison Plaza consists of a raised vehicular-free pedestrian level, bridging existing streets, capable of being extended with a pedestrian network to serve Edison Center (Doxiadis Associates proposed 24 ha. (60 acres) commercial and housing complex in the Detroit Central Functions Area) and joining future downtown pedestrian networks. A program was developed to:
a. functionally unite diverse Detroit Edison Company operations scheduled to occupy space in two existing buildings and the new 21-story Walker Cisler Building presently under construction;
b. upgrade the existing buildings;
c. offer safe all-weather interconnections;
d. provide a new computer and system control center; and
e. establish a focal point to stimulate growth of Edison Center.
The building program was phased as follows: Phase I (construction commencing immediately) a minimal cloister-like connection with structural provision to receive Phase II; Phase II, a climate controlled area offering restaurant, display, shopping, and public facilities; and Phase III, extension of the pedestrian level to serve Edison Center.
The solution is modest but dramatic. The existing 1922 General Offices Building has been used as the focus of an interconnecting plaza. Solid walls, contrasting the Phase II transparent roof enclosure, permits a sunlit outdoor-like atmosphere. The three office buildings both create and participate in the space which in turn synthesizes these disparate elements into a single spatial unity. Brick walls blending with the existing buildings and a strong landscaped plaza surface create a new ground level twenty feet above the existing streets, in effect reuniting the complex with Nature.
38   154   C.A. Doxiadis, *Ekistics: an Introduction to the Science of Human Settlements*, pp. 208-214.
39   154   C.A. Doxiadis, *Anthropopolis: City for Human Development*, pp. 149-157.
40   155   C.A. Doxiadis, *Emergence and Growth of an Urban Region: the Developing Urban Detroit Area*, Vol. 3, 1970, Figures 203-206.

No.	Page	
41	156	Jane Stein, "There are ways to help buildings conserve energy", SMITH-SONIAN, October 1973, pp. 29-35.
42	159	See note 1.
43	160	"Utopie architecturale à Evry", LE MONDE, May 18, 1973.
44	169	Doxiadis Associates, Inc., *Campus Planning in an Urban Area: a Master Plan for Rensselaer Polytechnic Institute*, Praeger Publishers, New York, 1971.
45	171	C.A. Doxiadis, *The Two-Headed Eagle: from the Past to the Future of Human Settlements*, pp. 11, 25, 72, 82. See also Part One, note 40.
46	171	C.A. Doxiadis, *Ekistics: an Introduction to the Science of Human Settlements*, Figures 179-182, 200. C.A. Doxiadis, *The Two-Headed Eagle: from the Past to the Future of Human Settlements*, pp. 78-79, 81.
47	171	C.A. Doxiadis, *Anthropopolis: City for Human Development*, pp. 136-140.
48	171	C.A. Doxiadis, *Emergence and Growth of an Urban Region: the Developing Urban Detroit Area*, Vol. 3, 1970, pp. 111-159. *Major Problems and Constraints*, The Northern Ohio Urban System research project, internal document by Doxiadis Associates Int., DOX-USA-A 89, September 1971.
49	176	C.A. Doxiadis, *Anthropopolis: City for Human Development*, pp. 185-187.
50	180	C.A. Doxiadis, *Emergence and Growth of an Urban Region: the Developing Urban Detroit Area*, Vol. 2, 1967, Vol. 3, 1970.
51	185	Ibid., Vol. 3, Figures 375-376.
52	185	Daniel Jack Chasan, "An answer to city traffic may be a horizontal elevator", SMITHSONIAN, July 1973, pp. 47-53.
53	199	C.A. Doxiadis, "Movement and City", EKISTICS, Vol. 37, No. 223, June 1974, pp. 377-380.
54	201	C.A. Doxiadis and J.G. Papaioannou, *Ecumenopolis: the Inevitable City of the Future*, pp. 425-434.
55	201	Ibid., pp. 281-283. C.A. Doxiadis, *Urban America and the Role of Industry*, report written for the National Association of Manufacturers, January 1971, pp. 44-50.
56	202	Robert Cassidy, "America Outside the Cities and Suburbs", PLANNING (The ASPO Magazine), August 1973, p. 9.
57	202	See Part One, note 8.
58	202	See Part One, note 9.
59	202	C.A. Doxiadis and J.G. Papaioannou, *Ecumenopolis: the Inevitable City of the Future*, pp. 140-145.

No. Page

60 204 C.A. Doxiadis, *Emergence and Growth of an Urban Region: the Developing Urban Detroit Area*, Vol. 3, 1970, pp. 276-286.
C.A. Doxiadis, *The Two-Headed Eagle: from the Past to the Future of Human Settlements*, pp. 110, 114.

61 206 C.A. Doxiadis and J.G. Papaioannou, *Ecumenopolis: the Inevitable City of the Future*, pp. 425-434.

62 206 *La Façade Méditerranéenne*, Schéma Général d'Aménagement de la France, 1ère partie, réalisé par EURDA, Société d'Etudes d'Urbanisme, de Développement et d'Aménagement du Territoire, "La Documentation Française", 29-31 quai Voltaire 75, Paris 7ème, Novembre 1969.

63 208 *Plan de Ordenación de la Provincia de Barcelona*, internal report by Doxiadis Iberica S.A., DOX-ESP-A 6 and DOX-ESP-A 7, November 1970, and *Plan de Ordenación de la Provincia de Gerona*, internal report by Doxiadis Iberica S.A., DOX-ESP-A 9, February 1971, prepared for the Diputación Provincial de Barcelona and the Diputación Provincial de Gerona respectively.

64 212 INTERNATIONAL HERALD TRIBUNE, December 1-2, 1973. National Aeronautics and Space Administration (NASA) photograph taken from a handheld camera aboard Skylab III. Reproduced by permission from the U.S. Geological Survey, EROS Data Center, Sioux Falls, South Dakota 57198, identification number: SL3-121-2445.

65 212 See note 53.

66 212 C.A. Doxiadis, *Anthropopolis: City for Human Development*, Fig. 46.

67 215 See Part One, note 9.

68 220 C.A. Doxiadis, "The Need for a Coordinated Transport System", European Conference of Ministers of Transport, Fifth International Symposium on Theory and Practice in Transport Economics, Athens, October 22, 1973.

69 224 *Development of the River Plate Basin: The Methodology*, internal document by Doxiadis Associates Int., DOX-AML-A 10, January 1969.

70 224 C.A. Doxiadis and J.G. Papaioannou, *Ecumenopolis: the Inevitable City of the Future*, pp. 188-204.

71 224 C.A. Doxiadis, "The Ecological Types of Space That We Need", ENVIRONMENTAL CONSERVATION, Vol. 2, No. 1, Spring 1975, pp. 3-13.

72 229 See notes 53 and 68.

73 231 C.A. Doxiadis and J.G. Papaioannou, *Ecumenopolis: the Inevitable City of the Future*, pp. 48-53.

74 231 "It's a Shrinking World", U.S. NEWS & WORLD REPORT, June 11, 1973, pp. 98-99.

75 232 C.A. Doxiadis, "The Forces That Will Shape the Ecumenopolis", EKISTICS, Vol. 15, No. 90, May 1963, p. 250.

No. Page

76 236 Arnold Toynbee, "Patterns and Predictions", THE AMERICAN WAY, August 1972, p. 20.
Copyright 1972 by THE AMERICAN WAY, inflight magazine of American Airlines. Reprinted by permission.

77 237 C.A. Doxiadis, "Marriage between Nature and City", INTERNATIONAL. WILDLIFE, Vol. 4, No. 1, Jan./Feb. 1974, pp. 4-11.

Part Three

1 242 Paul Weiss, *Dynamics of Development: Experiments and Inferences*, p. 25.

2 242 Ibid., p. 29.

3 242 E.W. Sinnott, *The Problem of Organic Form*, Yale University Press, New Haven, Conn., 1963, p. 136.

4 242 Loren Eiseley, *The Immense Journey*, Vintage Books, New York, 1957, p. 26.

5 242 Paul Weiss, *Dynamics of Development: Experiments and Inferences*, p. 43.

6 242 George Gaylord Simpson, *The Meaning of Evolution*, Yale University Press, New Haven, Conn., 1967, p. 344.

7 242 John W. Gardner, *Self-Renewal: the Individual and the Innovative Society*, Harper & Row, New York, 1964, p. 65.

8 242 George Gaylord Simpson, *The Meaning of Evolution*, p. 199.

9 244 Innokenti P. Gerasimov, "A Soviet Plan for Nature", NATURAL HISTORY, No. 10, December 1969, pp. 24-34.

10 245 "Man-Inflicted Scars on Earth Presented in Skylab Photos", INTERNATIONAL HERALD TRIBUNE, April 29, 1974.

11 247 C.A. Doxiadis, "Global Action for Man's Water Resources", paper delivered to the First World Congress on Water Resources on 'Water for the Human Environment' organized by the International Water Resources Association, Chicago, Illinois, September 24-28, 1973, Vol. I, pp. 3-28.
See also Part Two, note 77.

12 248 See Part Two, note 71.

13 252 C.A. Doxiadis, "Water and Human Environment", *Water for Peace*, International Conference on Water for Peace, Washington D.C., May 23-31, 1967, U.S. Government Printing Office, Washington D.C. 20402, Vol. I, pp. 33-60.
C.A. Doxiadis, "Water for Human Development", paper prepared for the American Water Works Association, 9th Annual Conference, Washington D.C., June 24, 1970. Abstracted in the AWWA JOURNAL under the title "World City of the Future", Vol. 62, December 1970, pp. 740-746.

No. Page

C.A. Doxiadis, "Global Action for Man's Water Resources", paper prepared for the First World Congress on Water Resources on 'Water for the Human Environment' organized by the International Water Resources Association, Chicago, Illinois, September 24-28, 1973.

14 254 See note 13.

15 254 M. Gayn, "For Water the Chinese Move Mountains", INTERNATIONAL WILDLIFE, November/December 1972, p. 25.

16 260 Alexis Carrel, *Man the Unknown*, Hamish Hamilton, London, 1961, p. 216.

17 263 Donald Broadbent quoted in *The Mind of Man*, Nigel Calder, Viking Press, New York, 1970, p. 28.

18 264 Arnold Toynbee, *A Study of History*, one-volume edition, Oxford University Press in association with Thames & Hudson, London, 1972, p. 43.

19 264 F.A. Hayek, *The Counter-Revolution of Science*, Allen & Unwin, London, 1952, p. 34.

20 265 C.A. Doxiadis, "The Urban Systems of the Future", paper prepared for the Conference on 'Technological Change and the Human Environment', California Institute of Technology, Pasadena, California, October 20, 1970.

21 266 C.P. Fitzgerald and the HORIZON MAGAZINE eds., *The Horizon History of China*, American Heritage Publishing Co., Inc., New York, 1969, p. 183.

22 271 C.A. Doxiadis, "Human Settlements and Crimes", EKISTICS, Vol. 39, No. 231, February 1975, pp. 73-76.

23 271 "Murder Rates in Venezuela, U.S. Highest", INTERNATIONAL HERALD TRIBUNE, July 10, 1973.

24 272 "The World's Safest City", NEWSWEEK, December 6, 1971, p. 32.

25 272 Oscar Newman, *Defensible Space*, Collier and Macmillan, New York, 1972.

26 272 See Part Two, note 32.

27 274 C.A. Doxiadis, *Ekistics: an Introduction to the Science of Human Settlements*, p. 31, Fig. 23, pp. 438-444.

28 275 The case of Fridley was well presented in *Modernizing Local Government to Secure a Balanced Federalism*, a Statement on National Policy by the Research and Policy Committee of the Committee for Economic Development, July 1966.

29 277 Grahame Clark and Stuart Piggott, *Prehistoric Societies*, Hutchinson, London, 1965.

30 278 C.A. Doxiadis, *The Great Urban Crimes We Permit by Law*, pp. 27-30.

31 278 Arnold Toynbee, "The Ancient World and the Modern World", EKISTICS, Vol. 35, No. 206, January 1973, p. 5.

No. Page

32 282 In other languages the corresponding terms will be TERMERAIR (Terre-Mer-Air in French), LANWALUFT (Land-Wasser-Luft in German), TER-MARIA (Terra-Mare-Aria in Italian), TIERMARAIRE (Tierra-Mar-Aire in Spanish) or ΓΗΝΕΡΑ (pronounce yinera, Γῆ-Νερό-'Αέρας in Greek).

33 286 C.A. Doxiadis, *Emergence and Growth of an Urban Region: the Developing Urban Detroit Area*, Vol. 3, 1970.
Feasibility of Utility Tunnels in Urban Areas, American Public Works Association, Special Report No. 39, February 1971.
Feasibility of Utility Corridors, Report No. 1, Technical Aspects by Utility Corridors Task Force, May 4, 1971.

34 291 C.A. Doxiadis, *Anthropopolis: City for Human Development*, pp. 187-190.

35 291 Ibid., pp. 167-168.

36 294 C.A. Doxiadis, "Ekistic Synthesis of Structure and Form", EKISTICS, Vol. 26, No. 155, October 1968, pp. 395-415, Fig. 33.

37 294 C.A. Doxiadis, *The Place of Value in a World of Facts*, p. 332.

38 294 See Part One, note 16.

39 294 C.A. Doxiadis, "The Structure of Cities", EKISTICS, Vol. 36, No. 215, October 1973, pp. 277-281.

40 295 C.A. Doxiadis, *Ekistics: an Introduction to the Science of Human Settlements*, pp. 287-288.

Index